KW-222-996

Contents

Illustrations appear between pages

120 and 121

THE SUBVERTERS
OF LIBERTY

THE SUBVERTERS
OF LIBERTY

J. Bernard Hutton

W. H. Allen · London & New York
A Division of Howard and Wyndham Ltd

1972

Printed and bound in Great Britain
for the publishers
W. H. Allen & Co. Ltd
43 Essex St, London, WC2R 3JG
by Butler & Tanner Ltd
Frome and London

ISBN 0 491 00209 2

Author's Note

Over a hundred years ago Karl Marx, the creator of the communist 'Class-War', wrote:

'We recognise our old friend, our old mole, who knows so well how to work underground, suddenly to appear: the Revolution.'

Today thousands of highly-trained Russian and Red Chinese under-cover master-subverters* live under respectable 'cover' occupations and professions in all countries of the Western democracies. International security officers estimate that at least thirty thousand under-cover subverters, paid by Moscow and Peking, are continuously undermining the Western democracies. They are aided by specially trained Communist Party members and fellow travellers. The conservative estimate by Western security experts is that at least half a million men and women are at work all over the world, bringing about the downfall of the profit-making economic system.

It has always been the aim of communist leaders to create revolutionary situations. Lenin favoured agitation to achieve his aim of communist world domination, and Trotsky advocated even more militant confrontation. But Stalin chose to train an army of undercover subverters to destroy Western democracy from within . . . a dangerous Red fifth column!

In this book, I present evidence that has been checked and counter-checked, and emanates from Soviet, Red Chinese and Western files. I expose the pattern of a world-wide conspiracy that threatens the peoples of the free world. I trace the birth of the Soviet fifth column, and reveal how selected Russian and Chinese communists have become leaders of a small army of undercover subverters. I show how they are assisted by selected Western communists to bring about demonstrations that develop into violent rioting, terrorism and guerrilla

* These are literal translations of the Russian and Chinese terms, as used in official documents.

warfare; how strikes, hijackings, kidnappings and inflation are brought about by studied planning and action; how powerful forces are striving to destroy the Western way of life.

Such a book as this can never be up to date, for every day new outrages occur. But I have included facts about Red undercover subverters' activities up to the time this book goes to press.

I take this opportunity to express my profound thanks to all those behind the Iron and Bamboo Curtains who helped me obtain documented facts from secret files, but who must, obviously, remain anonymous; and to the various Western security agencies and officers who helped me obtain, check and counter-check my facts. Without their valuable assistance I could not have written this story, never before told, of the men and women who are 'the enemy within'.

J. BERNARD HUTTON

I

The Tip of the Red Iceberg

It was the evening of the 24th of September 1971 when Sir Denis Greenhill, Head of the Foreign Office, climbed the steps of the Soviet Embassy in London to ignite the fuse of an explosive political incident that shock-waved into newspaper headlines throughout the world.

The Embassy staff had an inkling of the motive of the visit and Sir Denis was received with stiffer than usual Russian formality. Mr Ivan Ippolitov, the Soviet Minister, concentrated upon the niceties of diplomatic protocol to conceal the fact that he was as ill at ease as Sir Denis. Both men were acting out a charade and must have felt foolish doing so. Sir Denis solemnly handed the Russian Minister ten type-written pages dealing with Britain's expulsion of 105 Soviet diplomats, and while Mr Ivan Ippolitov acted out his astonishment and indignation at the allegations, Sir Denis prepared to deliver a speech expressing the deep shock of Her Majesty's Government at the extent of Russian espionage in Great Britain.

Any surprise voiced by a British Cabinet Minister about Russian espionage must be quite insincere. Espionage is a recognised branch of government activity, so popular and so heavily financed that it is almost an industry. There may not be as many British businessmen arrested in the Soviet Union while in the possession of secret documents as there are Soviet spies found within the British Foreign Office, but this may be because British spies are better trained. Spying is an unsavoury business, but it is an essential cog in the machinery of government. All publicans know that their barmen will dip into the till, and make allowances for it as 'losses'. Host-governments know that resident foreign diplomats will pick up military secrets and transmit them back home in code, as they themselves receive secret information from their own diplomats abroad. These are the 'perks' of diplomacy. But the perks must be kept within limits. The publican whose 'losses' exceed a reasonable percentage must start firing his barmen or go bust. The host-government which learns that resident foreign diplomats are engaged upon work normally undertaken by professional spies must call a halt, or suffer severe disadvantages.

The expulsion of 105 Soviet diplomats from Britain was a warning to the Kremlin that the reasonable limits of diplomatic espionage had been grossly exceeded. The tip of the Red espionage iceberg had thrust too high above the murky waters of diplomatic spying. It had been all but shouted from the rooftops that Russian agents are damaging Britain's aircraft industry and preventing the Concorde from becoming operational; that the disharmony fomented between France and Britain has disrupted the Concorde test flight programme; that the British trade union movement is undermined by subverters. British security agents have discovered long lists of names of trade union members who have been sounded out by Russian agents as possible sources of information and subversive action. British Army officers are studying the extent to which Soviet espionage has contributed to the sorely unsettled situation in Northern Ireland.

But now Russian diplomatic espionage had become too blatant; British prestige had to be preserved, so Diplomats were expelled. The Kremlin had erred and the British Government was obliged to rap knuckles, knowing that it was a face-saving, but otherwise totally useless gesture. With typical British staidness, the diplomatic protest was made, the Soviet diplomats went home and the attention of the world was riveted upon the tip of the Red iceberg. Its other nine-tenths remain submerged and virtually unassailable. British and Western intelligence services know it exists but cannot act. The established laws that protect the rights of the individual can be perverted into the protection of the guilty!

The Kremlin erred because Moscow is over-eager to transform the explosive situation in Northern Ireland into a civil war between Ireland and Britain. The Kremlin abandoned its customary caution and Russian diplomats in the United Kingdom were ordered to establish contact with undercover subverters, so as to be able to feel the pulse of Northern Ireland's simmering discontent and make split-second decisions.

High-ranking security officers in Belfast know that Soviet diplomats cooperated with subverters and arranged deliveries of arms to IRA Provisionals. They know that Soviet diplomats and KGB agents supplied terrorists in Northern Ireland with arms, ammunition and explosives, and planned their operations against British troops with the aid of Soviet military experts. The extensive activity of subverters in Irish politics is well known to security officers. The following case history is one of many.

Uglick Zbignew was a naturalised Pole, living in London. His credentials and cover story were sound, and he had found employment as a postman. Security officers know Zbignew was in Paris in 1968 and helped to inflame the student rioting that created a revolutionary situation in France.

On the 2nd of July 1971 Uglick flew to Belfast. His special services were needed to help stir up an ugly political situation. His subversive activities were short-lived, however. Soon after his arrival in Belfast, troops returned fire from a rooftop sniper and Uglick Zbignew was shot dead while scrambling over a rooftop. He was wearing a dark sweater and pants, his face was blackened and he was carrying a modern telescopic-sight rifle.

Moscow's tactical blunder was to implicate Soviet diplomats with subverters like Zbignew. It enabled British security officers to establish links between the Russian diplomats, the Angry Brigade, terrorists and Irish subverters; and to uncover large caches of armaments in the homes of Irishmen living in London and elsewhere.

* * *

There is an army of trained subverters at work in the Western world, and it has increased steadily over the years. Although the expelled Russians are now back in the Soviet Union, the insidious activity of subverters continues unabated, and as the discredited soviet diplomats undergo interrogation in Moscow by KGB officers, concerned to learn how deeply British security officers have penetrated the Russian sabotage networks, reports flood into the Kremlin confirming the unrelenting spread of the subverter cancer.

The following incidents occurred in the few days between the 5th and the 10th of October, 1971:

In the United States of America, where a nationwide dock strike threatened to cripple the country's economy, President Nixon invoked strike-breaking legislation against 15,000 West Coast dockers who had been on strike for three months. Another 45,000 East and Gulf Coast dockers continued to strike. Meanwhile, in California, raging bush fires destroyed fruit crops and houses, and caused an exodus of hundreds of residents. Fire experts discovered dozens of widely scattered incendiary devices with delayed-action fuses.

In Beirut, security guards foiled an attempt by an Algerian girl and a Jordanian man to hijack a Caravelle on a flight to Amman. The girl had concealed a hand-grenade under her wig. Another Caravelle, delayed for two hours at Beirut, miraculously escaped damage when a bomb exploded in a suitcase about to be loaded aboard it. 'If we had taken off on schedule, the bomb would have exploded in mid-air,' said the pilot. The previous day the Jordanian Government had confirmed the death sentence on Abdul Kader Hassen, who had attempted to hijack a Jordanian airliner in September, 1971; he had produced a hand-grenade and ordered the pilot to fly to Baghdad.

All the motorways into Paris were jammed over a seven-mile radius by traffic causing transport chaos, as the result of a strike of the Métro (underground railway) workers. Army trucks brought into emergency service could do little to ease the paralysis that gripped the city.

In Britain, it was officially reported that drug-smuggling had increased enormously, aided by the many new contraband methods adopted. Narcotics officers seized twice as much drugs in 1970 as in 1969.

All British Leyland's car plants in Birmingham were brought to a standstill by strikes. There was a one-day token strike of 1,200 workers at the British Steel Corporation's plant in Worcestershire, and publication of several magazines was prevented by a dispute between IPC Magazines and Trade Union members. Twenty key men of the Special Products department of LEC Refrigeration walked out, their action threatening to bring Bognor's largest industry to a standstill.

In Ireland the sniping, bombing and rioting took an uglier course. Not only were bombs planted in factories, police stations and public buildings by night and day, they also exploded indiscriminately in places and at times most likely to cause injury and death to innocent shoppers and passers-by. The mob weapons of sticks, stones and petrol bombs were augmented by submachine-guns, tracer bullets, sniping rifles with telescopic sight and 3-inch bazookas.

The following events which also occurred between the 5th and 10th of October 1971 vividly illustrate what is happening in Northern Ireland:

On the 5th of October twelve civilians were injured by bombs, a police officer in a patrol car was wounded by a sniper, and £11,000 was seized from a Post Office van by armed terrorists. Five caches of rifles, pistols, ammunition and explosives were captured by British troops in Belfast.

On the 6th of October a soldier and a civilian were wounded by submachine-gun fire, two shoppers were injured by a bomb explosion, and £3,000 was stolen from the Munster and Leinster Bank in Rostrevor by masked gunmen.

On the 7th of October ten bombs exploded in Belfast within the space of ten minutes, causing many injuries, and British troops were fired upon in Crumlin Road with tracer bullets.

On the 8th of October Roden Street Police Station in Belfast was raked by machine-gun fire; a bomb blew up its front door and shattered windows. An anti-tank rocket failed to explode in Belfast's Upper Springfield Road.

On the 9th of October employees of the Whitelock Road Reservoir Pump House were held up at gun-point while bombs were exploded in the machinery. Streets were flooded and thousands of homes will be without water for an indefinite period. A ten-pound gelignite bomb severely damaged a Belfast club. Forty-three women were evacuated from a Belfast maternity hospital and the area was sealed off; a bomb disposal team examined a suitcase that had been left outside the building.

On the 10th of October a woman was killed and nineteen injured when a bomb exploded in the bar of the Fiddlers Inn, Durham Street, Belfast. Yet another gelignite bomb exploded in Springfield Road Police Station, and shots were fired at it from a speeding car. The *Daily Mirror* and *Sunday Mirror* closed down its bomb-damaged Belfast printing plant; restoration was expected to take at least 10 months.

In August 1971 Peking's Special Division for Subversion transmitted the following directive to its master-subverters in Northern Ireland:

TOP SECRET!   MEMORISE!   THEN BURN!

1. SNIPING: British soldiers must be subjected to around-the-clock sniping. A handful of mobile snipers who shoot to kill can keep a large number of troops constantly on the alert and prevented from carrying out other duties. Take every precaution to prevent killed or wounded snipers falling into British hands. Camouflage all militant action so that it appears to be committed by the IRA or other Irish factions.

2. BOMBING: This should harass the enemy non-stop day and night. Political hotheads must be pressed into service for planting bombs. No network activist can risk involving himself in this activity. IRA Provisionals and similar Irish fanatics can be found who are eager to plant bombs and rig booby-traps. Youngsters and older children are ideal material for this work. They attract less attention and suspicion than adults, are more sensitive to monetary rewards and ask no questions. If captured by British Army or security officers they are unable to provide information about their employer. Children are used extensively in Vietnam, so use them too in your territory.

3. STREET FIGHTING: Whenever this is provoked it should lead up to throwing bricks, stones and bottles at British troops. More gelignite nail bombs and petrol bombs must be readily available for use by mobs. Killing British soldiers should be propagated as a praiseworthy target. British Army patrols can be lured into ambushes more easily when children, youngsters and women are the bait.

4. PRECAUTIONS: Every effort must be made to ensure that all acts of terrorism seem to be committed by the IRA, the IRA Provisionals or other Irish fanatics. *No clue must ever lead to any master operator or his undercover network! Network members must not personally engage in terrorist activity!* Their most valuable work is behind the scenes, inspiring obedience to these directives.

5. WEAPONS: To ensure that the IRA etc., are believed to be the

instigators and executors of terrorism, only Western-manufactured arms, ammunition and explosives should be used. Easily accessible small caches of arms, ammunition and explosives must be made known to all snipers and Irish militants.

6. BANK RAIDS: Bank and Post Office robberies must be staged, and propagated as fund-raising actions by the IRA and others, to purchase weapons. The supply of funds to network leaders for their networks activity will continue as previously, however.

7. EXPLOSIVES DIRECTIVES: Our directives on how to manufacture gelignite nail bombs, petrol bombs, time-bombs, booby-traps, etc., must be distributed widely. Encourage fanatics to duplicate and circulate them indiscriminately. Every bomb that explodes, no matter how inefficiently, adds to social disruption and harasses the enemy.

> THIS DOCUMENT MUST NOT FALL INTO UNAUTHORISED HANDS!
>
> MEMORISE!   THEN BURN!

The above listed schedule of events shows how these orders have been put into effect!

*   *   *

Sit-down strikes and sit-ins; 'Stop the Springboks', stop this and stop that; anti-nuclear bomb, anti-Vietnam War, anti-American hooliganism; work-to-rule and wildcat strikes! Such disturbances, which have become the way of life in the Western world, are promoted by subverters.

In the United States of America student subverters launched monster demonstrations that provoked appallingly violent rioting; militant Negroes terrorised cities and towns; public and private property was destroyed, innocent bystanders were injured and killed, and millions of dollars of property went up in flames. Only the National Guard could restore order.

A similar pattern of violence was simultaneously manifested in Amsterdam, Bonn, Paris, Rome, Tokyo and other cities of the free world. First, subverter students forcibly occupied their University buildings. Then, other trained subverters swung into action, provoking demonstrations, riots, sabotage, strikes, vandalism, violence and guerrilla warfare.

In Africa and Asia, Australia and New Zealand, Canada and South America, terrorist violence is a carbon copy of what has happened in the USA.

Demonstrations and strikes are the democratic way of life in the free world. They are a symbol of political freedom. But not until the 1960s did the increasing number of these incidents, synchronised with similar occurrences in many countries, transform political agitation into a *criminal* threat to world peace and security.

London's Grosvenor Square was the scene of rioting and violence in March 1968 when 10,000 demonstrators, including contingents of militant students from various European countries, marched upon the American Embassy after a mass rally in Trafalgar Square. More than 1,000 police officers were marshalled to protect the Embassy from a dangerous mob.

Dr Martin Luther King, the Negro leader whose influence and personality restrained Black Power violence, was shot dead. As his assassin fled, the Black Power leaders launched a wave of rioting and guerrilla warfare that synchronised with demonstrations organised by French students. Hundreds of French students, declaring themselves Anarchists, Trotskyists, Maoists and Castroites, burst into lecture rooms, disrupted classes and obstructed the functioning of the University until the authorities closed it down. Subverters skilfully inflamed the students' resentment against this closure into mob violence. The Paris streets became battlefields, the country was paralysed by nationwide strikes and the French government almost fell.

In Columbia University, as though geared to the French students' actions, American students occupied their University buildings. The disturbances that followed lasted weeks and caused deaths and injuries to students and police. The National Students' Association Survey reports that between the 1st of January and the 1st of June 1968 no less than 101 colleges and universities were subjected to major student demonstrations and protest meetings.

In Japan, riot police fought pitched battles for weeks against thousands of students and other militants. Many died.

In Mexico, clashes between police and students wrote the 'Night of Sorrow' into the country's history when twenty-eight died and 200 were injured in one single night of violence.

Following an attempt by the Guevarist terrorists to seize power in April 1971, the Ceylon Government still has thirty concentration camps imprisoning 14,000 suspected terrorists who are being interrogated.

In South Tyrol, rioting, bombing and terrorism created lawlessness that overflowed into Austria and Italy. Troops were compelled to use armoured cars, water cannon, tear-gas and firearms to cope with rioting mobs.

In West Germany, Holland, Scandinavia, Spain, the Middle East and elsewhere, strikes, riots, bombings and terrorism are commonplace.

In Britain, bans on overtime, work-to-rule, wildcat and official strikes and restrictive practices continually disrupt industry and increase inflation and unemployment.

In Northern Ireland, terrorism increases steadily. The Molotov Cocktails and gelignite nail bombs that kill British troops and Irish policemen are being replaced by automatic firearms, modern explosive devices, bazookas and rockets.

This increasing violence and terrorism is a direct result of an organised world-wide plot to destroy the Western democracies!

When many people of many nationalities simultaneously show *violent* defiance of authority it is a matter of grave public concern. When this world-wide challenge to law and order progresses from violence to terrorism, it threatens the entire structure of society.

Airliners and passengers have been blown up and hijacked. Innocent people have been kidnapped, held to ransom and assassinated. Governments have been blackmailed into releasing murderers to save the lives of women and children held to hostage. It is no coincidence that Dr Martin Luther King's assassination, the violent rioting in London's Grosvenor Square, the student riots in Paris and other places, and countless acts of violence, occurred simultaneously! It is not a coincidence that work-to-rule, strikes, skyjackings, kidnappings, rioting and bombing are increasing!

Influential men of all nations have repeatedly given warnings that there is a global plot to destroy Western society. The free world is being betrayed by an 'enemy within'—that enemy is an army of under-cover subverters, organised, trained and financed by Moscow and Peking.   *through stooges =>*

These warnings have been ignored by a sceptical public. People who enjoy individual liberty and freedom of thought are not easily convinced that men exist who are cold-bloodedly endeavouring to contrive the destruction of a democratic way of life, in order to replace it with Russian or Red Chinese totalitarianism.

When he was Prime Minister and seeking Emergency Powers to deal with the Seamen's Union's strike, Mr Harold Wilson explained to the House of Commons the difficulty of dealing with subverters in a free country, where it is legal for men to sway the opinions of others. Although Mr Wilson believed that the strike was inspired by foreign influences, it was painfully apparent how difficult it was to prove. He said:

> What we have to do is to distinguish between the genuine grievances and the genuine expression of these grievances, whether by rank and file or by elected representatives at all levels, on the one hand, and deliberate exploitation of those grievances by outside influences, on the other. Again, it would be wrong to suggest, and I shall not suggest, that members of the Communist Party—I think particularly of some dedicated communist seamen—are not deeply concerned about these grievances and about the problems which have to be settled.*

Later Mr Wilson said more bluntly:

> The House will be aware that the Communist Party, unlike the major political parties, has at its disposal an efficient and disciplined industrial apparatus controlled from Communist Party head-quarters. No major strike occurs anywhere in this country in any sector of industry in which that apparatus fails to concern itself. In special cases it has been seen at work, for example in the Electrical Trades Union, where it made a successful takeover bid, if not for the share capital at any rate for the management of the union, last-

* *Hansard*, 28th June 1966.

ing for some years. No other political party is organised on these lines.*

Although Mr Wilson named communists who had been vitally concerned in transforming the seamen's strike into a national crisis, their actions could not be legally condemned, and their underlying subversive motive could only be guessed. Members of the House, properly concerned with democratic rights, felt obliged to uphold the bastions of British freedom, behind which subverters can take unwarranted shelter.

Mr J. Grimond, the Liberal leader, said: 'I have some reservations about rushing into these inquiries which I think most people would agree when set up lately to investigate various allegations by this House have led to considerable damage to innocent people.'†

Sir Douglas Glover said: 'It may be that such an inquiry will show the whole of this trouble to be the result of the Prime Minister's imagination, I do not know.‡'

Some members of the House were ready to accept the circumstantial evidence of a Red conspiracy that Mr Wilson provided. Sir Edward Brown said: 'I am following the Hon. Gentleman's remarks closely. Doesn't he agree that the active interest of Tory trade unionists—and I am one—is nevertheless in the interests of the society of Great Britain, whereas the influence of the communists through infiltration— such as occurred in the ETU—is in the interests of a foreign power?'§

But many other members were too idealistic to believe there exist men so devious that they will work as Red fifth columnists within the British working men's most powerful organisations. Mr Manuel fumed: 'I therefore object to any tittle-tattle which suggests that this great movement will be destroyed because of the influence within it. Those influences are rare and do not count. This Labour Party grew out of the trade union movement, and the heart and soul and content of the movement are firmly established in a country which is committed to a democratic way of life and not to manoeuvres such as

not in 1995 any more!

* *Hansard*, 28th June 1966.

† *Ibid.*

‡ *Ibid.*

§ *Ibid.*

those about which suspicions have been thrown about the Chamber today.'*

Nevertheless a Red fifth column is operating secretly in all the countries of the free world. It is directed by Russian and Red Chinese master-subverters. These men and women, masked by excellent cover backgrounds, employ subtle techniques to induce law-abiding citizens to become their political tools.

This is not a fanciful, anti-Russian, anti-Red Chinese assertion. It is a factual statement. It is known to be true by Western statesmen, who are so bound by the laws which govern their free and decent communities that they are at their wits end to devise means to combat the menace.

Proof is also supplied by both Soviet Russian and Red Chinese secret documents. How the Red undercover subverter networks operate in the free world is shown in the following pages.

* *Hansard*, 28th June 1966.

How the Red Fifth Column was Spawned

While the Second World War was being fought, the bond of friendship between the Allies was strong. The Russians fought valiantly, and their battle for Stalingrad and subsequent victories over the German *Wehrmacht* earned them the unstinted admiration of the West. But when the war was won, and even before it was ended, suspicion and distrust began to disrupt the friendships between Soviet and Allied commanders, who disputed the military areas each should occupy, and the number of troops that should be employed to do so. Coldness slowly replaced the goodwill that the people of the West had felt towards Soviet Russia, and turned to hostility as more and more facts about Russian behaviour became public knowledge. Stalin had made two fundamental mistakes: he had shown the world to the Russians; and he had shown the Russians to the world.

Red Army occupation troops plundered, looted and raped mercilessly while their officers made little or no attempt to restrain them. There were reports of terrible Russian brutality, and of peasant soldiers, enrolled from primitive and remote villages, who behaved more like beasts than men. They displayed the sexual appetite of animals, chose their victims at random, stripped them in public and ravaged them with the encouragement and assistance of their companions. To the people of the West, the friendly, amiable, Ivan assumed a new image.

As soon as any German territory was occupied by Red Army troops, all German heavy industrial plant and all manufacturing machines, tools and raw materials which had escaped bombing, were dismantled and transported to the Soviet Union. The defeated Germans were forced to assist the Russians in this work; many German scientists, technicians and skilled workers were transported to the USSR where they 'disappeared'. The Russians shrouded all this activity in a secrecy enforced by cordons of special-task guards set up around the areas

involved. It was a long time before the Western Allies discovered that
the part of Germany occupied by the Russians had been stripped of its
means of production, and that its foremost scientists and technicians,
including many previously engaged upon rocket propulsion, had been
spirited away into the heart of Soviet Russia.

By 1948 the hostility between East and West had become the Cold
War. Controversy over Berlin and the Allied airlift (which maintained
the Western Powers' foothold in the former German capital) almost
sparked off another world war. There were men in the Kremlin who
believed that this was the moment for communism and capitalism to
engage in the inevitable armed confrontation. But Stalin did not share
their opinion and open warfare was averted. But this did not mean
Stalin had ceased to regard the Western Allies as Russia's enemy.

Stalin had good reason to avoid a shooting war. From analysis of
the reports gathered by his secret police about the mood of the Russian
people, he knew that the strain of world war had resulted in a widespread sense of desperation. His scorched-earth policy had placed an
unbearable strain upon Russia's economy; there was a serious shortage
of housing and consumer goods, and semi-starvation was commonplace. The fear of another war depressed the Soviet people. They had
lost the will to work and lived only for today, convinced that to-
morrow an American atom bomb would liquidate them all.

The severe mauling that the Red Army had received from Hitler's
disciplined *Wehrmacht* had reduced Russia's military strength to a very
low ebb. Although three years had elapsed since the end of the Second
World War, the Red Army was still reorganising and re-equipping.
In contrast, the Western Allies still possessed a massive, geared-up
armaments- and troops-producing machine that was being allowed to
run down, but slowly. It was clear to Stalin that a shooting match
between communism and capitalism would be fatal for Russia, and
that was what made him decide on a different type of warfare—the
subversive undercover destruction of capitalism . . . *from within*!

* * *

Introducing subversive activity into capitalist countries was not a new
political policy. Back in March 1919, all the communist parties of the

capitalist world had received precise instructions from the Kremlin on how to cause the downfall of the capitalist regimes. Lenin had sum- marised the methods in 1920:

> The communists in Western Europe and America must . . . strive everywhere to awaken the masses, and draw them into the struggle . . . It is very difficult to do this in Western Europe and America but it can be done and *it must be done*. Propaganda, agitation and organisa- tion inside the armed forces and among the oppressed must be coordinated in a new way. The communists must exert every effort to direct all working-class movements and social development along the straightest and quickest road to the universal victory of Soviet power and the dictatorship of the proletariat.

Twenty-eight years later Stalin advocated a more dynamic and forcible policy. In March 1948, at a secret meeting of the Kremlin's Inner Circle, he said:

> Comrades, it is imperative that we create an entirely new type of fighting force. It will operate first in the most advanced capitalist countries, and later in other countries. This fighting force will con- sist of devoted and trained comrades who will have no outward connection with the Communist Party whatsoever. These comrades will operate under cover, as do our intelligence officers and spies who are working abroad. This special fighting force will control networks of other undercover comrades, who will also have no outward connection with the Communist Party of their country.
>
> The objective of this fighting force is to speed up the development of revolutionary situations and spread awareness of how unrest, public disturbance, disorders and industrial dissatisfaction can bring about a breakdown of the capitalist system. This will lead to the revolutionary overthrow of governments, and the establishment of Soviet states.

With these words Stalin launched a new type of warfare. The Red fifth column was born, and the establishment of a network of highly- skilled, trained undercover subverters became a mighty weapon in the Kremlin's war against the Western democracies.

Stalin directed that these undercover subverters should be controlled by the Action Committee of the *Cominform*, and he appointed Mikhail Suslov as the Supreme Commander of the future undercover subverters.

Suslov, respected as one of the most capable men in the Kremlin hierarchy, undertook his task with enthusiasm. But even before his secret coded messages could be despatched by the Action Committee to Communist Party leaders throughout the world, informing them of the important role the Red fifth column would play in the future, Stalin changed his mind. He decided that the new fighting force of undercover subverters would work much more effectively if it was controlled directly by Moscow's Secret Service Headquarters.

But in April 1948, at another secret conference of the Kremlin's Inner Circle, Stalin announced:*

The way to assure success is for us to create not one, but *two* undercover subverter networks. They will operate simultaneously in all the countries of the Capitalist World. The undercover subverters of the first network will operate quite independently of the second.

In each capitalist country one undercover subverter network will be composed of tried and trusted communists who are *nationals* of that country. Their activities will be directed by Comrade Suslov, who will be responsible to the *Politburo*. This network of undercover subverters will comprise men and women of ability and intelligence, especially selected for these qualities. As soon as they undertake this undercover subverter-work, they will sever all their contact with the Communist Party—and dedicate themselves to working for the Party by indirect methods. They will be called upon to join and operate within organisations and societies that are bourgeois and opposed to communism and the Soviet Union. They will engage in undercover subverter activities within these organisations and societies on behalf of the Communist Party. It will be necessary for them to conceal their previous and present connection with the Communist Party. They will create the impression they are opposed to the ideology of communism . . .

* I have given a condensed translation of his speech.

The second network of undercover subverters will consist of operators of Soviet nationality. These comrades will be under direct orders from our Secret Service Headquarters. A new department at Secret Service [KGB] Headquarters will be created forthwith, to be named the 'Special Division for Subversion'. The directors of this Special Division will select and train recruits of Soviet nationality for this professional undercover master-subverters' network, in the same way that they select and train Soviet comrades for work abroad as Secret Service Network Operators . . .

This decision to create *two* parallel undercover subverter networks was unanimously accepted by the members of the Kremlin's Inner Circle. Moscow KGB Headquarters immediately set up the 'Special Division for Subversion' and this became responsible for international professional fifth column activities, coming under the control of the Second Directorate of the Soviet Secret Service.*

Immediate preparations were made to train Soviet undercover master-subverters who were to penetrate the Western democracies, provoke disturbances and stimulate revolutionary situations; they would receive the same stringent training as was given to Russia's master-spies.

Meanwhile, under the direction of Mikhail Suslov and his lieutenants, hard-core Communists in the Capitalist countries were selected as fifth columnists. They severed all connection with the Communist Party and assumed a new way of life. They became religious fanatics, members of the Conservative or Liberal parties, or members of other right-wing organisations where they could declare themselves as antagonistic to the political ideology of communism.

The Red fifth column was born.

---

* The Second Directorate trains professional murderers and saboteurs, and organises kidnappings and acts of terrorism.

3
The Training of Western Hard-Core Communists

Mikhail Suslov's undercover subverter network was officially classed by the Kremlin as *Institute 631's Subversive Cadres*.

In the spring of 1948 Institute 631 sent out its first directive in code to communist party leaders throughout the world:

> The leaders of all communist parties must select completely trustworthy comrades who will take up undercover subverters work *outside* the Communist Party. Their activity will be revolutionary and subversive. It is essential that these chosen comrades sever all connections with the Party. It is desirable that they become regarded as antagonistic to the Party, and in conflict with its policy.

This same directive described in great detail how secret training establishments should be set up to school communist undercover subverters in sabotage, the instigation of social discontent, violent rioting and industrial espionage. The directive concluded with these words: 'Undercover cadres must appear to be anti-communist, they must never reveal that they are working for the communist cause and they must pursue their subversive work as though motivated by personal incentives.'

The introduction of undercover subverter networks into capitalist countries was classified by the Kremlin as a priority political measure. All Soviet Embassy Second and Third Secretaries, Attachés, Vice-Consuls and other officials enjoying diplomatic immunity were enrolled in a special unit controlled by Mikhail Suslov. This unit coordinated the recruitment of undercover subverters. Embassy and Consular officials, cloaked from arrest by diplomatic immunity, worked hand in glove with trusted communist party members. They built up strong and smoothly functioning undercover subverter networks.

The Soviet diplomats also arranged for the training of the recruits, and subsidised them generously to enable them to live in the meantime under respectable 'cover' occupations. Mikhail Suslov believed it a major tactical error to hamper the growth of the Red fifth column by restricting funds. Stalin agreed, and sanctioned all his demands for economic subsidies. Enormous sums in dollars, pounds, marks, francs and other currencies were smuggled into Western countries via the diplomatic bag. By the early summer of 1948, the first batch of Red fifth-column recruits were receiving training from Moscow-taught experts.

*   *   *

The first undercover subverter training centre set up in the United Kingdom was established in July 1948 in Purley, Surrey. The training centre was a large residential dwelling in a long tree-lined street of semi-detached houses. It masqueraded as a Guest House, and the men and women who stayed there for three or four weeks at a time appeared to be quiet and well-behaved boarders. Nobody suspected they were Red fifth-column recruits being taught the art of political intrigue, sabotage and subversion. A second secret training establishment was set up a few weeks later in Edgbaston, Birmingham, and soon afterwards other training centres were established in Maidstone, Cardiff and Glasgow.

In the USA the first training centre was established in the early summer of 1948 in Chicago. This secret school remained in active use for seven years and turned out a very considerable number of competent undercover subverters. By July and August 1948, other secret Red fifth-column training centres were functioning in Boston, Detroit and New York. None of them was ever detected while they were in operation.

Also in the summer of 1948 training schools were set up in Paris and Marseilles. Both of these secret centres occupied such large residences that the French Communist Party opened no others.

West Germany's subverter training centre was established in Munich in August 1948. The German communists had learned in the hard school of war how to operate under cover, and were already highly skilled in subversive activities, so the West German Communist Party leaders considered that one training centre would be adequate.

In Italy, however, centres were set up in four cities: Rome, Milan, Torino and Palermo. Three months later, two other establishments were opened in Genoa and Naples.

In Japan, a secret training centre was opened in Tokyo in July 1948. Japanese Communist Party members had also engaged in extensive undercover activity during the Second World War and had gained so much practical experience that only one training establishment was considered necessary.

Similar training centres were opened in all other countries of the capitalist world, where Red fifth-column recruits were trained and generously subsidised by Soviet Russia.

The recruits attending these secret undercover subverter centres were hard-core communists, men and women who were prepared to dedicate their lives to the cause. They abandoned their relatives, friends and the environment in which they were known, and travelled hundreds of miles to other parts of the country to begin life over again. But a new type of life. The subverters cultivated new circles of friends and acquaintances wherein they proclaimed themselves anti-communist and anti-Soviet. Many subverters chose the 'cover' of being respectable business people. With the funds provided by Moscow they were able to set up in business and become employers. They voted for the Conservative Party, supported the local church, took a leading part in charity activities and in every possible way disguised their true loyalty to the Communist Party and the Kremlin.

Those recruits who distinguished themselves during training were selected as possible leaders of the subverter networks and given special schooling in the Soviet Union. Their trips to Moscow were arranged in complete secrecy. The recruit would announce his or her intention of taking a vacation in France, Italy or some similar foreign holiday resort. When he arrived in the chosen foreign country, he or she was whisked away by a waiting contact and put on an airliner to the Soviet Union. The contact provided an air ticket, money and a new passport containing all the necessary visas and official seals to satisfy the airport authorities. It looked so genuine it could never be challenged.

On arrival in Moscow, Soviet Communist Party officials escorted the future subverter network leaders to one of their special training institutions in Kuchino, near Moscow, in Dietskoye Selo, Leningrad, in Maiskoye or Sigulda, near Riga. The intense training schedule lasted from two to four weeks. Attendance was from 7 a.m. until 9 p.m., including Saturdays and Sundays. This cramming course gave the future network leaders training in every field of undercover activities: provoking strikes, inciting demonstrations and riots, sabotage and terrorism; and taught them how to communicate by means of coded radio messages and establish secret contact with Moscow Headquarters.

An enlightening account of these special training schools has been given by a trainee:*

Our four weeks' stay at Kuchino was an unforgettable experience. Accommodation, food and treatment were first-rate. The seventy-two male and female students from various English-speaking countries were exceptionally fine people. We all became close friends from the start, and memories of those most enjoyable four weeks will remain with everyone forever.

All the instruction courses were very strenuous. They lasted many hours each day, but the subjects were so challenging, and the instructors so pleasant, that we relished every minute. We were taught how to drug someone, if necessary; rifle sniping; the making and handling of explosives; coding and communicating with network members without risking detection; and transmitting and receiving coded radio messages to and from Institute 631 Headquarters.

The emphasis was upon the most effective tactics to employ in undercover agitation. We all knew that it is not easy to bring all the workers of a huge factory out on strike, even when the majority bear a grudge against the management. We learned that it is often much easier to bring out a few workers in a key plant of a huge factory. This causes the laying-off of non-striking workers. We

* Extract from the secret Kremlin publication *Party Bulletin*, Moscow, November 1948.

discovered that there is a great difference in knowing something in
theory only, and in practice. But by creating artificial situations, and
practising to persuade workers to take industrial action, we acquired
the know-how to achieve spectacular successes. We were taught that
when inducing people to demonstrate, strike or obstruct the police,
our one and only hope of success lies in the way the people are
approached. We learned which issues are best suited to convince
law-abiding people that militant action is the only way to safeguard
their families' personal interests. We were also taught that all young
students and white-collar workers, and all other working youngsters
of a community, are the most malleable material. Most young
people will oppose authority if the right methods of agitation are
adopted.

At Kuchino we learned that industrial and social disruption can
bring about the eventual downfall of the capitalist system. People
from all walks of life can be made into excellent tools for paving the
way to the eventual creation of Soviet régimes, and we now know
how to induce these people to carry out our aims . . .

After the crash course the future subverter network leaders were
flown back to the countries where they were supposed to be holidaying. On arrival there they relinquished the false passports they had
used to visit the Soviet Union, and returned to their own countries
with their real passports, betraying no sign of their travels, and with
souvenirs, perfume and other presents, which they had taken care to
buy, to enhance the impression that their holiday had been spent
properly and enjoyably.

*   *   *

There are three types of subverter: the open member of the Communist Party; the undercover hard-core Communist; and the Russian-
born, specially trained undercover master-subverter.*

The objective of the Communist Party in all democratic countries
is to form a nucleus of tried and trusted comrades whose idealism has
been transformed into fanaticism, and whose loyalty does not waver
when there is conflict of opinions. Any idealist who becomes such a

* Pages 59–69.

fanatic through long membership of the Communist Party accepts all directives from Moscow without question. He will finally believe that black is white, if the Kremlin so directs.

Recognising that all independently thinking people will eventually leave the Party, and only fanatics will remain devoted members, each Communist Party cell lets the system be its own filter, and grows a hard core of fervent comrades who blindly obey all Head Office directives. This nucleus has not been forged and tempered overnight. Countless people have joined the Communist Party during the last half century; it is only a small percentage of them that has remained inextricably trapped, among them many dedicated, intelligent and highly-respected men and women.

All Communist Party Head Office administrators are installed by the Kremlin. Only those who have convinced Moscow of their unshakeable loyalty to the Soviet Union are permitted to be leaders. Even then, Russian master-subverters keep watch on them and send secret reports to Moscow.

Within democratic countries the Communist Party operates openly, campaigning against this or agitating in favour of that. Its policy is published widely in its Party newspapers, and there are always enough young enthusiasts in the process of passing through the Communist Party filter to provide adequate support for protest meetings and demonstrations. The hard-core members do not hide themselves. They are well known in their area. They address street corner meetings, press Communist Party policy at Trade Union conferences and accept nomination for election as officers of many left-wing organisations. They make no attempt to conceal their loyalty to the Communist Party. Only the undercover subverters work secretly.

The British Communist Party, like any other in the free world, does not recognise any loyalty to its own country. It is a branch of the Kremlin's Communist Internationale and receives all its policy direction from Moscow. When it suits the Kremlin that there should be widespread industrial unrest in any of the Western Democracies, the Communist Party labours to achieve that—heedless of the hardship caused to the people.

It is indeed a Red fifth column.

4

Red Fifth Columnists Inside the United Kingdom

From the start Mikhail Suslov's Institute 631 undercover subverter networks in the United Kingdom worked hard to incite chosen victims to damage Britain's economy. Institute 631 issued its basic orders to undercover subverters in the form of the following directive to the British network leaders:*

1. Comrades must infiltrate into public life, and into all spheres of political activity. Instigating demands for wage increases, better working conditions and the shortening of the working week must be given priority. No suspicions must be aroused that these demands are caused by Communist Party agitation. The pressure should be applied by workmen who have no political affiliations or who are known to be anti-Communists.

2. Comrades whose membership of the Communist Party is secret must infiltrate *every* field of Britain's social life and activities.

3. It is recommended that women members infiltrate the Churches and other religious organisations. The scope for undercover activity in these fields is extensive.

4. Once comrades have infiltrated into the Liberal Party, the Conservative Party, sports organisations and other social institutions, their position must be consolidated. This is best done by other, known, Communist Party members accusing them of being anti-Communist and opposed to the interests of the working class.

5. A comrade who has successfully infiltrated into other organisa-

---

* For the convenience of readers this is a shortened summary of the directive. The original, like all orders issued by the Kremlin, is painfully detailed, and larded with such phrases as 'war-mongering capitalists and lickspittle fascist reactionaries', etc.

tions is forbidden to have any direct contact whatsoever with the Communist Party or any of its members.

6. Comrades who have infiltrated into places giving them access to technical or military information must pass this on to their selected contacts.

7. It is imperative that the class-enemy be discredited. Consideration must be given to what the class-enemy is obliged to do in '*given circumstances*'. Then, when a clear line of action has been decided upon, our activists must forge ahead and commit such acts as the class-enemy would himself commit. For example: A bomb explosion could be caused in an English town or village in such a way that the I.R.A. or some other organisation will be blamed. This will cause the authorities to impose martial law or take other unpopular action.

8. In nuclear research establishments sabotage must be committed whenever possible.

9. Wherever a nuclear establishment is to be built, or is already in the process of construction, the population must be alerted to its dangers and encouraged to demonstrate in protest.

10. *All* activist action is valuable. It can range from sabotage and damage of property to action which has merely nuisance value. The objective is to make the public discontented. This can be brought about by cutting power cables, the dislocation of railways at rush-hours and the interruption of other essential services, and lightning strike action, to inconvenience the public.

This directive could be widely interpreted, as the following examples show.

In September 1958, in the Notting Hill district of London, a neighbourhood with a large coloured population, violent rioting broke out between coloured and white people on a scale which startled the British public.

It must be acknowledged that some whites resent coloured immigrants; but that this could cause bloody rioting seemed unbelievable at the time. For weeks journalists, radio and television commentators, writers and social workers, endeavoured to discover the root cause of these riots. They were mystified. They could find no strong racial hatred of a kind that could lead to such violence, but where there is smoke there must be fire.

It was finally realised there was no fascist or other influence at work. The riots had no *obvious* political basis. The terrorism had been sparked off by young, teenage hooligans whose only motive was to create disturbances. These youths were in those days called 'teddy-boys'. Their modern equivalent might be called 'beatniks', 'drop-outs', 'hippies' or 'skinheads'. They roamed the streets of Notting Hill Gate in gangs, abusing and fighting the coloured people. At West London Magistrates' Court, a number of young hooligans were found guilty of violent behaviour. Police investigations found that the youths had no association with any political party; their violence seemed without motive, apart from an inexplicable desire to 'see a bit of action'.

But a secret Kremlin publication threw more light on the matter:*

> The outstanding success of the British Communist Party's under-cover cadres in initiating widespread fighting between white and coloured people in the London district of Notting Hill Gate and adjacent areas, has deeply disturbed the British nation. Our British undercover cadres have proved that it is possible and practical to obtain excellent results by following the directives issued by In-stitute 631.

Hooligan violence in Notting Hill Gate was not an isolated incident. Encouraged by undercover subverters, teddy-boy gangs roamed the streets of London armed with bicycle chains, knives, axes and knuckle-dusters. The authorities grew increasingly alarmed about gang violence. The police uniform became a despised symbol of law and order, and attacks upon the police increased.

One cold night in December 1958, a fight developed among a gang of young men outside a north London dance hall. A young policeman intervened to restore order, was stabbed in the back and fell to the ground dying. Subsequently Henry Marwood, a young scaffolder, was accused of murdering the police officer. He was found guilty at the Old Bailey in March 1959, and sentenced to death. Marwood was a young

* *Party Bulletin*, Moscow, September 1958.

man with an attractive wife. Sympathy for him was aroused in the neighbourhood where he lived; a reprieve petition was organised and hundreds of signatures obtained. Members of Parliament, clergymen and other respectable and influential personalities were drawn into the issue. The campaign to reprieve Henry Marwood gained strength; it was argued that he was guilty only of manslaughter, and not of murder. But the petition failed and young Marwood was hanged at London's Pentonville Prison. Outside the prison gates and all over the country, protest demonstrations proclaimed that Authority had committed a brutal act of injustice. Injustice always arouses disquiet in a community and the Marwood affair was widely publicised.

The Kremlin's interest in the Marwood affair was revealed in a directive issued by Institute 631 in May 1959.

SECRET!   STRICTLY CONFIDENTIAL!

UNDERCOVER WORK IN THE UNITED KINGDOM

1. Strike tendencies in all branches of industry must be exploited, and strikes precipitated. It is unimportant if the strikes are originated by trade unionists or by undercover subverters. A united effort must be made now to bring about the obstruction of Britain's productivity.

2. The recent Marwood campaign is an excellent example of how demonstrations and petitions against Government decisions can be organised. The aim of all such demonstrations and petitions is to publicise the public's discontent with its government and to spread discontent.

*   *   *

On Saturday the 6th of December 1958 a lunch-hour meeting was held in the market place of Swaffham, a village in Norfolk. It was organised by the Direct Action Committee Against Nuclear War. After the meeting, two hundred demonstrators marched with banners to nearby North Pickenham, where a rocket base for Thor Guided Missiles was under construction, their objective to impede the building of the missile site.

On their arrival at the site, forty-six demonstrators climbed over the barbed-wire fence and staged a sit-down. Officials asked them to leave; they refused. The police were summoned; then the fire brigade was called and hoses were directed against the demonstrators. They still refused to move.

Tension developed. The building workers' livelihood was threatened. A climax was reached when the demonstrators sat down in front of a cement-mixing truck and prevented it working. There were angry words, jostling and finally some vigorous manhandling, during which a number of men and women demonstrators fell into a six-inch deep mixture of mud and wet cement. But the demonstrators, undaunted, still refused to move away, although some had to receive medical treatment. Eventually, police reserves were brought in and the demonstrators were forcibly ejected from the site; but not without many policemen also falling into the mud and wet cement.

The demonstrators were not deterred. They regrouped, built fires to warm themselves throughout the long night, heated soup in tins and maintained a picket line around the area.

The following morning they made another determined assault upon the site. They gained access to a concrete-mixing plant and prevented its use. Some demonstrators climbed onto its roof; a woman climbed inside the mixing-hopper and resisted all the efforts of RAF police to remove her. More demonstrators arrived and lay down across the roadway, preventing the arrival and departure of trucks. Others talked to the workmen, persuading them to down tools.

Moscow sent the following coded acknowledgment of this operation to its undercover-subverters in Britain on the 10th of December:

> The action taken at the Thor Rocket Base shows an excellent understanding of last month's instructions. It is regrettable it was impossible to stop *all* work on the building site, but the publicity has been invaluable. This action has become an impressive nation-wide and international manifestation of the people's determination to halt the nuclear war that is threatening the USSR. More actions of this type must be organised all over Britain.

On the 23rd of December a 'Ban the Rocket Bases' demonstration marched through the streets of London, declaring solidarity with the

Swaffham demonstrators. Before the procession reached Downing Street there were scuffles in Trafalgar Square between the demonstrators and police.

In January 1959, an obstructive demonstration took place on a rocket launching site at an airfield near Watton, Norfolk.

On the 15th of April 1959 the Amalgamated Union of Building Trades Workers told its members not to work on the construction of guided-missiles factories. These factories were to be built for De Havilland Propellers and English Electric at Stevenage, Hertfordshire. Twelve hundred trade union members struck the following day and staged a protest demonstration against the manufacture of nuclear weapons. 'The bourgeois Trade Union of Building Workers in Great Britain bars its members from working on British nuclear factories and requests them to strike and demonstrate in protest against nuclear weapons,' joyfully reported the Soviet Press and Radio on the 16th and 17th of April.

On the 18th of June 1959, at Melton Mowbray in Leicestershire, another rocket building site was occupied by demonstrators. 'We intend to stay here all night,' one demonstrator told a reporter; 'we should have been sleeping in tents, but the police have taken them away from us; fortunately we have blankets; some of us will sleep in cars and others in the fields.'

Nuclear weapons threaten the existence of mankind, and the stopping of war is a praiseworthy human ambition shared by all intelligent men and women, but by infiltrating into organisations opposed to war, Moscow's undercover subverters found rich and fertile fields for exploitation. It should be remembered that while the communists organised obstruction to the building of rocket missile bases in Britain, the men in Moscow were applying pressure to ensure that Soviet rocket missile bases were constructed in the shortest possible time.

*   *   *

Just before President Eisenhower's visit to Britain in 1959, Institute 631 transmitted, on the 18th of August, the following directive in code to the British communities:

In preparation for the American President's visit to England, the following instructions must be passed on to Party District Secretaries, and through them to individual Party cell leaders:

1. Demonstrations, protest meetings and open-air rallies must be organised, protesting against the transfer of American air bases from France to England. The British must resist any attempt to turn their country into a US atom-bomber base.

2. Demonstrations against the manufacture and testing of nuclear weapons must take place in Britain during the President's visit.

3. Leaflets on this subject must flood the country, especially those areas which the President will visit. The use of balloons to scatter leaflets is recommended. Acts of sabotage and violence must be carried out with great care so that the Party cannot be accused of responsibility for them.

4. Official Party policy must be toned down and the importance of friendly relations between the Soviet Union and the USA must be stressed.

At the General Elections following President Eisenhower's visit to Britain, the Macmillan Government received an overwhelming vote. This surprised the Kremlin. Its undercover subversion had been so successful that it had been misled into believing there was widespread opposition to the Conservative government. The Kremlin leaders had to rethink. They decided that more energetic tactics were needed to 'revolutionise the Britishers'. Institute 631 sent another directive in code to London. It arrived four days after the General Elections. The burden of the text was as follows:

SECRET! MUST NOT FALL INTO UNAUTHORISED HANDS!

1. The election results prove that the Party tactics are not flexible in Britain. The excuse that the British people are conservative, and not ripe for revolutionary ideas, does not explain the decline of support for the Communist Party. In future, Party activity must *synchronise* with the work of undercover subverter networks and must create situations that seriously disturb everyday life and bring stress upon the government.

2. The British elections show strong support for the Conservative

Party. Our undercover subverters must infiltrate much deeper into the Conservative Party and set up subversive cells.

3. The trade unions, the Labour Party and other organisations must be infiltrated on a much bigger scale than hitherto. This should be easier now the Labour Party is concerned about regaining political power in parliament.

4. Increased penetration into Churches and other religious organisations is essential. Protests have been received from comrades who believe that church work is a waste of time. This is a deplorable attitude. It cannot be tolerated. Churches are influential and involved with all walks of life. From within the Church organisations our undercover subverters can perform invaluable services for the Party.

5. Industrial obstruction and the instandgation of strikes must never cease. Never forget that a handful of key workers can bring an entire industry to a standstill.

6. There are strong influences in the British Government that are bitterly opposed to Anglo-Soviet friendship. They wish to maintain the 'Cold War'. Discontent and unrest in the community will weaken the power of these men and contribute to Anglo-Soviet friendship.

7. Full and detailed reports on all activities must be reported immediately.

8. There must be no contact whatsoever between any of the comrades, and any officials of the Soviet or other People's Democracies' Consulates and Embassies.

*   *   *

As the British man-in-the-street went about his work, his willingness to live in harmony with his neighbours was aborted by communist subverters who worked like beavers to disrupt industry, law and order, and social life.

5

The Knife in the Back

Only a year prior to his visit to the USA, Nikita Khrushchev told the leaders of the Communist Parties of the world at a secret meeting in the Kremlin:

> It is of vital importance to cripple the armaments industry and all the other important industries of all capitalist enemies. It is of still greater importance to accomplish this within that cradle of aggression—war-hungry America! The Americans are feverishly preparing for war against the peace-loving bloc of the Soviet Union and other People's Democracies . . .

He then referred to directives which had been issued by Institute 631 telling the leaders of the world's communist parties: 'Because the United States of America is our Enemy Number One, even more ruthless action is called for in that country.'

The secret orders to which Khrushchev referred, stated:*
1. The new, flexible and revolutionary strategy must be studied and put into practice at once.
2. The main targets in the United States of America shall be wherever scientists and technicians are engaged upon research and perfection of nuclear weapons. Acts of sabotage must be organised. Such nuclear development work *must* be obstructed and, if possible, brought to a standstill.
3. All armaments factories must receive similar disrupting treatment.
4. As many strikes as possible must sweep through the USA.
5. Whenever a class enemy must be eliminated, it is preferable to employ a professional gangster, instead of the task being undertaken by a comrade. Under no circumstances must the Communist Party

* For the convenience of readers this is a summary of the directive.

be associated with violent crimes. Party propaganda shall specifically condemn all physical violence used for political ends.

Detailed instructions on fermenting disorder, disruption and discontent followed.

*   *   *

Communists tend to believe that anyone who does not agree with them is against them. The fanatical communist often sincerely believes himself surrounded by enemies. When carrying out Institute 631's directive, the elimination of class enemies was practised so vigorously in America that by late summer 1958, Khrushchev was alarmed and tried to apply the brakes. He ordered Institute 631 to transmit the following coded warning to the US comrades:

> America is notorious for the number of killings that occur every year. But there must be reason in all things! Elimination of class enemies may occur only in cases of extreme urgency!
> Reports indicate some comrades have formed strong alliances with the bosses of dangerous gangster organisations. This must cease! Comrades must not think in the *rubbing-out* terms of gangsters. Also, such men must not be given the opportunity to blackmail our comrades . . .

But the rubbing-out of class enemies continued despite this warning, and three months later Suslov was obliged to issue a sterner warning:
'Despite orders to discontinue alliances with gangsters, some comrades have disobeyed. Anyone discovered disobeying this order in future will be expelled from the Party.'
And a secret Kremlin publication had this to say:*

> The decision of the District Party Secretary in Chicago to employ professional killers to deal with those who make it their business to investigate the activities of undercover comrades, was doubtless right. No other steps could have been effectively taken to safeguard the work of the undercover comrades in question. But the amounts paid to the hoodlums for their services were excessive. This comment

* The *Party Bulletin*, Moscow, October 1958.

applies equally to the expenditure of the District Party Secretariat in Boston and New York . . .

On the industrial front there was equally vigorous compliance with the Institute 631's orders.

At the end of September 1958 a paralysing strike broke out at Fords, organised by the United Automobile Workers' Union. A week later, a new wage agreement was being sought by the workers at Chrysler. On the 2nd of October 1958 a quarter of a million employees at General Motors downed their tools.

A man who is praised for his efforts works with increased enthusiasm. The Kremlin leaders know this and give praise when it is justified:*

'Our American undercover comrades concentrated their efforts upon those key products which are vital to keep factories operating. The walk-out of 7,100 Chrysler key workers ensured that the other 33,000 workers were brought to a standstill. This is an excellent lesson for comrades to learn . . .'

* * *

The posthumous mud-slinging campaign against Stalin seemed to remove the barrier to East–West friendship. Nikita Khrushchev, the Head of the Soviet State, told the Russian people and the Western world that Stalin's realm had suffered a reign of terror. He said the dead dictator had instigated a cult of hero-worship and set himself up as a 'God'; he had suffered persecution mania and subjected the people of the Soviet Union to the tyranny of secret police executioners; not only had he falsely accused his friends and comrades of plotting against him, he had also falsely accused them of crimes against the State; he had fabricated reasons to remove them from positions of political influence, and imprisoned or executed them.

This open acknowledgement by the Kremlin leader of the evils of the past seemed to promise improved relations—even, perhaps, the end of the Cold War. These hopes were accelerated when Khrushchev announced that his purpose in visiting the USA in 1959 was 'to encourage friendly relations between the Soviet Union and America,

* The *Party Bulletin*, Moscow, October 1958.

and demonstrate that peaceful coexistence is not only possible, but necessary'.

The great dictator Stalin had never dared set foot in the West, where he was beyond the protection provided by his own private army of secret police. The fact that the new head of the Soviet Union was willing to travel to the United States was a grand gesture of trust and friendship.

The McCarthy era had bred distrust of communists in the USA. Khrushchev knew he would have to face a luke-warm American reception. To offset this, he planned a propaganda coup. Soviet scientists launched *Lunik II* on the 12th of September—just three days before Khrushchev's departure for New York. *Lunik II* landed on the Moon exactly where the Russians predicted.

Before his departure to the USA Khrushchev told his Kremlin Inner Circle comrades:

I am convinced Mr Ike will think twice before he continues his aggressive warmongering policy against us. He and his trigger-happy generals know that if we can send *Luniks* to the Moon we can hit any target on this world with accuracy, using short-range, medium-range or intercontinental rockets.

Let us drink to our research workers. They are the people behind the scenes who have helped to avert another murderous war. I will talk a great deal about our strength in America. I will make it clear we can destroy the capitalist world before it has a chance to attack us. But I will also make it clear we want peace, peace, peace!

War does not get anyone anywhere. It destroys what has been achieved. When we are the leading power in the field of guided missiles, and when we have more than enough of everything to wipe any enemy off the face of the Earth, we must not overlook the fact that nuclear weapons are boomerangs. Radioactive fall-out is so dangerous that even if the Western Powers never get a chance to fire a single H-bomb, the radioactive fall-out from our own bombs can devastate whole countries . . . Everything must therefore be done to avert a nuclear war. For armed confrontation we must substitute organised, large-scale undercover warfare . . .!

Nikita Khrushchev, when seen on television, was a stocky, fun-loving man with a twinkle in his eye. He was intelligent and played the role of a great humanitarian. He had the heart of a clown and showed contempt for stiffnecked traditions. Wherever he went in America, he won the goodwill of the people. The whistle-stop election campaigners of the USA learned a great deal from this happy, ever-smiling, man who was always ready with a quip to delight journalists, and radio and television commentators. At the United Nations Assembly he had once gained notoriety by kicking off a pair of pain-fully new shoes and placing his stockinged feet upon his desk. He'd earned the approval of all working men who like to kick off their shoes comfortably at home after a hard day's work. Now he shook hands with factory workers, kissed babies and flattered wives as en-thusiastically as any Presidential candidate.

Khrushchev's mission of goodwill produced a number of highlights worthy of recording. At a dinner given by the *Journal of Commerce*, he said the impression he'd gained from his tour of the United States was:

'The American people are peace-loving; it remains to be seen whether the American Government also is!' Later, when discussing trade relations between the two countries, he said, solemn-faced: 'We want to trade with you because we believe trade is a litmus paper which indicates whether you want to live in peace with us.' He added piously: 'May God give us strength to solve our problems with reason, instead of with force. That is what the people expect from us.'

President Eisenhower was disturbed by hostile demonstrations to-wards Khrushchev during his visit. The American President had no wish to endanger goodwill between the two countries, and he gave discreet orders for less baiting of the Soviet leader and more con-ciliation. Khrushchev responded to this butter as a cat responds to cream.

'You magicians of charm—you captivating charmers, my true and loved friends,' he said when he addressed his audience in San Fran-cisco. 'I hope that friendship between the United States and the Soviet Union will be as bright and inextinguishable as the southern sun of California.'

'Let's quit talking about the things which divide us and concentrate on things which unite us,' said one American speaker. The sentiment warmed Khrushchev. He leaned over backwards to find common ground for friendship.

'There is much in common between the Sermon on the Mount and communism,' he preached. 'We have absorbed many of Christ's precepts—Love for one's neighbour, for example. We want no enmity among men; we want complete equality, as preached by Christ. We wage the struggle for a communist society without recourse to arms; we use only words. As for those who differ from us, we always respect their opinion.'

When he was presented with a gavel made from the wood of one of California's famous Redwood trees, Khrushchev said:

I will use it for the first time when I strike it, in triumph, on the table, the day we sign a Pact of Non-Aggression and Eternal Love between the Soviet Union and America; and a second time when we sign a Treaty of Disarmament with all the nations of the world. I await with impatience my talks with your President, hoping that our two hearts will be prompted to reach agreement and establish conditions of peace and friendship.

In an off-the-cuff kerbside interview with American reporters outside his hotel in Iowa, Khrushchev said:

'It is much better to talk man to man than exchange distant messages which are not always friendly in tone. Man-to-man talks are the best. Nothing can replace them. One conversation between Heads of State is better than a hundred cables . . .'

Nikita Khrushchev and President Eisenhower conferred in secret. Afterwards, a communiqué was issued: 'We have agreed that outstanding international problems should be settled not by the use of force, but by peaceful means through negotiations.' The communiqué called for a better understanding between the Soviet Union and the United States, and the achievement of a just and lasting peace.

By the time he left the United States, Khrushchev had succeeded in winning the hearts of a great many people, as a person. He attained more popularity than many American politicians could ever hope to win. He left behind the impression of a jolly, warm-hearted man, and

the hope of a thaw in the Cold War between East and West seemed
justified.

*   *   *

The American communists sighed with relief when Khrushchev's aircraft took off for Moscow. They had not rested since the Soviet leader
had set foot on US soil. They had followed out long and painfully
detailed orders issued by the Institute 631; some of these directives are
summarised here:

1. Comrade Khrushchev's visit to America *must* be a success. He
must take America by storm. The following instructions must be
regarded as the most important ever given. They must be complied
with obediently, persistently and ruthlessly.

2. All hostile demonstrations against Comrade Khrushchev *must*
fail.

3. The American security forces are anti-Soviet. They will protect
Comrade Khrushchev *without* enthusiasm. Therefore the Party must
provide its own security measures. Squads of loyal communists
must be formed to act as an additional bodyguard. Training and
exercising must begin at once.

4. A great welcome must be prepared for Comrade Khrushchev.
Open-air rallies, mass meetings and demonstrations must be held in
all the cities and towns that Comrade Khrushchev visits. Resolutions
shall demand American-Soviet friendship, an end to the 'Cold War'
and the banning of nuclear warfare.

5. While a campaign is waged for disarmament, it must also be
stressed that the Soviet Union's rate of armament production is
vastly superior to America's.

Khrushchev and the American communists had worked hard for
friendship and goodwill between the Soviet Union and the United
States.

How sincere was the Soviet leader and his Kremlin comrades?

*   *   *

After Nikita Khrushchev's return from the US not one change was
made in the undercover activities employed against America. The

following is a summary of a secret Institute 631 directive received by the American undercover subverter leaders as the New Year of 1960 dawned:

1. Comrades working in telegraph, teleprinter and telephone services must organise an effective monitoring system to intercept important communications, and enable the Party to learn what is going on inside the US government, the security forces, industry, and in all other important establishments of the USA. Such information must be passed on through already established links to undercover network leaders. It is vitally important that they shall make *no* communication whatsoever direct to Communist Party Headquarters or Secretariats.

2. Comrades working in armament factories or in nuclear establishments must memorise all charts, blueprints, production lists, etc., that they come upon through their employment. If it is possible to photograph such documents without risk of detection, this is preferable.

3. Comrades must make a determined effort to infiltrate into all sections of the US Armed Forces. The American GI is not a stubborn militarist. In most instances he prefers comfort and peace to the dangers and hardships of war. He should be converted to a determined opponent of war between the United States and the Soviet Union. Special pressure must be applied upon units connected with the launching of space rockets. Acts of sabotage at nuclear missile bases are invaluable. If the well-publicised launching of a space rocket results in failure, this is of tremendous propaganda value.

4. In addition to the above special tasks, everyday life in all parts of the USA must be disrupted as often, and as effectively, as possible. Every opportunity must be taken to create disturbances. Racial riots are the most easily provoked disorders. If they are brought about in a way which makes it seem that the ruling class has precipitated the riots, this is valuable propaganda. But activity should not be concentrated solely upon racial riots. *Every* opportunity must be seized to disrupt the peaceful flow of everyday life. The class enemy must be discredited, hit often, and where it hurts most.

A secret Kremlin report shows Institute 631's official acknowledgment of the work performed by American undercover-subverters:*

> The mass demonstrations in support of peaceful coexistence between the Soviet Union and the rest of the world, which took place in Chicago, and which ended in fierce clashes between the police and large numbers of demonstrators, is a remarkable example of how American undercover comrades are able to convince non-political citizens that if they do not want to risk their cities being destroyed in a war against the USSR by Soviet nuclear bombs and guided missiles, they must demonstrate their opposition to war.

And another *Party Bulletin* account proudly announced:

> Due to the excellent work of our undercover comrades in the American steel industry, 12,000 steel workers at the Pittsburg plant of the Jones & Laughlin Steel Corporation, the third largest of the nation's steel producers, walked out on strike. The final shut-down of this important steel plant came twenty-four hours after the Corporation had been forced to close down a battery of open-hearth furnaces because the men employed on them had left their jobs.

> This strike, however, was only a beginning. Later, a confrontation between the American steel workers and the mighty steel tycoons came when 450,000 steel workers stopped production and drastically cut off ninety per cent of US steel production. Within forty-eight hours tens of thousands of workers in other industries connected with steel production—railways and river barges, coal mines and the trucking industry—were laid off.

While Khrushchev preached peace and goodwill to America, Mikhail Suslov's Institute 631 undercover subverters were working like beavers throughout the United States to cause economic disruption and social despair.

* The *Party Bulletin*, Moscow, February 1960.

6

Undercover Subverters Everywhere

America and Britain are the Kremlin's major potential targets. But because West Germany occupies a very important strategic position in world affairs, it is also subjected to intense Red undercover activity. Any weakening of the Bonn Government automatically increases the relative strength of East Germany and hence that of the Soviet bloc.

West Germany is extremely vulnerable to infiltration. Undercover subverters, trained in East Germany and aided by East German border guards, find it easy to slip under the Iron Curtain. The activities of these undercover subverters are more violent than in Britain and the United States of America. The pre-war atmosphere of Germany encouraged political violence. Before the rise of Hitler, members of the German Communist Party and the Nazi Party frequently clashed in violent street fighting, armed with truncheons, knives and pistols. As Hitler's party gained political strength the communists were hounded, imprisoned and executed. Physical violence was a political way of life and the Second World War intensified its savageness. The Red undercover subverters in West Germany unhesitatingly murder to gain a political advantage. Influential men in power who oppose communism and the Soviet Union are taken at night, beaten close to death or assassinated, and left in dark alleyways. The victims are coldbloodedly selected, their movements studied and attacks upon them carried out with military precision. These methods were used by the German Communist Party during Hitler's Third Reich, when especially vicious Nazi stormtroopers were singled out for execution. These methods are still used today. *Anybody* in West Germany who obstructs the communists can fall victim to political gangsterism: a police officer thought to be too repressive in maintaining peace and order; a Town Council secretary who withholds permission for an assembly hall to be used for a political meeting; a factory foreman who favours the management against the workmen; or even a stubborn workman who resists being stampeded into a wildcat strike.

West Germany is a rich sea of red herrings. The Allied Powers are as wary of the growth of neo-Nazism as is the Soviet Union. It is always possible to arouse alarm by crying 'Nazi!' Almost any security measure adopted by the Bonn Government can be challenged by well-disguised Red undercover subverters as 'leaving the way open for a re-emergence of Fascism'.

A continuous stream of East German refugees flood into West Germany. Most are genuine, but many are undercover subverters who mingle with the true refugees and are accepted by them. They learn which refugees are politically undesirable to the Soviet Union, learn the names and addresses of their nearest relatives and pass back the information to Moscow. Many genuine refugees are blackmailed into undercover subversion inside West Germany because their relatives in East Germany are held as hostages. Some refugees who possess knowledge important to the Kremlin are kidnapped by undercover subverters and transported back into East Germany by various means. Not infrequently the Kremlin decides that a particular refugee must be liquidated. Such assassinations are camouflaged so that it seems the victim met his death by accident.

The secret Kremlin publication made this startling reference to communist kidnapping activities in West Germany:*

The excellent work of the Transport Department of the German Undercover Network deserves particular praise for its efficient and methodical action. We must give thanks to these comrades that certain elements who were dangerous and obstructive to the Soviet Union could be torn free from the West German fascist stronghold, and returned to those People's Democracies interested in them. These people thought they were perfectly safe in the midst of West Germany . . .

The *Party Bulletin* continued further on:

Accordingly, dangerous troublemakers were thus silenced. On the other hand, those people who could be of importance to the Soviet

* The *Party Bulletin*, Moscow, September 1958.

Union's scientific, or technical research development, and who had stubbornly refused to work in the USSR, <u>were persuaded to change their minds</u> and take an active part in research. Thus they ultimately served the cause of lasting world peace and friendship between all the peoples of the world . . .

*   *   *

Each country has its own way of life. Institute 631 took this into consideration when issuing orders to undercover subverter network leaders. How completely this was done can be gauged from the following directive, issued to the local network when <u>the Soviet Union tried to bring the whole of Berlin under Russian domination</u>:

STRICTLY CONFIDENTIAL   MEMORISE, THEN BURN

Each member of a Party cell and undercover network must be in constant readiness. The following instructions must be obeyed to the letter:

An immediate propaganda campaign is to be set into motion. Workshops, tenement blocks, stores and all other suitable places must be converted into centres of propaganda.

The population must be convinced that West Berlin must be freed from foreign occupation troops.

On no account must it be suspected that the Party is behind this action.

All available comrades are to be assigned to Stormtroops, and <u>must be ready for combat operations.</u>

Key workers in industry, the railways, postal services and other sectors of public life must be ready to act in accordance with the instructions they are given.

<u>It is imperative that every comrade knows exactly what is to be destroyed in order to paralyse public life in his sector.</u>

Combat action shall take place *only* when orders have been issued by the Central Committee. Such instructions will be given by the use of the following passwords:

Tuesday: Mass demonstrations.

March: Strikes.

October: Sabotage leading to the paralysis of industry and
           public life.
Friday: Riots in the streets.

Combat action will take place only when cell and network
leaders receive the password direct from the district Organisation
Leader.

The above instructions are for Organisation and Political Leaders
only. They *must not* be passed on to comrades in the cells and networks.

Not all the comrades obeyed the instruction to burn this treacherous
directive. Copies of the document fell into the hands of Western
counter-intelligence, and security measures were adopted which
robbed the plot of its sting. At a subsequent election, when West
Berliners were given the opportunity to choose between Allied occupation and the 'Free Berlin' desired by the Kremlin, they gave a clear-
cut decision. Ninety-eight per cent voted for continuation of the Allied
occupation of Berlin.

Institute 631 therefore decided that it must change its tactics in West
Germany and focus its activities upon discrediting the Allied armies.
In March 1959 a secret directive, 'Instructions Berlin', set out a pattern
of political activity for Communist subverters. This is a summary of
the directive:

1. It must be shown by propaganda that the Western forces in
Berlin are kept there for the purpose of using the city for espionage
against the Soviet Union. Berlin is a jumping-off ground for Allied
spies, saboteurs and wreckers who smuggle themselves into the
German Democratic Republic. Undercover subverters must induce
all ranks of the US Armed Forces, as well as civilians, to cross the
border into the German Democratic Republic, then advise the
authorities so that they can arrest them and prove their espionage
activities.

2. Women comrades are useful for the following work: attractive
women can easily persuade love-hungry Americans to accompany
them. But no attempt should be made to persuade GIs to cross the
border at the first two or three meetings. Only when confidence has

been established should an American be persuaded to cross the border for sightseeing or other purposes.

3. If the American cannot be persuaded to cross the border, he should be encouraged to accompany the woman to an apartment where a reception is prepared. When the woman screams, her friends will run to her assistance. Most Americans, when accused of rape, wish to avoid being involved with the police. They will usually compromise and pass on information of a military nature. Their written agreement to do this turns them into proven traitors. The threat of disclosing this written agreement to their Army Headquarters enmeshes them even deeper. They can be led on to ever greater indiscretions. If their resistance finally hardens, a full report of all their indiscretions can be lodged with their superior officers. This serves the purpose of discrediting American soldiers.

4. When a woman has gained the confidence of an American soldier who cannot be induced to compromise himself, arrangements can be made to transport him across the border. The woman will persuade him to dine in a restaurant of her choosing, where his drink will be doped. A car will be waiting outside the restaurant when he is led out. Care must be taken to ensure that the American leaves the restaurant *before* he becomes unconscious. Most Americans habitually get drunk, and no suspicions will be aroused if he is unsteady on his feet. It must be remembered that when the American is arrested in the People's Democratic Republic, the US authorities will try to prove he was drugged, kidnapped, and carried across the border.

5. Prepared incriminating documents can be placed in an American soldier's pocket and be discovered by our undercover subverter. She can accuse the soldier of being a spy and threaten to inform the authorities. This threat should ensure his cooperation. He must be persuaded to handle these documents so that his fingerprints are on them.

6. The use of violence is to be avoided, except when specific instructions are given. The US Army has warned all soldiers to be on their guard against attractive German women. Nevertheless there are many soldiers and civilians who disregard these orders.

!!! STRENG VERTRAULICH !!!

AUSWENDIG LERNEN   DANN VERBRENNEN

Um aufzuzeigen,daß die Westmächte aus dem einzig und alleinigen Grund in Berlin bleiben wollen,um Berlin als ihren Ausgangspunkt für Spionage in der Sowjet Union zu benützen,um von Berlin Saboteure and Schädlinge in die Deutsche Demokratische Republik,und von dort in die anderen Länder der Volksdemokratien zu schicken,ist es unbedingt notwendig Beweise hierüber beizubringen. Unsere Tarnkader müssen demzufolge ihr Möglichstes tun,Angehörige aller Ränke der amerikanischen Wehrmacht und amerikanische Zivilpersonen in vorzugsweise wichtigen Stellungen,zu bewegen die Grenze in die Deutsche Demokratische Republik zu überschreiten,denn dies ermöglicht den Behörden zu beweisen,daß diese Leute ausschließlich zwecks Spionage u.s.w.über die Grenze schlüpfen.

1.

Obwohl sowohl Genossen,als auch Genossinnen,diese Arbeit auszuführen haben, fällt es hübschen Genossinnen natürlich leichter liebesdurstige Amerikaner zu überreden auf ihre Pläne einzugehen. Trotz der Tatsache,daß keine kostbare Zeit verloren werden darf,ist es dennoch wichtig auf keinen Fall während des ersten oder zweiten Zusammentreffens auf ein Überschreiten der Grenze anzuspielen,da ein derartig unbedachter Vorgang möglicherweise Verdacht erwecken könnte. Persönliche Weitsichtigkeit muß in jeder Hinsicht walten und erst wenn die betreffende Genossin wirklich davon überzeugt ist,daß ihr der Amerikaner voll und ganz vertraut,darf eine Einladung für einen Rundschauausflug über die Grenze gemacht werden.

2.

Falls irgendeine der vorerwähnten Arten fehlschlägt,müssen die „Freundinnen" alles dransetzen ihre Amerikaner zu überreden in ihre Wohnungen (oder andere geeignete abgeschlossene Orte) mit-

dann beschuldigt wird versucht zu haben das Mädchen zu vergewaltigen oder sogar zu ermorden,und wenn man ihm droht ihn der Polizei auszuhändigen,falls er nicht gewillt ist mitzuarbeiten,werden sich die meisten von ihnen bereit erklären vertrauliche Nachrichten preiszugeben, und werden allmählich zu brauchbaren Werkzeugen unserer Bewegung werden, vorausgesetzt natürlich,daß sämtliche notwendigen Vorsichtsmaßregeln,die in Lehrgang „Werbung von Angebern" aufgezeigt wurden,angewendet worden sind. Falls das Opfer jedoch unerwartet auf die Vorschläge nicht eingeht,ist es ratsam die Polizei zu rufen und den Amerikaner in allem Ernst mit versuchter Vergewaltigung,Mord,oder ähnlichen Gewalttaten anzuklagen. Obwohl dieser Vorgang unserer Bewegung nicht hilft,trägt er dennoch zu dem schlechten Ruf,den die Amerikaner allgemein haben,bei. Und deren möglicherweise Enthüllung,daß sie in eine Falle gelockt wurden,um gezwungen zu werden als Spitzel zu arbeiten,dürfte nurmehr als eine gute Verteidigungsgeschichte betrachtet werden,hauptsächlich deshalb da es allgemein bekannt ist wie sich Amerikaner benehmen wenn sie mit einer Frau allein sind.

3.

Falls der Amerikaner ablehnt in eine Privatwohnung (oder einen anderen geeigneten abgeschlossenen Ort) zu gehen,müssen alle Anstrengungen gemacht werden ihn in ein Restaurant oder ein anderes Vergnügungslokal zu locken,wo es möglich ist unbeachtet Betäubungsmittel in sein Getränk zu mischen. Gleichzeitig müssen natürlich auch notwendige Maßnahmen getroffen werden erforderliche Transportmittel bereit zu haben,um den betäubten Mann unbehelligt über die Grenze zu bringen. Allergrößte Vorsicht muß hierbei jedoch gewahrt werden,und man muß vollkommen sicher sein,daß sich niemand dessen bewusst sein kann,daß ein betäub-

Photograph of a top-secret directive sent to Moscow's undercover-networ

zukommen. Bevor dies jedoch getan wer=
den kann,müssen alle notwendigen Vor=
sichtsmaßregeln getroffen werden,um si=
cherzustellen,daß Genossen bereit sind,
die darauf warten sofort hereinzustür=
zen wenn das betreffende Mädchen plötz=
lich um Hilfe ruft. Wenn der Amerikaner
falls jedoch kein Anhaltspunkt hinter=
lassen wurde,ist es für sie unmöglich
zu beweisen,daß er die Grenze nicht
freiwillig überschritt.

4.

Falls es sich herausstellt,daß der be=
treffende Mann nichts trinken will,und
daß es somit unmöglich ist den vorer=
wähnten Plan zu verwirklichen,können
„verräterische Schriftstücke",die von
der Abteilung für Taktische Strategie
erhältlich sind,geschickt in seine Ta=
sche geschlüpft werden. Unsere diesbe=
zügliche Genossin kann dann „ganz zu=
fällig" herausfinden,daß ihr Begleiter
ein „Spitzel" ist und kann ihm leicht
drohen ihn von der Polizei verhaften
zu lassen,falls er nicht bereit ist zu=
sammenzuarbeiten. Ein solcher Schach=
zug muß jedoch überaus sorgfältig vor=
bereitet werden und „vertrauenserwek=
kende Zeugen" müssen handlungsbereit
sein,um der Polizei mit genügendem Be=
weismaterial versehen zu können,falls
der Amerikaner ablehnt zusammenzuarbei=
ten. Alles erdenkliche muß getan werden
um sicherzustellen,daß Fingerabdrücke
des Betreffenden auf dem Schriftstück
vorfindbar sind,und hierbei sollen
ebenfalls die mannigfaltigen Anwen=
dungsarten des Lehrganges „Werbung von
Angebern" angewendet werden.

5.

Gewalttätigkeiten sollen unter allen
Umständen vermieden werden. In beson=
deren Fällen mag es jedoch unumgänglich
sein einen Amerikaner zu knüppeln und
ihn dann besinnungslos über die Grenze
zu transportieren;aber es soll nur
dann getan werden,wenn es besonders

ter Mann abtransportiert wurde;der Ein=
druck muß auf jeden Fall erweckt werden,
daß er sinnlos betrunken ist. Diese Vor=
sichtsmaßregel ist überaus wichtig,da
hiermit vermieden wird,daß die amerika=
nischen Behörden irgendwie herausfinden
könnten,daß der Mann entführt wurde;
wichtig ist,und wenn alle anderen Mit=
tel fehlschlugen. Obwohl es bekannt
ist,daß das amerikanische Oberkommando
seinen Leuten genaue Anweisungen gege=
ben hat auf die selbst verführerisch=
sten Freundschaften mit deutschen Frau=
en nicht hereinzufallen,und vor allem,
darauf zu achten,die Grenze in die
Deutsche Demokratische Republik unter
keinen Umständen zu überschreiten,sind
dennoch immer noch genügend Soldaten
und Zivilpersonen bereit-keine Notiz von
diesen Warnungen zu nehmen,falls diese
Leute richtig angegangen werden.

6.

Gleichgültig ob Nachrichten,die Amerika=
ner preisgaben,nur allgemeinwichtig sind
oder ob sie sich auf das Alltagsleben im
amerikanischen Lager beziehen,müssen sie
sofort an die Abteilung für Taktische
Strategie weitergeleitet werden. Die Ab=
teilung benötigt diese Angaben dringend
für ihre Arbeit,da sie ihr ermöglichen
genau festzustellen was bei den Amerika=
nern vor sich geht. Wenn möglich,sollen
Photographien von Amerikanern mit deut=
schen Frauen geknipst werden;die wert=
vollsten Bilder sind die,die darauf hin=
schließen lassen,daß diese Pärchen intim
miteinander sind. Diese Photographien
sind hauptsächlich dann von größter
Wichtigkeit,falls der betreffende Ameri=
kaner verheiratet ist.

Die vorerwähnten Anordnungen müssen in
weitgehendstem Maße in die Tat umgesetzt
werden und müssen unverzüglich in Arbeit
genommen werden. Es muß jedoch wieder=
holt werden,daß nur die fähigsten und
erfahrensten Tarnkader Genossen für die=
se Tätigkeit ausgewählt werden dürfen.

!!!STRENG VERTRAULICH!!!
AUSWENDIG LERNEN DANN VERBRENNEN

activists in West Berlin. A summary of this directive is on pages 44, 45, 48.

7. Any information relating to American camps, military headquarters or troops movements must be reported in detail. When
possible, photographs of Americans with German women should be
obtained, preferably showing them embracing intimately. These
photographs are of great value if the American soldier is already
married . . .

Confronted with this planned assault upon their natural weaknesses,
many young American soldiers found themselves in difficulties with
superior officers, and the West Berlin authorities. Many young American soldiers woke up with a splitting headache in a prison cell in East
Germany, charged with espionage or sabotage.

A secret Kremlin publication reported a typical case:*

Corporal Brooke and Private Allerson disappeared from Berlin on
the 7th of May 1959. Both men were vamped into a trap by their
German girlfriends. They found themselves accused by angry friends
of their girlfriends, of attempted rape and murder. Both men agreed
to cooperate with the Germans rather than be handed over to the
West Berlin police. They were instructed to obtain various types of
information and they cooperated.

Before long it was learned that the two soldiers had come under
suspicion. It was feared they would be arrested by Allied counter-
intelligence and interrogated. To forestall any cross-examination
which might induce the soldiers to betray their Communist contacts, the two young men were brought over the border into East
Germany. Both men signed a request for political asylum, and that
was the last their authorities knew of them.

A more imaginative method was devised to lure Allied pilots into
communist territory. Radio Guidance Posts transmitted radio signals to
assist a pilot to check his bearings. The radio guidance posts in communist territory were manipulated to give false signals and lured
Allied pilots over Soviet territory. Waiting Red Air Force fighters then
scrambled and forced the disorientated Allied pilots down; they were
then accused of flying over Soviet territory to take aerial photographs,

* The *Party Bulletin*, Moscow, June 1959.

or drop saboteurs and spies. A substantial number of Allied pilots were caught in this trap before an Allied control tower picked up one of these false signals. Nowadays all communist radio guidance posts are continuously monitored by the West and pilots instantly warned if they are heading into trouble. Nevertheless, some pilots are still trapped by false signals which have not been detected by the monitoring stations, and are lured into Soviet territory. Fortunately these occurrences are rare.

* * *

Institute 631 has encouraged the use of physical violence in West Germany.

Radio Free Europe is an American-financed, anti-communist broadcasting station, operating in Munich. It has its own staff cafeteria. In November 1959 the management called in the police and invited them to inspect the salt-cellars on the cafeteria tables. The police took them away for laboratory analysis. They had been filled with atropine.* If this had not been discovered it could have poisoned many of the radio station's staff.

Mr Eric Hazelhoff, the European Director of Radio Free Europe, had received a timely tip-off about the murder attempt. Such tip-offs were not unusual, since some men and women found it profitable to be double agents, working simultaneously for the Americans and the Russians.

Shortly afterwards, an attempt was made to blow up the radio station. Another friendly tip-off and a search of the building revealed a time-bomb that could have destroyed the building and killed its staff.

Institute 631 issued the following reproachful directive to their undercover subverters about these two abortive attempts at violence:

> Our undercover subverters are to be commended for their attempt to silence the fanatical communist-haters who operate Radio Free Europe. But it was criminal negligence to permit an easily identifiable communist to fill the salt-cellars with atropine. This task should have been performed by a man or woman who could not possibly be suspected of having any contact with the Party.

* Deadly Nightshade.

This grave tactical mistake was repeated by the known Communist Party members who prepared and later installed a bomb in the building.

FAILURE TO FOLLOW INSTRUCTIONS HAS BROUGHT THE PARTY INTO DISCREDIT. MORE FAILURES OF THIS TYPE CAN DO IRREPARABLE DAMAGE TO THE PARTY AND THE SOVIET UNION.

*   *   *

Following up a wave of strikes that paralysed industry throughout Belgium, Institute 631 gambled on what it believed was a revolutionary situation. Orders to 'adopt the strongest measures' were sent out to communist undercover subverters.

Once again a double-agent tipped off the Allied authorities in time. The Belgian police swooped on selected pit-strikers' homes near Mons, the heart of the trouble area. Enough arms, ammunition and explosives were found to support an armed uprising.

Mikhail Suslov fleetingly mentioned the Belgian failure at the same time as he gave the following general report on Institute 631's successful activities throughout the world:*

During winter 1958–1959 our undercover subverters in Australia, the Benelux countries, Canada, Cuba, France, Great Britain, India, Italy, Japan, Nyasaland, Pakistan, Rhodesia, Scandinavia, North and South Africa, West Germany, the United States of America and other Capitalist countries throughout the world, managed to stop vital production by:

1. Calling the workers out on strike.
2. Causing rioting and armed clashes with the police following demonstrations.
3. Dislocating traffic and transport.
4. Derailing trains.
5. Damaging bridges and roadways.
6. Blocking waterways.
7. Starting fires in key factories and warehouses.

* The *Party Bulletin*, Moscow, March 1959.

8. <u>Practising revolutionary acts</u> which cause the class enemy serious economic problems.

Institute 631's determination to wage aggressive undercover warfare against the Western democracies was clearly expressed in the following report:*

It is evident that an early showdown between the Soviet Union and the Western Powers is inevitable. Therefore every precaution must be taken to support the struggle of our Party and its secret undercover subverters in their work within the countries of the Capitalist World.

Our undercover subverter network leaders will be reinforced by our Division for Tactical Strategy, which will be behind our comrades abroad, and support them at all times.

It is vitally important that close contact is maintained between the Division for Tactical Strategy and all our undercover subverters.

It is vitally important that communications are made only through one individual contact, and with the use of the Party Code.

Any class enemy who is a danger to the Party and its undercover subverters' networks and to the Soviet Union must be reported. He will be dealt with by the KGB.

* The *Party Bulletin*, Moscow, August 1959.

7

Expert Forgers

Institute 631 set up a department to specialise in forgery. Unlimited funds were provided, and in spacious premises in Pankow*, experts installed expensively-equipped photographic studios, laboratories, printing shops and even a paper mill. During the 1950s, this factory was able to supply Institute 631 and the Soviet secret service with all the falsified identification and other documents they required. The expert forgeries that have issued from Pankow have caused the West enormous problems.

Mein Liebster

Endlich kann ich Dir heute den versprochenen Brief senden. Ich habe mir schon Vorwürfe gemacht, weil ich Dich so lange warten ließ. Unser letztes Zusammensein war so schön, ich kann es gar nicht vergessen.

Ob Deine Frau etwas gemerkt hat? Ich grüble darüber nach. — Du hast mich ganz verändert und trägst allein die Schuld. Ich fühle mich seit ein paar Tagen nicht recht wohl. Ob Du eine Dummheit gemacht hast? Wenn es so ist, bitte ich Deine Frau, Dich freizugeben, denn Du sagtest mir doch, daß Eure Liebe weit (nicht) hof sei.

Sehen wir uns bald wieder, Liebster? Ich hoffe es und erwarte Dich wie immer. — Lasse mich nicht umsonst warten.

Deine Dich liebende,

Inge

Komme bald !!!

Photograph of an actual Perfumed Love Letter.

In their efforts to make life uncomfortable in all ways for the Western democracies these forgers have practised many ingenious hoaxes. The most bizarre is known as Operation Perfumed Love Letters, and the armed forces of West Germany were its first victims.

* Pankow is a district of East Berlin in the closely guarded Soviet Sector. The area is cordoned off and patrolled by KGB officers. The headquarters of the Division for Tactical Strategy in Moscow are Pankow's head office.

The forgers first obtained the names and addresses of all married officers and men serving in the West German army. Then women were employed to write hundreds of love letters on perfumed notepaper. These love letters, carefully phrased, divulged that intimacy existed between the female writer and the male recipient of the letter. The letters usually referred to a baby that was on the way and expressed delight that the recipient of the letter had agreed to divorce his wife.

These letters were mailed so that they would arrive at soldiers' homes when they were absent on duty. The wives' suspicions were aroused by

Wehrbezirkskommando Essen V.

Wehrstammrolle 08/15 56

Tag der Ausstellung 1. April 1956

Einberufungsbefehl

Gleichzeitig gültig als Fahrausweis III. Klasse auf der Bundesbahn

Nach Bundeswehrdienstgesetz vom 15. März 1956 §§ 3 und 4, Absatz 1 und 2 haben Sie sich am ...15. Juli... ...1956 bis spätestens ...10.. Uhr, bei NATO-Regiment I (zbV.) in Andernach; Theo-Blank-Kaserne; Mac Cloy-Straße 100 zur Ableistung Ihrer Wehrpflicht zu stellen

Mitzubringen sind:
1. Einberufungsbefehl und Wehrpaß.
2. Alte Wehrmachtspapiere und Auszeichnungen, die sofort auf der Schreibstube abzugeben sind.
3. Eine Bescheinigung des Arbeitgebers, daß das Arbeitsverhältnis, bezw. der Lehrvertrag unwiderruflich gekündigt ist.

Wir erwarten, daß Sie Ihrer Einberufung pünktlich Folge leisten. Der Aufbau der Wehrmacht ist ernsthaft gefährdet, da sich ein großer Teil Wehrpflichtiger der Einberufung entzog und sich in die Deutsche Demokratische Republik begab, weil es dort keine Wehrpflicht gibt und Schutz vor Verfolgung durch die Organe der Bundesrepublik gewährt wird!

Bill Wolter
Colonel
Unterschrift und Dienstgrad

Matzky
Oberst
Unterschrift und Dienstgrad

Photograph of forged Call-up Order and rail-fare voucher sent to men throughout West Germany and creating havoc for the West German military authorities.

the strongly scented, brightly coloured envelopes and unmistakable women's handwriting. Many wives opened the letters, fell for the trap, jumped to hasty conclusions and, in many instances, left their homes. It is impossible to assess the moral damage caused to many married couples by the suspicion, bitterness and sense of betrayal that these love letters engendered, but the effect of the operation was certainly widespread and long-lasting.

The West German armed forces also fell victim to another well-

AMT FUR SICHERHEIT DER BUNDESWEHR
DER LEITER

Abt. III/5 – Ka Tgb. Nr. 2378/58

Dortmund, den 24.10. 1958
(Ort)

Herrn
S:
1

/Weser

| Unbedingt beachten! |

Betr.: **Sicherheitshinweis**

Da Sie zu den kürzlich erfaßten Wehrpflichtigen des Jahrganges 1938 gehören und somit vor der Musterung stehen, sehen wir uns zu folgendem Hinweis gezwungen:

Die Aufforderung zur Musterung erging bisher auf schriftlichem Wege. Da aber von gegnerischer Seite zu wiederholten Malen gefälschte Musterungsbescheide in Umlauf gebracht wurden, die nur von einem Fachmann identifiziert werden konnten, wird mit Wirkung vom 1. 10. 1958 angeordnet:

Die Aufforderung zur Musterung erfolgt ab sofort ausschließlich auf dem Wege der persönlichen Benachrichtigung.

Im Interesse eines ordnungsgemäßen Ablaufs der Musterung erhalten Sie als Verhaltungsmaßregel:

Schriftliche Musterungsbescheide sind als Fälschungen zu betrachten. In diesem Falle ist eine persönliche Benachrichtigung unbedingt abzuwarten.

Hochachtungsvoll

gez.:

Beglaubigt:

Photograph of forged security instructions, advising West German conscripts to ignore any call-up orders received by post and to take call-up orders only from members of the armed forces who called on the conscripts personally. To create as widespread upheaval as with the counterfeit call-up orders, scores of fake army officers wearing genuine army uniforms called upon the conscripts and sent them to recruiting centres.

planned Pankow forgery that all but totally disrupted the functioning of the West German army.

Pankow printed large quantities of West German Call-up and Demobilisation papers. Over a period of time many serving men prematurely received Demobilisation Orders and returned home. Other disgruntled male citizens found themselves unexpectedly ordered to report to barracks. The West German army administration almost collapsed under the strain of coping with thousands of men who had inexplicably deserted, and thousands of others who reported to barracks without being conscripted. Eventually, the West German military command realised that it had been hoaxed.

For the Pankow department of the Institute 631's Division for Tactical Strategy the hoax was merely a practice exercise; for West Germany the forgeries were a grim warning of what can happen during a time of national emergency, when dozens of similar administrative hoaxes are launched at the same time. A country could swiftly suffocate under an over-abundance of false red tape.

The printing of counterfeit currency keeps an entire department of Pankow working full time. The fake currency produced by Moscow's master forgers is the work of experts. It is so good it is never challenged. The only way it became known that Pankow currency was being circulated was because currency notes bearing the same numbers appeared at clearing banks. Even then, currency experts were unable to decide which of the two notes was the forgery.

Smuggling counterfeit money into various countries and putting it into circulation created no problems for Institute 631, with the facility of the diplomatic bags, and other smuggling methods, through undercover subverters and established go-betweens, false banknotes quickly find their way into circulation. In many cases undercover subverters have enlisted the help of petty crooks to distribute the fake banknotes at race courses, betting shops and market places.

This steady distribution of forged currency has had an insidious inflationary influence upon the countries of the Western World. Too much money in circulation results in too much money chasing too few goods. This causes prices to rise. Higher prices result in demands for wage increases. Very considerable damage has been caused to the *details?*

Western democracies because counterfeit currency has invaded their economy on a large scale.

Fake currency provides another fringe benefit for the Kremlin, for it is used to finance communist activity throughout the world. Within reasonable limits Communist Party members, undercover-subverters' networks and go-betweens can squander money for the cause and at the same time increase inflation.

Western authorities are uncomfortably conscious that this distribution of counterfeit currency is merely practice. If the East and the West are ever involved in a bloody conflict, then hidden stocks of fake currency will flood out from hidden storehouses and swamp the markets of the Western democracies. The purchasing value of all money could be destroyed overnight.

Meanwhile the printing presses of Pankow never stop. Day and night they produce forgeries that cause damage to the Western democracies.

Most of Pankow's products are stored and are not used except as experiments to test their usefulness. For example, all the shop stewards of the Dutch Transport Union recently obeyed instructions from their head office to call out the men on a two-day token strike. These orders were subsequently found to be counterfeit.

Tons of forged material is held in reserve all over the world, ready for use during an appropriate emergency. Hard-core communists and undercover subverters, when ordered, can deluge any country with forged demobilisation papers, perfumed love letters, misleading bus and train timetables and a hundred similar forgeries.

One ingenious type of Pankow forgery, which causes the West a great deal of embarrassment, is the method of introducing false information into Western newspapers and magazines. For political reasons, Moscow frequently wishes the West to be discredited, and Pankow arranges for this.

An entire edition of a Western newspaper—the London *Times*, for example, or the *New York Herald Tribune*—will be completely reproduced, except for one column. This column is replaced by a carefully prepared news item which makes the required damaging admission discrediting the West. Copies of the newspaper containing these false statements are widely circulated from hand to hand, and attention is drawn to the false news item. Thus it becomes widely known—in Czechoslovakia, Hungary or Poland, or perhaps in the Middle East, Africa or other countries where Western newspapers are difficult to obtain—that the West has failed to keep faith with its principles.

Quite often the Pankow forgers are called upon to provide specialised counterfeiting, as on one occasion when the Kremlin's foreign policy demanded that Monsieur Paul-Henry Spaak should be discredited.

Spaak was Secretary-General of NATO. Two letters were secretly circulated among NATO members; they had been written and signed by Monsieur Spaak when he was the war-time Belgian Foreign Minister. Both letters made it clear that he had written secretly from London to friends in Vichy, asking them to help him make a separate peace treaty with the Germans. The letters also revealed that Spaak had tried to make a secret deal with the German occupation authorities in Belgium, *without* the knowledge of the Allies.

Handwriting experts had no doubt that it was M. Spaak's signature at the bottom of the letters. The printed notepaper was tested. It had undoubtedly been manufactured in England during the war.

Grave doubts were aroused about M. Spaak's loyalty. But Western security officers, systematically sifting all evidence, were able to prove that the first of the letters was a forgery. The Pankow forgers had made a serious blunder. They had dated the first letter 'London, the 24th of June 1940'. The Western investigators were able to prove to everyone's satisfaction that M. Spaak had been in France, and on the run from the Germans, until October 1940, before underground channels could transport him safely to Britain. Since the first letter was a forgery, it was evident that the second letter, on the same subject, was also counterfeit, and M. Spaak was vindicated.

Many similar forgeries prepared by Pankow have been successful, however. Hundreds, perhaps thousands, of politicians, administrators, diplomats, industrialists or social workers, have had their lives and careers seriously disrupted by false documents or letters that have been strategically planted where they would cause most damage to their reputations.

*　　*　　*

The Pankow counterfeiters department of the Institute 631's Division for Tactical Strategy has caused the Western democracies immense damage. So, although it was originally created to serve the Institute 631's undercover subverters, it was not abolished when the 'professional' undercover master-subverters of the Soviet Secret Service's Special Division for Subversion took over. The Pankow counterfeiters department was instead incorporated into the Soviet secret service Berlin-Pankow Branch Headquarters, and continues from there to damage the Western democracies.

8

Subverter Schooling for Work Abroad

Throughout the 1950s, while the Institute 631's networks, supported by the foreign communist parties everywhere in the world, were doing their utmost to disrupt everyday life in the Western democracies, the 'professional' Russian master-subverters were undergoing training in various spy-schools. The selection and training of these special agents began in the early spring of 1948—immediately following Stalin's decision to create two separate forces of undercover subverters.

The population of the Soviet Union is 246,471,000. From this enormous reserve KGB draws its master-subverters and master-spies.

Every Party Organiser throughout the USSR has standing orders to 'report fully about each comrade's private life, relatives, friends and acquaintances; their habits, hobbies, and all other details that throw light upon their character and way of life outside the Party'. In this way, an official 'brotherly eye' is fastened upon all Soviet citizens. Everybody's degree of loyalty to the State, and to communism, is accurately assessed and recorded. Occasionally a citizen is observed to possess those special qualities which indicate an aptitude for espionage or undercover activity. From then onwards, concentrated attention is paid to this possible recruit. For a period of time, the citizen is placed under such intense KGB surveillance that his or her private life becomes an open book to the State.

If the possible recruits satisfy all these searching enquiries, of which they are quite unaware, they are recommended for an espionage or undercover career and are officially classed as 'a possible trainee'.

The first stage of training begins at the Marx–Engels School at Gorky, near Moscow. The recruits are given no hint that they are being schooled for undercover activity; they believe they are being groomed for a Party career.

The Marx–Engels School stands well back from the street and is surrounded by high walls. All entrances are guarded by State security police. Nobody can enter without presenting a special pass.

On arrival at the school all recruits surrender their Party membership cards and all other identity documents, and fill in a long questionnaire. Next comes a general-knowledge entrance examination, aimed at ascertaining the educational level and mental alertness of the recruit. For those who pass the examination, all private life comes to an end; for the duration of their training, which lasts four months, they become boarders, and are forbidden to leave the school grounds. They live collectively, sleep in dormitories and sign an undertaking they will at no time communicate to anybody, in any way, anything about the school. They undertake: 'to work to the best of my ability and spare no effort nor energy to become an outstanding specialist in the fields to which I may be transferred'.

Everyone at the Marx–Engels School works to a strict timetable; beginning at 7 a.m., every minute of the day is accounted for until bedtime at 10.30 p.m. There are recreation breaks of fifteen minutes' duration, and half an hour is allotted for breakfast, for lunch and supper. All other time is devoted to physical training, lectures, study-preparation and educational film shows. The specific object of this stringent training schedule is to ensure that every recruit is 'thoroughly schooled in communist ideology, and grows accustomed to thinking and acting like a classic bolshevik'.

*   *   *

Recruits who pass their preliminary Marx–Engels School training course are transferred to the Lenin Technical School at Verkhovnoye, some ninety miles from Kazan. It is in a desolate area near the border of the Tartar Autonomous Soviet Republic, and can be approached only by a private road. It consists of a large complex of buildings, sprawling over seven square miles, and is enclosed by a high brick wall. All entrances are guarded by State security police and no one can enter without producing a special pass.

The recruits are transported to the Lenin Technical School in KGB vehicles and are prevented from making any contact with the outside world en route. Upon arrival they are once again billeted in large dormitories, and their lives dominated by a formidable study-schedule. Their life is spartan, directed with military precision and discipline. However, those who have survived to this stage of training are already so conditioned to discipline and dedication to the communist cause that they have no thought of complaining. They are forbidden to inform anybody where they are or what they are doing, but are permitted to communicate with their relatives and friends through an accommodation address. They are still quite ignorant that they are possible recruits for undercover training by Moscow Secret Service Headquarters.

Training at the Lenin Technical School lasts twelve months. Both male and female students undergo strenuous combat training: they climb steep hills, scramble under barbed wire and over obstacles, jump from heights, traverse muddy marshes, rivers and rough terrain, climb over rooftops, scale treacherous mountain paths and tramp for long distances over rock-strewn ground while laden with heavy equipment. They learn to delight in 'steeling their bodies' to serve their country's cause.

They learn self-defence, ju-jitsu, judo, karate and most other forms of defence and attack, including unconventional boxing and wrestling styles. They are taught to handle firearms, shoot with pistols, revolvers, rifles and submachineguns. They practise how to destroy bridges, buildings and military installations with dynamite, TNT, gelignite and plastic explosives; how to make bombs and how to look for concealed timebombs and boobytraps and render them harmless. This phase of training also covers the blowing of locks, strongroom doors and 'burglarproof' safes. They learn which type of explosive is suitable for any particular job, and how to muffle the explosion. Training for waging guerrilla warfare is also included.

There follows a comprehensive course in doping or poisoning drinks, sweets, food, cigarettes and cigars. The use of drugs for specific tasks is illustrated and how long these drugs take to be effective, and what symptoms the victims suffer. The recruits are also taught what antidotes to take if ever they are forced to take a particular drug themselves.

Another specialised course teaches the recruits to tap telephone lines and to utilise high-power limpet microphones. All forms of radio reception and transmission are studied thoroughly, and microfilming, microdotting and coding and decoding are practised.

At the conclusion of this course all recruits undergo a final examination. Then, while the Selection Board studies the examination results in conjunction with the instructors' weekly progress reports, the recruits are transported to the Oktyabr Recreation Centre in the Caucasian Mountain Spa of Kyslovodsk. There they enjoy a well-earned holiday, lasting a month or more.

*   *   *

Those recruits finally selected as 'suitable for undercover master-subverters' activities abroad' now spend another year with instructors who test them for aptitude in specific branches of subversive work, and adaptability to any particular country. This 'assessment period' is even more strenuous than the previous training, but worse trials are still to come.

The next stage tests the recruits' fitness for field work abroad. The Soviet teachers try to break down their own pupils under simulated interrogation pressure.

A recruit is arrested in all earnestness by the secret Police and taken to State Security Headquarters as though he has been suddenly discovered to be a foreign agent. Expert interrogators submit him to brainwashing, third-degree and all the other modern methods of extracting information and confessions. Some interrogators have been so carried away while acting out their role, and have submitted the accused victim to such physical violence, that it became necessary for the directors of the Special Division for Subversion to restrain them Almost all recruits so accused manage to resist this strenuous interrogation and do not break.

Having survived this test, the recruit is brought before his interrogators and it is explained that this nightmare-experience was 'just another test'. The interrogators praise the recruit for the resistance he has shown, but before he is 'set free' oblige him to pledge himself to keep the nature of this special test a secret from his fellow-recruits; those still to undergo this test must be taken unawares.

Now the recruit has *proved* himself suitable for undercover work abroad. His loyalty to communism and the Soviet Union cannot be shaken, he is in excellent physical condition, he has received a solid training and he has proved himself adaptable, intelligent and qualified for further training as an undercover master-subverter. He is now deemed fit to start his final course of training at one of the Soviet Ace spy schools. This training lasts ten long years.

* * *

Soviet citizens selected for work abroad as undercover master-subverters receive their training in special sectors of the same schools that turn out master-spies.

The best known of the Soviet Ace spy schools is Gaczyna. It is situated a hundred miles south-west of Kuibyshev and is an enclosed area of some 425 square miles, stretching along the border south of the Tartar Autonomous Soviet Republic to the Bashkir Autonomous Soviet Republic. The entire zone is guarded by State security police and is sealed off for a radius of thirty miles. No one can approach it without a special Secret Service permit. It is not shown on any map and only the elite of Russia's Secret Service know of its exact location.

Gaczyna is the ace school for master-spies and master-subverters who have been selected for work in the English-speaking world. It is divided into four sections: the North-American Division is in the north-west; the Canadian Division is in the north; the United Kingdom Division occupies the north-east; and the south is devoted to Divisions for Australia, New Zealand, India and South Africa. Each sector is a completely independent zone that has no communication with the other sectors.

From the moment of their arrival at Gaczyna, students are ordered to speak only English. They are given an English name, and are pledged to forget their Russian tongue and Soviet nationality. They must immerse themselves completely in their new Anglo-Saxon identity.

The ten-year indoctrination period at Gaczyna is considered by the Soviet Secret Service directors as the essential minimum time to condition the human brain to its new language and its new way of life. After this conditioning, during which the students are frequently awakened at night and subjected to snap question tests, any master-spy or master-subverter will stick to his or her adopted identity as though it was truly his or her own. The Soviet Secret Service directors boast that neither torture, brainwashing, nor truth drugs can break their agents.

*   *   *

The United Kingdom Division of Gaczyna contains accurate replicas of typically English streets, buildings, cinemas, restaurants, snack bars, public houses and other similar establishments. British clothes are worn, and the way of life is typically and totally English. The students live in boarding houses or hotels, apartments, or detached or semi-detached houses; they eat good old English dishes—roast beef with baked potatoes and Yorkshire pudding, and fish and chips; they ride on London buses, spend English money, read English newspapers and watch recorded English television programmes. They speak only English, no matter how slowly and falteringly. Heavy fines and penalties are imposed upon any student overheard speaking Russian.

The language masters are hand-picked Communist Party members, former United Kingdom nationals who have spurned the country of their birth to become Soviet citizens. Other British-born nationals help to create an authentic English environment; they are waitresses, policemen on the beat, bus conductors, hotel receptionists, shop assistants and so on. The students are encouraged to conduct long conversations with these British people, whom they meet every day. They also spend a great deal of time in the cinema, watching American and British films brought in from the West.

Learning to speak the English language fluently usually takes less than five years. But the Soviet Secret Service directors are thorough. They insist that the first five years of a student's training at Gaczyna shall concentrate on perfecting his or her speech. Hours are spent daily in listening to recorded BBC broadcasts, and afterwards repeating the phrases over and over again, being continuously corrected by their teachers until accent and pronunciation is accurate. No Gaczyna student arrested by Scotland Yard's Special Branch or the FBI has ever betrayed himself by a language imperfection. Gordon Lonsdale, the notorious Soviet master-spy who stood trial at the Old Bailey in London, never ceased to insist he was Canadian; only secret documents in the possession of Scotland Yard finally proved his Russian origin.

The United Kingdom Division at Gaczyna occupies approximately sixty square miles. There is a city section and a rural area. Students live in turn in a typical city suburb with a High Street lined with shops, cafés, public houses, banks, a post office, etc.; then in a provincial town; and finally in a village. They receive a weekly salary of £40 in English currency and use this to pay rent and buy food, clothing and the other necessities of life, at prices currently applying in Britain. They are as acutely aware of the rising cost of living in Britain as any British housewife. These true-to-life surroundings, coupled with expert tuition, enable the Gaczyna students literally to speak English, think English and live English.

The second five years' training at Gaczyna directs the students into more specialised fields of knowledge. They learn and practise the modern techniques of undercover activities. They memorise code systems which Moscow knows cannot be broken by experts; they practise radio communications, dismantle and assemble short-wave radio receiver/transmitters and use modern equipment that can transmit and receive long messages in mere seconds; they learn to handle ultra-modern photographic equipment which can reduce a large blueprint or a long document into microdot photographs; they are taught how everyday articles can be converted into containers for microfilms.

They also learn all the well-tried methods of making contact with other agents—through coded classified advertisements in newspapers; through coded telephone signals; and through the use of 'dead-drops'. Training for waging guerrilla warfare is given by Red Army experts; the students are able to later pass on this knowledge to their undercover network subverters.

When Gaczyna students have completed their ten years' training they are more British in speech, mannerism and knowledge than most native-born British people.

*　　*　　*

Apart from Gaczyna, there are other, similar establishments that cater for other countries and other languages. They all function on identical lines.

In the West of the Soviet Union is the Prakhovka Spy School.* It lies seventy miles north-east of Minsk, the capital of the Byelorussian Soviet Republic. Its 220 square miles stretch along the border of the Latvian Soviet Republic. Like Gaczyna, the territory is sealed off by State security police and every precaution is taken to ensure that its existence remains a secret.

In the northern sector of the school, Prakhovka trains master-spies and master-subverters to operate in Norway, Sweden, Denmark and Finland. The master-spies and master-subverters for the Netherlands are trained in the south-west. Austrian and Swiss operators are housed in the south and German master-agents are trained in the south-east. As in Gaczyna, each sector is a true environmental replica of the appropriate country, and the students at Prakhovka undergo an identical training with their comrades at Gaczyna.

The Stiepnaya Spy School lies about 110 miles south of Chkalov and extends along the northern border of the Kazakh Soviet Republic. This establishment turns out master-spies and master-subverters intended to operate in Latin countries. Stiepnaya has a French Division in the north-west; a Spanish Division in the north; an Italian in the north-east; and a Portuguese, Brazilian, Argentinian and Mexican in the southern zone.

Vostocznaya Spy School caters for Asiatic and Middle East countries. It is situated about 105 miles south-east of Khabarovsk.

Novaya Spy School, which is ninety miles south-west of Tashkent, trains master-spies and master-subverters to operate in Africa.

None of these spy schools is as large as Gaczyna, but each year

* During the Second World War, when Hitler's *Wehrmacht* seized Byelorussia, Prakhovka was evacuated to further Stalin's scorched-earth policy. An emergency school was set up near Ufa, in the Bashkir Autonomous Soviet Republic. After the war Prakhovka was rebuilt on the original site and reopened in 1947.

each turns out a formidable number of well-trained master-spies and master-subverters who are an ever-increasing menace to the Western democracies.

*   *   *

Undercover master-subverters are *not* spies, but they do need to maintain contact with the Special Division for Subversion at Soviet Secret Service Headquarters in Moscow. For this reason they receive comprehensive espionage training at Gaczyna and the other spy schools. They are forbidden, however, to take part in any active spying without specific instructions from their Moscow superiors.

When the students finish their training, they remain in their spy school until the directors of the Special Division for Subversion in Moscow order the Transport Department to smuggle them into their 'country of birth'. Sometimes the new master-subverters wait for months, but they are not allowed to leave the confines of the spy school. The Soviet Secret Service directors will not risk allowing them to mix with their fellow-countrymen again, for fear their ten years of mental conditioning and linguistic conversion might be disrupted. Many master-subverters never see their families again, and few ever again speak their mother tongue.

*   *   *

All master-subverters leaving Gaczyna and other spy schools are provided with perfect 'cover' documents. Until the late 1950s the Pankow counterfeiting department supplied these forged documents. But even undetectable forgeries of personal documents are of limited value, for they cannot stand up to a thorough Security investigation. A forged birth certificate, for example, will serve for routine social purposes, but if Security suspicions are aroused a more searching investigation will reveal that the information it contains does not link up with the registry files. Driving licences, National Insurance cards, passports and other personal documents can be forged to perfection by the Pankow counterfeiters. But they can be checked! Western Security is so good that a considerable number of Russian-controlled undercover subverters were detected during the 1950s by the simple process of checking documents against registry files.

When Moscow realised that increasing numbers of their undercover subverters were being arrested, counter-measures were adopted. All subsequent documentation was supplied by the Third Division of the First Directorate of the Soviet Secret Service Headquarters. All Russian master-spies are supplied with genuine documents, not forgeries and, the undercover master-subverters, too, since the early 1960s, have been issued with genuine documents.

The Soviet Secret Service's Personal Documents Strongroom is stocked with genuine documents, painfully acquired over many years, and by many ingenious means. Third Division agents are continuously on the lookout for genuine documents, and the Soviet Secret Service will pay lavishly for suitable material. It also has infinite patience, as is shown by the case of Aleksandr Karyn.

At the beginning of the century the daughter of a well-to-do Swiss couple, on holiday in Tsarist Russia, married a young Russian teacher. In 1903 she gave birth to a boy; but she died in 1910. Her Swiss parents kept in touch with their son-in-law and grandson until the 1917 revolution caused a mass migration of Russians, when they lost touch.

A Russian agent, Aleksandr Karyn, was ordered to impersonate the grandson. He wrote to his 'grandparents' and learned that his 'grandfather' had died and his two 'uncles' were wealthy, respectable businessmen. The Soviet Secret Service provided Karyn with archive photographs of his mother, which he sent to this 'grandmother'. He wrote to her that he would like to emigrate to Switzerland, to be 'reunited' with his 'family'.

The Swiss family contacted all their influential friends in Switzerland and other European countries, begging them to use their influence to persuade the Soviet authorities to allow their 'grandson' to leave Russia. The Soviet authorities eventually 'yielded' to pressure, and exit permits were eventually granted for the 'grandson', his wife and little daughter to travel to Switzerland. He was welcomed by the Swiss family and in due course obtained a genuine Swiss passport. Karyn's deception was never discovered. After living for some time among sincere friends his conscience was pricked and he confessed to Swiss Security. But hundreds of other Russian agents, successfully infiltrated, have been conditioned not to suffer conscience qualms.

Gordon Lonsdale, the Russian master-spy sentenced to a long term of imprisonment at the Old Bailey, London, in March 1961, almost escaped being detected as a Russian. 'Gordon Lonsdale' was the identity given to Lieutenant Vasiliy Vasilyevich Pakhomov, better known as Molodyi,* when he entered Gaczyna Spy School to be converted into a 'genuine' Anglo-Saxon.

The genuine Gordon Lonsdale was born in Canada in 1924. His father was a half-breed Cree Indian named Jack Emmanuel Lonsdale, his mother a Finnish immigrant to Canada named Alga Bousu. Two years after Gordon was born his parents separated, and six years later Alga Lonsdale took her son to her native Finland. During the winter of 1939–1940 she and her sixteen-year-old son were both swallowed up in the Soviet-Finnish War. They were never heard of again. But the birth of Gordon was documented in the Canadian registry files.

When the fake Gordon Lonsdale was smuggled ashore at Vancouver from a Soviet grain ship, he lodged in a respectable boarding house, took out a driving licence and obtained other Canadian indentification documents. Later he applied for a Canadian passport and eventually landed in England with unchallengeable documents.

Moscow's Secret Service directors take such pains to ensure their master-spies and master-subverters possess 'genuine' documents that even when captured redhanded, and found guilty of spying or subversion, it is often never suspected that their true nationality is Russian. The Personal Documents Strongroom contains thousands of authentic records of people, dead and missing, that will be used as a 'cover' for the Russian master-spies and master-subverters now undergoing training.

* Russian for 'The Young One'.

9

Master-Subverters in Action

It was in the spring of 1948 that Stalin initiated the undercover sub-verter programme, but it was December 1960 before the first master-subverters were classed as ready to go out into the field. By then the Special Division for Subversion of the Soviet Secret Service had ready for despatch forty-five master-subverters in Gaczyna, the Prakhovka Spy School also had forty-five, Stiepnaya had prepared forty and Novaya and Vostocznaya had each turned out fifty.

Every year new recruits enrol in the spy schools to replace those thoroughly trained and going out on active service. Classified records extracted from the Kremlin files reveal how some master-subverters have operated.

*   *   *

Richard Cecil Cooper was a respectable London businessman. He had a West End flat and owned a one-man import–export business. He was prosperous and had no financial problems. He had inherited a small fortune from an uncle in Colorado, USA, and increased it dramatically by a run of good luck at the gambling tables. He was a jovial, good-natured man, a free spender who made friends easily. He met, and became attached to, a woman whose first name was Helen. She worked as a secretary in Thomas Cooks, the travel agency owned by the British Government. Cooper also met Helen's brother, a strong friendship developed and Richard provided Helen's brother with the finance to launch his own business. Richard took no active part in it, but Helen's brother worked hard, and also prospered.

Time passed and Richard's fondness for Helen cooled as he developed a passion for a married woman. This love affair had to be secret because she was the wife of a VIP. Her indiscretions could have resulted in unpleasant front-page publicity.

In 1967 Cooper decided that the only solution was for him to leave London and seek another way of life. He sold his business, bade farewell to his friends and set sail for Bermuda, where he intended to 'look around' and perhaps settle. Two years later, friends of his, visiting Bermuda, were unable to find any trace of him.

In fact Richard Cecil Cooper was neither British nor a businessman. He was born in Leningrad in 1927 and his name was Klim Andreyevich Kushnikov. He was educated at Moscow University, where he showed such promise that he was selected for special training as an undercover master-subverter. He stayed ten years in Gaczyna before his instructors felt he was qualified to undertake undercover activity in Britain.

He was transported by a Red Navy submarine that slipped its moorings at Kronstadt and surfaced by night just off the British coast. Kushnikov-Cooper, wearing woollies under a rubber frogman's suit, slid down into the water, while sailors lowered a tiny rubber boat into which was dropped a suitcase labelled 'Made in England'. Then Cooper made the long, cold swim to the shore, pushing the tiny rubber boat before him.

A KGB officer travelled with Cooper and watched through night-glasses as the master-subverter reached the deserted shore and stripped off his rubber frogman's suit, flippers and woollies, which he placed in the rubber boat. While he dressed in the clothes he took from the suitcase, the tiny rubber boat was drawn back to the submarine by a fine nylon line. When Cooper was fully dressed, he looked around to make sure he had not been observed, signalled to the KGB officer and set off inland. The submarine re-submerged.

Richard Cecil Cooper reached Newcastle-upon-Tyne without arousing suspicion. He stayed a few days in a businessmen's hotel and then travelled to Glasgow, where he remained for two weeks. He then made a slow, leisurely journey to London, stopping at Leeds, Manchester, Oxford and other towns, meanwhile acclimatising himself to life in Britain. He already spoke and wrote English as though British-born and educated, but he did not reach London until he was confident that he was behaving in every respect like an Englishman.

He rented a flat in London's West End, acquired a small office in the City and set up his import–export business. For six months he devoted himself to developing his business, making acquaintances and orienting himself. Then, using his cover as a businessman to give him sound reasons for airing his dislikes of all left-wing organisations, he set about his secret work.

For the following six years Richard Cecil Cooper masterminded many industrial disputes, remarkable for the disproportional amount of disruption they caused.

He operated with great deftness through British Communist Party pawns, who obeyed his orders with blind faith. They never met him. He had only one contact, to whom he issued his instructions, and these filtered outwards through many political tributaries.

The main targets of his undercover disruption were the Ford Motor Company, the London Docks, and Vauxhall Motors as well as a number of other large and small concerns. His speciality was creating an injustice and using this grievance to spark off wildcat strikes. His technique was to concentrate upon key workers, the withdrawal of whose labour brought thousands of workers to a standstill. He used great ingenuity in devising schemes which aroused discontent among key workers; later came resentment, anger and finally strike action. He used hard-core fifth-column communists skilfully, planting them as anti-trade unionists in factories where they curried favour with the management. Such men are disliked by their workmates; and such men can easily provoke workmen to excesses. Some trade union working rules are so complicated that even shop stewards have difficulty interpreting them. When goodwill exists this need not cause complications; but when an undercover hard-core communist intends to cause disruption, the rule-book can become a terrible weapon.

Cooper burrowed deeply into the British way of life. His import-export business flourished, he was a silent partner in another business and he lived gaily. He took no active part in politics, apart from expressing extreme right-wing opinions, and he would probably still be operating in Britain today if it had not been for his private love life.

The Soviet Secret Service uses Control Agents to spy upon all its master-subverters. In due course it was reported to Moscow Headquarters that Cooper was having an affair with the wife of a VIP. It could only be a matter of time before the husband, or a reporter, discovered the wife's adulterous association and caused a scandal. Moscow was alarmed. The Soviet Secret Service cannot afford to have its operatives involved in publicity of any kind. So Cooper received new orders: he was to retire and settle down in Bermuda.

Sadly, the master-subverter said his farewells and departed from London. After a few months of idleness in Bermuda he was quietly transported to Moscow. He disappeared from the British scene as gently as a small and wayward cloud. Within a few weeks, another master-subverter was landed in Britain with orders to establish himself as a British businessman, and resume work where Cooper left off.

The same year* that Richard Cecil Cooper was smuggled into Britain, eleven other Russian master-subverters illegally entered the United Kingdom. Between 1962 and 1966 an additional twelve master-subverters were secretly landed in Britain every year. In 1967, 1968 and 1969 the numbers were increased to fifteen; if any master-subverter had to be recalled, he was replaced within weeks. In 1970, the number of master-subverters smuggled into Britain was increased to nineteen. A small army of highly trained Russian master-subverters is now working within the British Isles; and its numbers increase yearly.

*　　*　　*

Russian undercover master-subverters have infiltrated all the Western democracies.

Kurt Zimmermann was just another East German who found Russian domination intolerable. Risking severe punishment, he escaped into West Germany hidden under the tarpaulin of a loaded truck. He at once asked for political asylum.

West Germany receives refugees from communist East Germany with sympathy and understanding, but also with suspicion. West German Intelligence officers are efficient; they have no illusions about the methods of espionage and undercover subversion employed by the Russians and their satellites. Herr Zimmermann was subjected to a thorough security examination. He understood that these precautions were necessary and assisted his interrogators in every way. He told his life story, told of his suffering at the hands of the East German

* 1961.

police, of his restricted liberty and the political discrimination used against him. He possessed documents and papers that corroborated his story, and he satisfied his interrogators he was a genuine political refugee.

Herr Kurt Zimmermann's true name was Vladimir Maksimovich Mironov. He was born in Tula in 1927, the son of a trade union secretary who was also a member of the Russian Communist Party, and a brother of one of Moscow's Secret Police interrogators.* Mironov's father and brother had been loyal and reliable Party members, and Vladimir stepped into their shoes.

Vladimir first attracted the attention of Soviet officialdom when he was a member of the Russian Communist Party Children's Movement. A big-brotherly eye was fastened upon him when he graduated into the Communist Youth League. Later, when he was training to be an engineer at the technical college in Kharkov, the Soviet Secret Service decided he was ideal material for training in its Special Division for Subversion. Vladimir was sent to Prakhovka Spy School where he adopted the name of Kurt Zimmermann. He received ten years' training for work as an undercover master-subverter in West Germany. His 'escape' to West Germany was engineered by Moscow's Secret Service, which supplied him with all the necessary documents and papers.

Zimmermann was a trained engineer, and once he had been okayed by the West German intelligence officers he had no difficulty in finding employment with the Siemens Group. He worked hard and his workmates found him likeable. But at times his resentment towards the Soviet Union was expressed so bitterly that the mention of Russia had to be avoided in his hearing. On one occasion, when the men were discussing working conditions in the factory, Zimmermann became so incensed by his workmates' left-wing opinions that he launched into a frenzied, unreasoning denunciation of everybody. He accused some of his mates of being Soviet spies and subverters, which naturally caused deep resentment. During the next few days he received many anonymous telephone calls, warning him to give up his anti-communist

* This very much older brother had participated in Stalin's 'Treason Trials' in the 1930s.

attitude, or stay away from the factory. Zimmermann ignored the threats, but wisely guarded his tongue. The incident was smoothed over, but not forgotten.

Zimmermann had deliberately provoked this incident. He had been cleared by West German Security but knew he was still under observation. At the cost of earning the dislike of his workmates he had destroyed any lingering doubts about himself. Nevertheless he waited another few weeks before he made his next move. He provoked another incident between himself and his workmates, and was sent to Coventry. At this he threw up his arms in disgust and resigned his job. He couldn't stand working with bigots, he declared; he'd find work elsewhere. That same night, when he was returning home, he was jumped by a gang of men and beaten up so badly that he spent the next few days in hospital. Moscow's special agents had carried out the attack to provide the master-subverter with an additonal and very convincing reason for leaving the factory. His workmates were believed guilty of this brutal attack and nobody was surprised that Zimmermann looked for work a long way away.

Zimmermann went to Frankfurt-am-Main. He had no difficulty in securing a good, well-paid job. He inspired the management's confidence and was soon promoted. Now, at long last, he began work as an undercover master-subverter. No longer under suspicion by West German Security, he planned and issued orders to West German hard-core communist undercover-subverters who formed his fifth-column network. Scrupulously guarding against betrayal, he made contact through only one person. Even this contact was indirect— through coded advertisements in newspapers, and by the use of dead-drops.

This Russian master-subverter's activity inside West Germany was extensive, but short-lived. He masterminded lightning strikes, protest demonstrations and political rioting, but his activity came to an abrupt end.

Like many hard-working West Germans, Zimmermann went abroad for his holiday when the factory closed down for a month in the summer. He chose the sun and beaches of the Mediterranean coast. He was a strong swimmer and loved the sea.

One night he left his hotel for a midnight swim and did not return. It was a warm night without a hint of a breeze. The sea was as still as a lake. The next morning his body was found floating by the water's edge. His lungs were full of water. It was very odd that a strong swimmer should succumb in still water, so close to shore, but there was no doubt about the cause of death. The autopsy report said 'death by drowning'.

The Special Division for Subversion of the Soviet Secret Service had its own theory about Zimmermann's death. Three years previously, Red China (which also has training schools for undercover master-subverters), had sent its first batch of master-subverters to West Germany. Zimmermann soon reported to Moscow Headquarters that one of Mao Tse-tung's agents had somehow penetrated his cover disguise. The Chinese agent had proposed to Zimmermann that he should work solely for Peking, or else work for Peking *and* Moscow, passing on any useful information he might receive from his Special Division for Subversion directors to Peking. Zimmermann knew the risks a double-agent runs: he is distrusted by his new superiors because he has proved he lacks loyalty, and can expect none in return. He wisely reported the offer to his Moscow directors and received orders to turn down the Chinese offer. However soon after this the Peking master-subverter was arrested by West German security officers. It was obvious that the Red Chinese master-subverter had been betrayed; but not by Zimmermann. It was Moscow that had betrayed him. But Peking believed Zimmermann was the guilty man. The swift silencing of a Judas on a warm Mediterranean night could have seemed to Peking the best way to deal with a master-subverter so unethical as to betray another master-subverter.

Zimmermann was one of eighteen master-subverters who passed out from Prakhovka Spy School in 1960, and were smuggled into West Germany. Every year after that until 1967 eighteen Prakhovka-trained master-subverters eased their way into West Germany. From 1968 onwards, the number of master-subverters smuggled annually into West Germany from Prakhovka was increased to twenty-five. These men's order were to:

'*Undermine the foundations of the West German Federal Republic; wrest power from Capitalist reactionaries; and unite all Germans in one powerful consolidated State under a Communist Government.'*

*   *   *

Norma Sullivan was the American name given to Vira Borisovna Smirnova when she entered Gaczyna Spy School. She was born in Tiflis in 1926, the daughter of a Georgian Communist Party official, and a Polish mother. She was slim, attractive, well-proportioned and of above-average intelligence. She was attending the Academy of Arts in Moscow when she was informed that she had been selected for special training. Three years later she was speaking American and living in a simulated United States environment. She was earmarked to operate as an undercover master-subverter in America.

When Norma was ready to begin her new life she was concealed aboard a Soviet merchant vessel that docked at Vancouver, Canada. Smuggled ashore, she made her way to the left-luggage office to retrieve two suitcases that had been deposited for her. The suitcases contained everything to prove that she was a young American woman holidaying in Canada, including a United States passport.

Norma booked in at a modest hotel in Vancouver, did some sight-seeing and then leisurely toured across Canada. When a suitable lapse of time had convinced her she was not under surveillance, she 'returned' to the American border and entered the United States as easily as any other carefree young American woman who was enjoying her holidays.

Norma Sullivan was to operate in New York. She travelled there without haste, by airliner, bus and train, stayed overnight in small cities and acclimatised herself. Two months after her arrival in Vancouver, she stepped off a bus in New York. Her cover story was that she was a native of Michigan, lured to the bustling activity of a great city where she wanted to find temporary employment.

She was attractive, self-possessed, intelligent and exactly right for the job she obtained as a receptionist in an airline office. Although she had never set foot in America until a few weeks earlier, she soon settled down, was liked by her boss and the rest of the staff and was happy at work. She soon learned adroitly to ward off the office

* *KGB Information*, Moscow, March, 1961.

Romeos' advances with cheerful American self-assurance. She was sad when after a month she had to give notice and leave all her new friends. But she was still acclimatising herself and it was Moscow's instructions she should engage in a succession of different employments. This not only gave her useful experience, it was also a security precaution.

In turn she worked for a secretarial agency and an advertising agency that produced films for the American television network. She moved on as receptionist to a public relations concern, and finally became assistant manageress in a high-class New York nightclub. The club paid good wages. Its clients were mainly from the entertainment profession.

The directors of the Special Division for Subversion then decided that Norma had worked around long enough and could now begin her work as a master-subverter. Her swift succession of jobs and several changes of apartments had thoroughly covered her tracks.

Norma rented a comfortable apartment in Manhattan, settled down to her job in earnest, and made her first, and only, personal contact with a carefully selected American hard-core undercover communist. He passed on her orders to a network of hard-core undercover subverters. Thereafter she contacted him only through coded classified advertisement and dead-drops.

The Special Division for Subversion was well satisfied with Norma's efficiency in organising disruption and subversion. Her remarkable successes were partly due to the human raw material with which she worked. Americans tend to have strong political opinions. Many Right-wingers smell a Red plot every time there is a public protest against injustice, others are emotionally prejudiced against black pigmentation and when confronted with a 'Nigger' lose all sense of proportion. Such emotional volatility provides excellent fuel for undercover subverters. With it they calculatingly provoke disturbances that are triggered off by emotional outbursts. The skilful use of prejudiced hot-heads can spark off racial riots, arson and bloodshed, and gain headline publicity.

Norma exploited racial feelings. She set the Italians against the Irish, the Jews against the Gentiles and the Catholics against the Protestants. Through her, American hard-core undercover communist pawns sowed the seeds of hatred between men. Wherever a small grievance rubbed into a sore, Norma's masterminding transformed the sore into an ugly wound.

Meanwhile she worked so well in the nightclub that she was promoted to manageress. It was a pleasant, well-paid occupation and Norma found many sincere friends among the nightclub's clients, as well as many admirers.

And Norma Sullivan failed the Kremlin.

She possessed a built-in weakness that all the specialised brainwashing and training of the Soviet spy school could not eliminate. She was a woman. *She fell in love at first sight.*

She met the lucky man in the nightclub. The moment she set eyes on him, the pattern of her life instantly changed. The long years of master-subverter training in Gaczyna, and the brainwashing that had made of her an intelligent robot dedicated to the commands of the Special Division for Subversion, lost all significance. She was in love. She wanted this man for herself. Nothing could sway her from her purpose. The man was a diplomat, vaguely connected with the Intelligence Service. He had no suspicion that Norma was a master-subverter. Learning the truth might well have set him against her. Yet, for reasons that are unknown, Norma confessed to her lover. She told him every detail of her selection and training, and about her transportation to the United States. The only secret she did not betray was the name of her American contact. She withheld that until she'd warned the man to 'disappear'. And with him vanished all hope of tracking down Norma's widespread network of hard-core undercover subverters.

When Norma married the diplomat they left the United States. Her deliberate betrayal of the Special Division for Subversion merited severe punishment. Norma knows that the threat of death overhangs her, but so much time has elapsed without retribution that she hopes her offence may have been forgiven. Perhaps somewhere in the Soviet Secret Service is a compassionate Controller who can understand that a woman can be so dominated by her emotions that she will give up everything for love. Is such a man, or woman, holding the avengers in check and permitting Norma, 'the traitor', to escape her punishment?

The Gaczyna Spy School provided fifteen master-subverters to be transported to the United States of America in 1961. Every year after that until 1966 another fifteen joined the team. In 1967, 1968 and 1969 the number of master-subverters was stepped up to eighteen, and in 1970 to twenty. This formidable army of professionals has at its disposal many widespread networks of native-born hard-core under-cover subverters who obey orders unquestioningly. These men and women work ceaselessly to provoke strikes and work-to-rule, riots, bomb explosions, arson, kidnappings and killings.

*   *   *

Jacques Martinez began operating in Paris in 1961, in the Clichy district. He was a merchant and the French authorities had no suspicions about him. His documents showed that his forefathers had been of Spanish nationality; they had established a business in Spanish Morocco and later transferred it to Algeria, and they had prospered. The political disruption between Algiers and France had caused the son, Jacques, to open a branch of the business in Paris, as a security measure for his family.

Jacques Martinez' real name was Mikhail Gregoryevich Tamarov. He was born in Odessa in 1926, attended the University of Moscow and was studying literature when the Soviet Secret Service selected him for special training and sent him to the Stiepnaya Spy School. But this was not known to French Security until after Martinez mysteriously disappeared from Paris.

Martinez set up a number of business enterprises. One was a secretarial agency to which he devoted most of his time. There, behind the locked door of his private office, Jacques plotted industrial strife and student disorders. Western counter-intelligence now possess his dossier, but his unexpected disappearance from France in 1967 prevented the Security Police from rounding up the network of subverters that Martinez had manipulated so successfully.

In 1961, when Jacques Martinez was transported from the Stiepnaya Spy School to Paris, eleven other master-subverters from the same school had already established themselves in other parts of France. From then until 1966 another twelve master-subverters filtered into France every year. From 1967 onwards the annual number was increased to fifteen and in 1970 to eighteen.

France, like all other Western democracies, has suffered an increase of internal disruptions, strikes and riots that is directly in proportion to the influx of Russian master-subverters.

*   *   *

When converted Russian undercover master-subverters established themselves in the Western World in 1961, they took over full control of all existing subverter networks that had previously operated under the direction of Institute 631. The former undercover subverter network-leaders retained their positions, but from then on took orders from the Russian master-subverters. For security reasons, the Russian master-subverters never make direct contact with the undercover network leaders. They issue their instructions through various safe communication methods: coded advertisements in newspapers, telephone signals or dead-drops.

In 1961 about eighteen Russian master-subverters had been smuggled into America, Europe and overseas countries. Each immediately took charge of at least one existing Institute 631 fifth-column network. According to the classified information bulletin issued to Kremlin and Soviet Secret Service dignitaries,* these Institute 631 undercover subverter networks each comprised fifteen to thirty-five national members. This meant that an estimated three thousand, fairly experienced undercover subverters then became operational under the direct control of Russian-born and Russian-trained master-subverters.

In succeeding years Russia's spy schools were geared up to turn out an increasing number of undercover master-subverters every year, and by the mid-1960s they had become a very formidable danger to the Western democracies.

The steadily mounting number of strikes, workings-to-rule, demonstrations, riots and terrorist outrages occurring simultaneously in most countries, convinced Western Security that an international communist conspiracy was at work. Intelligence officers were instructed to infiltrate the undercover subverter networks and detect the identity

* *KGB Information*, Moscow, July 1961.

of the master-subverters, but Moscow Secret Service 'Control Agents'
learned of this Western Security action and immediately flashed a
coded high-speed radio warning to Moscow Soviet Secret Service
Headquarters. The Special Division for Subversion was able to warn
all its master-subverters to be alert for Western Security agents trying
to penetrate the networks.

To frustrate Western Security officers the Special Division for
Subversion imposed stricter security rules, and the Kremlin ordered
the communist parties in the West openly to advocate and instigate
wildcat and official strikes, and protest demonstrations. Every Communist Party member in the West became an open and declared
agitator and wrecker of the peace. By focusing the attention of the
press, radio and television upon known communists in the public eye,
the Kremlin hoped that their Russian master-subverters and undercover
networks would avoid drawing attention to themselves. But Western
Security experts were not hoodwinked. A number of intelligence
officers succeeded in penetrating some of the undercover subverter
networks, and were able to list the names of hard-core communist
fifth columnists. However, the security measures adopted by the
Russian master-subverters were so efficient that only one or two of them
were ever in danger. None were caught; those who came under suspicion were at once whisked back to the Soviet Union.

IO

Red China's Master-Subverters

When Mao Tse-tung first firmly established himself as 'Leader of the Great Chinese Revolution' in 1949, very strong bonds of communist brotherhood united Peking and Moscow. Stalin had found an ally to help fight the wicked capitalist countries that threatened his power; and Red China was used to help destroy the Western democracies from within.

Moscow gave every assistance to Peking's secret service to build up its own spy force. At first Mao Tse-tung's master-spies were trained in Soviet spy schools, but soon Russian espionage experts were sent to Red China where they set up spy schools on identical lines to those in the USSR. Within four years Peking Secret Service Headquarters were turning out their own trained master-spies, having cut down the training period from ten years to ten months.

The first graduates from Peking's spy schools were master-spies who operated in Chiang Kai-shek's Nationalist China and other Asiatic countries. They went to work as soon as they left Red China, lacking the ten years' training that all Russian master-spies undergo, but nevertheless proving themselves remarkably capable.

In 1964 an icy wind blew over the swiftly cooling friendship between Soviet Russia and Red China. It was at last publicly admitted that there was a violent ideological conflict between Moscow and Peking. The hostility that had grown up between the two communist countries became aggressive, resulting in troop movements and bloody border skirmishes.

The rift between Moscow and Peking caused the Kremlin and Mao Tse-tung to compete in trying to win the support of all foreign communist parties. A determined struggle for domination of the world communist parties began, and Mao Tse-tung decided to increase his operative master-spies and master-subverters inside the Western

democracies. The Red Chinese spy schools were already established and
the training of master-spies and master-subverters was stepped up.
Secret Peking records reveal that by December 1970 Red China had
at least 300 undercover master-subverters at work in the field; they
were assisted by 7,500 hard-core communist fifth columnists.

When the Peking Secret Service Headquarters' Special Division for
Subversion decided to train undercover master-subverters to work in
America, Europe and other Western countries, they encountered certain fundamental difficulties. The Soviet Secret Service can easily find
Russians who look like natives of their respective country; tall, fair-
haired men and women with blue eyes who can pass as Swedish, British,
German or American. But Red China's citizens are Asiatic. Their slant-
ing eyes, smooth black hair, high cheekbones and yellow skin pigmentation cannot fail to attract attention in the bustling business life of
London, New York, Paris or Berlin. Some Red Chinese could find a respectable 'cover' in a Chinese laundry or restaurant, but Peking believes
that any Chinese national living in the West is a 'natural Red Chinese
suspect'. It is only seldom, therefore, that undercover master-subverters
of Asiatic origin are allowed to operate in a 'White' country.

Peking Secret Service Headquarters were obliged to develop special
techniques for infiltrating spies and subverters into the West. They
adopted the tactics of British, American, French and West German
intelligence services and searched for their undercover master-subverters in the target area.

Most countries of the West have many citizens who have long been
residents in the Far East. Hong Kong, Singapore, Tokyo, Bombay and
other Far Eastern cities are the homes for many emigrant British,
French, German and other nationals. But now that colonialism is dying
fast, many of these citizens face grave economic problems. Peking's
Secret Service prepares dossiers on all these Europeans, records all the
details of their economic difficulties, and their ability and efficiency.
Among the many thousands of European residents in the Far East, Red
Chinese recruitment scouts have found many willing spies and undercover subverters. Surprisingly, the most fruitful field for recruiting is
among middle-aged women. Many are widows and deeply worried
about their economic future. They jump at the chance to undergo

secret training, provided they can return to the land of their birth with adequate capital to start a business and a guaranteed monthly income, secretly paid in cash.

Recent arrests of self-confessed Red Chinese master-subverters prove how deeply the Western world has been penetrated by spies and sub- verters. Günther Linke, who was arrested while in possession of secret directives from Peking's Special Division for Subversion, eventually confessed he was in charge of a widespread undercover subverter net- work. Mademoiselle Maria Rhodez, trapped while coding instructions to her undercover network agents, broke down and admitted she was employed by Red China. So did Jonathan Webster when he was arrested with secret Peking directives and forged currency in his pos- session.

* * *

It makes no difference to the West if the master-subverters under- mining its society are Moscow- or Peking-directed. But it does make a great difference in the degree of violence provoked by the subverters.

Soviet-directed undercover master-subverters are content to bring workers out on strike, stage protest demonstrations and disrupt every- day life by comparatively 'mild' methods, although they also encourage rioting and limited terrorism. But Red China's subverters are sent out specifically to instigate vicious violence. Asiatics are notoriously in- different to the sanctity of human life. The use of terrorism against innocent men, women and children is prescribed by Peking's Special Division for Subversion. Mao Tse-tung is not concerned with justice, only with the destruction of the capitalist Western world. Peking has no scruples. Red China's undercover master-subverters have orders to 'instigate unrestrained terrorism and guerrilla warfare'.

The Irish Republican Army, the Basque Nationalist Movement, the American left-wing and Black Power groups have all spawned break- away bodies that use the same mixture of Maoist and Che Guevara slogans, phraseology and violence. They exchange ideas through train- ing cadres in Havana, Peking, Hanoi and Algiers. They speak but one idea in a dozen languages.

* * *

The early coded Red Chinese directives sent to undercover master-subverters in the field followed the Moscow pattern. They were lengthy political diatribes and gave painfully detailed orders about the way to disrupt society. But these coded orders soon took on a much more virulent tone. The directors of the Red Chinese Special Division for Subversion issued clear-cut instructions for the perpetration of terrorist acts, as is shown in the following extract from secret coded Peking orders.

Strike action must increase continually, and factories must be brought to a complete standstill. All profits lost to the imperialist exploiters hits them where it hurts most. Widespread strike action damages the economy of any country if manufacturing plants producing export goods are forced to shut down. If any country is unable to maintain its export schedule, vital foreign currency is lost and the downfall of imperialism is brought a step nearer. Therefore all-out efforts must be made to increase strike action until so many industries are affected that the country is close to paralysis.

Strike action is, however, only part of your dedicated task. Much more harmful to the imperialist industrial tycoons is the destruction of their plants. If a factory is blown up or burned down, it is not only the building that is destroyed. The imperialist also loses his stock, machinery, tools and raw materials! This is much more effective and long-lasting damage than strike action. This can so damage imperialist exploiters that they never fully recover. The destruction of vital factories can be a mortal wound to the imperialist regimes.

Burning down or blowing up warehouses, bridges, airliners and public property not only creates huge losses for imperialists, it also disrupts the capitalist way of life. It is imperative to remember that all acts of destruction must be carried out in such a way that our master-subverters never come under suspicion. Malcontents, arsonists and criminals must be blamed for the crimes. Our specific orders on how to incite, organise and execute destructive activity must be complied with precisely to avoid arousing suspicion that it is planned, or with political intent . . .

These coded secret directives from Peking duplicate—almost verbatim—instructions that Moscow Secret Service Headquarters had already transmitted in code to their own subverters: reactionary elements and other hotheads had to appear to be the culprits for destructive activity.* The Red Chinese recommended the enlistment of hoodlums and petty crooks for subversive activities, as did Moscow. But Peking went further and clearly recommended the exploitation of 'easily influenced' or 'bought' delinquents, and criminals.

Mao Tse-tung's undercover master-subverters in America, Britain, France, Italy, West Germany and the rest of the free world followed their orders. The rioting, looting, arson and terrorism that has occurred all over the globe shows that they work diligently. Political reactionaries, nationalists, irresponsible hooligans and racialists have all been blamed for instigating outrages which have caused loss of life and enormous damage to property. The Red Chinese master-subverters have skilfully used pawns to do the job and get the blame.

* * *

Allied and Red Chinese secret files contain many case histories about Mao Tse-tung's undercover master-subverters operating in the free world. James Rose, a young South African jack-of-all-trades, was leading a monotonous and not very rewarding way of life in Johannesburg when he met by chance a middle-aged man in a public house he frequented. A friendship developed and James's new friend suggested that there was money to be made in Hong Kong. The young South African paid no serious attention to the suggestion. All he knew of his new acquaintance was that his name was Robert Bush, and that he was a Hong Kong industrialist visiting South Africa to explore export and import possibilities. He appeared affluent, but James was more than surprised when, a few days later, Bush said he'd communicated with his Hong Kong office and could offer James a very good job. He was even authorised to pay James's passage from Johannesburg to Hong Kong.

The offer appealed to James and he accepted. He found everyone in the Hong Kong office very friendly and settled down happily in the bustling harbour city. When, soon after his arrival in Hong Kong, he enjoyed a whirlwind romance with lovely Chin Mong-foo, he felt life for him was making a fresh start.

* See pages 24, 25, 39

But thunderclouds soon appeared on his horizon. Some weeks after his arrival in Hong Kong, Robert Bush told him that unforeseen cancellations of large export orders had brought the business to the point of ruin. The directors faced bankruptcy and were compelled to dismiss everybody instantly; they could not even pay James's return fare to Johannesburg.

James tried to find alternative employment, without success. The high salary he'd earned during his few weeks' employment had enabled him to save a little money; but this rapidly dwindled away. He was facing starvation when Chin Mong-foo, his lovely Chinese girl friend, came to the rescue. She introduced him to a Mr Wang, who offered to help the young man. In a day or two, Wang promised, he would make some useful suggestions. The next evening he invited Chin and James to a lavish dinner and proposed that James should become a highly paid Government officer, with a secure future, excellent working conditions and high remuneration. It was all dependent upon James's ability to pass a special training course; but Mr Wang did not doubt James could do this easily. James was enthusiastic, until he learned his employers would be the Red Chinese Government, and that after he'd passed his training course he'd be expected to work abroad for Peking.

'What have you got against the Chinese People's Government?' Wang asked bluntly. He argued that James as a white South African, should have a grudge against his country, which had never given him an opportunity to make a good living. Did he not believe that all men should have an equal opportunity to get on in life? If so, what *could* James have against the Chinese People's Government? Peking was fighting for the underdog against the oppressors. If James agreed that the poor should be helped to better themselves, here was a golden opportunity to help mankind, and himself. He could become a respected and trusted officer of the Chinese People's Republic.

More coffee and liqueurs were consumed, the discussion continued for hours, and eventually James was persuaded by Wang that it was an honour to be offered a responsible position in the Peking Government. The very next day, Wang arranged for James to be smuggled into Red China. The girl Chin accompanied him.

On his arrival in Peking James was welcomed with great hospitality

by officers of the Recruitment Division of Peking Secret Service Headquarters. They skilfully brainwashed him into believing Red China's
cause was a just one, and that the sacred duty of all honest men and
women is to destroy the capitalist régimes. Before very long James was
eager to start training as an undercover master-subverter in Peking's
spy school.

The Chinese spy school to which James was sent was a well-guarded
establishment in the Kiangsu Province. Together with other English-
speaking recruits who had been smuggled into Red China from many
Anglo-Saxon countries he learned all the theoretical and practical
techniques of undercover work.

During the nine-month course, great emphasis was placed upon
practical experience in promoting industrial unrest. Spy school instructors posed as shop stewards and workmen who were contented
with their wages and working conditions. The future undercover
master-subverter knows that frequently shop stewards and workmen
have no good reason to strike; nevertheless, his orders are to induce the
men to down tools.

The following is an account of a rehearsal of the instigating of strike
action, given by a recruit who underwent training as an undercover
master-subverter in the Kiangsu Province spy school.*

The shop stewards and the men I faced were so typically petit-
bourgeois it was impossible to hammer sense into their bigoted
brains. Whatever argument I used, they countered. They made it
clear they wouldn't strike without good reason. This is how it
went:

I argued: 'You are exploited by the management and paid in-
adequate wages. The factory directors are laughing because you lack
the guts to fight for your rights while they make fat profits.'

A shop steward replied: 'We are well treated and paid better than
trade union rates. The factory profits don't concern us.' A workman
was abusive: 'Keep out of our way, big-mouth. We don't want
communist propaganda around here.' Everybody was solidly against
me. A shop steward said: 'If we take unjustified strike action, we only

* Extract from the classified publication *Action Reports*, Peking, July 1965.

D

harm ourselves. The factory can well afford a long strike, even if it lasts months. The trade union wouldn't recognise it; but even if they did, and we got strike pay and increased wages, at the end of the strike we'd *still* lose. It'd take a bloody long time to make good what we lost during the strike.'

I knew I had to use other tactics. 'You dare accuse me of using communist tactics,' I lashed out. 'You know I hate the Reds. That doesn't mean I put up with exploitation! No matter what you all say, it's a fact that we are all underpaid. I'm an ordinary chap like the rest of you, I'm not a trained speaker; but I know that the accident rate in this factory is too high, and so do you!'

A shop steward contradicted me: 'New safety measures are continuously introduced and the accident rate is getting lower!'

I'd learned it's bad tactics to oppose. It's better to blend into the opposition. 'You're right about continual safety-measure improvements,' I said. 'But they don't *stop* accidents. What happens when one of us has an accident that prevents him from doing his old skilled job? He has to take a lower-paid job! Either that, or live on a pension that's a pittance.'

A workman cut in: 'That's not the management's fault. They comply with the safety precautions. And if somebody is hurt and can't return to his old job, the management finds him a job he *can* do!'

I wasn't getting anywhere. Yet, I had to find *some* angle to arouse discontent. 'But all men are entitled to security,' I said. 'Pressing for higher wages by strike action is striving for security. If we get higher wages we can start a voluntary fund for the men who get injured. Then we'll all know that if we're injured and have to take a lower-paid job, we can get our money made up.'

At long last I'd found an angle. I argued strongly and finally got a majority vote for strike action. I'd learned that working men have a weak spot. They're concerned with their own personal selfish interests.

I knew all along that I was faced with more difficult conditions than I'd ever encounter under real circumstances. Our instructors, acting as hostile shop stewards and workmen, were skilled teachers.

They used strong counter-arguments which factory workers are rarely capable of using. They did their utmost to teach us the correct psychological tactics to adopt towards strong opposition, and know the value of emotional and humanitarian appeals.

At the end of the nine-month course James easily passed his examination and was brought back to Peking Secret Service Headquarters for final instructions. After a fortnight's holiday he was smuggled back into Hong Kong.

During his absence from the British Crown Colony Chin had paid the rent for his apartment, and had maintained appearances that he was still in Hong Kong. She'd obtained documentation, provided by a large respectable Hong Kong Trading Corporation, which showed that James had been employed by them in their head office all the time he'd in fact been away in Red China. This same Trading Corporation now appointed James their representative in South Africa and he returned to his native country with a plausible 'cover'. He set up an office in Johannesburg to promote large-scale exporting and importing.

With the very adequate funds available, James expanded his business rapidly. He employed efficient clerks who knew the trade, and employed a good manager who participated in the profits and was capable of running the business with little reference to James. James seemed to be directing a prosperous business that gave him an excellent profit, and enabled him to lead a life of luxury.

James enjoyed his luxury living and he remained loyal to Peking's Special Division for Subversion. He contacted an undercover hard-core communist who became his subverter network leader. Soon a small army of subverters were following out James's orders. While apparently living the respectable life of a prosperous businessmen, he secretly devised and directed subversive campaigns of every description. He controlled his network subverters so skilfully that fifth-column activity was widespread throughout South Africa, damaging the country's economy and discrediting the Pretoria government.

In January 1970, Peking's Special Division for Subversion decided that James's undercover subverter leader was so well established as a master agent in South Africa that James could branch out, and open an export and import business on the American continent.*

*   *   *

Another equally revealing illustration is the case history of Liam Murphy, a Dublin clerk.

Murphy was disgruntled with his job, but unable to find a better one. His family was poor, his father crippled and unable to work full-time, and Liam, the eldest of the family, gave up his wage-packet to his mother, who returned him only a few shillings for his own requirements.

He decided to try his luck in England. But despite the post-war boom, he was unable to find well-paid work and had to accept a low-paid job in a London office. In desperation to escape the deadly monotony of the office he responded to tempting advertisements offering an adventurous and secure life in the British Army, and joined up. His Army career eventually brought him to the British Crown Colony of Hong Kong.

Liam Murphy liked the Far Eastern harbour city. During his off-duty hours he easily made friends with the young and pretty local Chinese girls. He was an easy-going young man with considerable Irish charm and soon formed an intimate association with a very attractive girl named Lin Pao-yen. It was not long before they were sharing an apartment.

When his army service ended, Liam returned to England. Once again he tried to find reasonably well-paid work in London, but despite his good army record could find only low-grade employment. However, he corresponded with Lin Pao-yen, confided to her his dissatisfaction with life in England and regretted ever having to leave Hong Kong. To his delight, Lin wrote him she had found him a post in Hong Kong. The managing director of the firm was a remote relative of Lin's. He had accepted her valuation of Liam's ability, would give him employment and would even pay his passage from London to Hong Kong.

Liam jumped at the opportunity and was soon back with Lin in

* The secret files do not yet state whether it was Canada, the USA or South America, and whether or not he used the same identity.

Hong Kong. Yet, like James Rose, his enthusiasm cooled when he learned he was to be employed by the Red Chinese Government. But Lin was persuasive—the prospects were dazzling, and Liam was soon brainwashed and working for Peking's Special Division for Subversion. He trained to be an under cover master-subverter at a spy school in the Kiangsu Province and then returned to Hong Kong. During this interval of ten months Lin had paid his rent and concealed his absence from the British Crown Colony. He was provided with documentation showing that he had been employed continually by a Hong Kong company and his passport showed that he'd been in the British Crown Colony from the day he had first arrived until the day of his departure to Europe as the Company's sales representative.

In London Liam posed as a prosperous businessman while he set up a network of undercover subverters. The name and address of a reliable hard-core communist was provided by Peking and this operative maintained indirect contact with Liam through code advertisements in the personal columns of London evening newspapers.

Liam's undercover subverter network successfully fomented strikes, demonstrations and rioting, and notably disrupted the London and Merseyside docks, the motor industry and mining; it transformed anti-war demonstrations into riots, and instigated bomb outrages for which various Arab nationalistic groups were blamed.

In February 1970 Liam received orders from Peking to transfer command of his network to his lieutenant and proceed to Ireland. At first he operated in Eire organising the training of saboteurs, with the emphasis upon instruction in the use of explosives and sniping. The trained terrorists were then smuggled over the border into Northern Ireland where their terrorist activity was directed with political strategy.

The last entry in Peking's secret files shows that Liam Murphy had set up a number of terrorist training centres in remote farmhouses not far from the Northern Ireland border.* More than a hundred terrorists received training there and were smuggled over the frontier. Bomb explosions, sniping, the use of gelignite nail bombs and renewed outbreaks of rioting, arson and murder in Northern Ireland can be correlated with Liam's arrival in Eire. However Peking's secret files do not

* See page 176.

reveal if Liam Murphy is still operating in Eire, or if he has been transferred to Northern Ireland to direct subversive activity personally.

* * *

Owen Davis was an American citizen of Welsh origin and an automobile salesman before he joined the Merchant Navy. His ship was held up for repairs for some weeks in Singapore and during this time Owen met a Peking agent. Owen was brainwashed and agreed to become a Red Chinese undercover master-subverter. He signed an undertaking to become a master-subverter for Peking's Special Division for Subversion and was given a large sum of money. His orders were to return with his ship to the United States, spend some time drifting across the country, getting many odd jobs to cover up his tracks, and then return to Singapore. Owen followed out these instructions, returned to Malaysia, reported to a Red Chinese agent and was smuggled into Peking.

Owen received his nine months' training in a spy school in the Kiangsu Province, passed his 'finals' and was classified for work as an undercover master-subverter in the USA. When he returned there, his documents gave no hint that he had ever set foot in the Chinese People's Republic. He bought a restaurant in Chicago.

Like all Red Chinese master-subverters Owen had substantial funds at his disposal, which enabled him to live well while he made contact with the hard-core communist whom he appointed leader of his network. Soon Owen's organisation was inciting negroes and students to demonstrate and riot. Pitched battles took place between the police and rioters, millions of dollars of property was damaged and destroyed, culminating in students and negroes being shot dead by National Guardsmen on the University Campus and in the streets.*

Owen's network spread far beyond Chicago. His subverters were active in Detroit, Washington, Jacksonville and California. But Owen himself never took any active part in subversion.

Eventually, Peking's Secret Service Control Agent in Chicago reported that Owen Davis had come under suspicion. The FBI began to investigate him after the arrest of an operative who had planted

* See pages 134–136.

explosives in a government building. Peking's Special Division for Subversion promptly and secretly transferred Owen from the US to Peking. The Red Chinese file on Owen Davis has been closed. But he was one of Peking's most efficient undercover master-subverters and it is almost certain he has been smuggled back into the United States and is operating again in a different part of the country and under another cover identity.

*   *   *

The Special Division for Subversion of Peking Secret Service Head-quarters recruits master-subverters from all parts of the free world. Recruits are smuggled into Red China and are trained for subversion in various spy schools. There are special spy schools for Africans, Arabs and Asians; for the French, Italians and Spaniards; and for the Germans and Scandinavians, as well as for other nations. Information is available about only a few of these training centres: the one for West German, Swiss and Austrian nationals in Chekiang Province; the one for the French, Italians and Spaniards in Honan Province; and the one for the Japanese and other Asiatic nations in Chekiang Province. The training centre for Arab undercover master-subverters and guerrillas is believed to be in Shantung Province.

All these spy schools brainwash men and women of nearly every nationality. Less than a year's schooling turns out qualified master-subverters ready to be smuggled out into the free world. They are seldom detected. They are provided with a good 'cover' and *never* take an *active* part in subversive activities. If any undercover subverter or network leader is detected and interrogated, little information can be squeezed out from him. The subverters' only communication with the master-subverter is through indirect methods which protect him.

Western security officers are well aware that Red Chinese undercover-subverter networks operate throughout the free world, and they have occasionally unmasked master-subverters, but enough legal evidence to gain a conviction is rarely available, and it is very seldom that a detected master-subverter will talk and incriminate himself and his network.

There have been some exceptions however. A Red Chinese master-subverter in France for example, decided to defect, and she told

Western security officers all she knew about the recruitment and training of master-subverters in the French-speaking world. Master-subverters in the United States, West Germany and Japan have also defected. Through these defectors, Western intelligence has been able to corroborate the information they had already obtained from Peking's secret files.

Red China's recruiting agents operate everywhere. Secret case histories show that they are continuously recruiting national master-subverters in New York, Chicago and other North American cities; London and other important British centres; in Paris, Marseilles, Algiers, Tunisia and other places where French is spoken; in Frankfurt, Stuttgart and other West German cities; in Rome, Amman, Cairo, Beirut, Tokyo, Sydney, Bombay, Antwerp, Rotterdam and Montreal. Algiers, Tunisia, Marseilles, Singapore and Hong Kong are the confirmed 'clearing centres' for the transport of subverter recruits to Red China. Allied Security has reason to believe that active 'clearing centres' also operate in many other parts of the globe.

The number of Mao Tse-tung's master-subverters already smuggled into all parts of the free world constitutes a serious danger to all democratic régimes. But the Special Division for Subversion of Peking Secret Service Headquarters is still not satisfied. It plans to continue annually to step up its output of master-subverters.

The Spread of Student Violence

By the mid-1960s both Moscow's and Peking's subverter networks were established in all countries of the free world, operating independently of each other. A concentrated onslaught against the Western democracies was thus launched by two disconnected subversion forces. Millions of working hours were lost to the countries of the West by work-to-rule, wildcat strikes and official stoppages. The ever-increasing number of demonstrations, riots and terrorist outrages threatened to destroy the foundations of all democratic régimes. Yet, although subversive acts were escalating, the directors of the Special Division for Subversion in Moscow and Peking were still not satisfied with the results. Moscow flashed coded orders to master-subverters, instructing them to step up the industrial disputes and protest demonstrations. Meanwhile Peking instructed its own master-subverters to 'sharpen political conflict by instigating destructive rioting and lawless action'. Both Moscow and Peking directed their master-subverters to 'concentrate upon the young, the most malleable and most gullible section of the population'.

Moscow advised:*

> It is the idealistic young who most violently resent injustice. This is natural. The young are experiencing new emotions and have not yet learned to control them. The young feel strongly about everything: about love, sex, art, poverty and beauty. The universities where young men and women gather and discuss world economics, history, social revolution and politics, is the ideal seeding ground for revolutionary ideas. New ideas take root swiftly and flower abundantly . . .'

* The *Party Bulletin*, Moscow, January 1967.

Peking summarised it thus:*

> Outspoken political disagreement and protest marches have long been a student activity in the capitalist world. The young are enthusiastic and zealous; they are anxious to be heard and they express themselves loudly. In recent years they have forsaken reason, law and order and resorted to militant action to express their political discontent. Under expert stimulation by master-subverters they will even resort to criminal violence . . .

The infiltration of subverters into the student communities has resulted in disturbances quite out of proportion to the grievances that spark off disorders.

*   *   *

In Britain subverters provoked student discontent, demonstrations, sit-down strikes and confrontations with the police. But the British are not prone to criminal violence and students' militancy has rarely expressed itself in violent rioting. Peking's directors of the Special Division for Subversion were disappointed. They wanted to see violent student rioting in the United Kingdom. Their master-subverters used as a pretext the London protest demonstration against the Vietnam war.

British students, joined by contingents of students from other European countries, held a meeting in London's Trafalgar Square on the 17th of March 1968. The 10,000 demonstrators were protesting against American military intervention in Vietnam. From the plinth of Nelson's Column the organisers called upon the students to form up and march to the US Embassy in protest.

The police acted swiftly with radio messages and speeding police vans, and built a three-deep defence cordon around the American Embassy building. More than 1,000 police officers were employed for this task only; many of them were mounted.

For many hours the police resisted a determined assault upon the Embassy by a mob that hurled stones, bottles, fire-crackers and smoke bombs. They scattered thunder-flashes under the hoofs of police officer's mounts, causing them to rear up and unseat the riders.

* Extract from the classified publication *Action Reports*, Peking, February 1967.

Fireworks and smoke bombs cannot be bought in London's West End on a Sunday afternoon. There were individuals who had gone to Trafalgar and Grosvenor Squares with the specific intention of instigating violence. It was evident to the public that a proportion of the demonstrators came to the Trafalgar Square meeting primed to riot and clash with the police.

At one point during the rioting the mob came within a few yards of the American Embassy building steps. It broke many windows and caused considerable damage to steps, railings and walls. A total of 170 policeman were injured; four of them were detained in hospital and one officer suffered a serious spinal injury. Only forty-five demonstrators received hospital treatment, showing that the police acted with great restraint and resisted provocation. 246 demonstrators were arrested.

'There is evidence that a not insignificant number of people went to this demonstration with the intention of provoking violence,' said Mr Callaghan, the Home Secretary, who had been provided with Intelligence reports. He told Parliament that a number of foreign nationals had entered Britain solely for the purpose of taking part in this demonstration; he also commented: 'The demonstrators were determined to stay until they had provoked a violent response of some sort from the police. This intention became paramount once they had entered Grosvenor Square.'

This first large-scale riot of British students was planned by under-cover master-subverters and implemented by their networks. When it was realised that British students could not be induced to use force in demonstrations, other militants were imported to mingle with the student-inspired demonstrations and provoke rioting. The plan was successful. The Grosvenor Square riots received widespread publicity, and launched a new fashion.

Later that same year,* the Vietnam Solidarity Committee organised another anti-Vietnam war demonstration in Trafalgar Square. The VSC chairman, a former president of the Oxford Union, emphasised that the demonstration would be peaceful. He strongly opposed the use of violence and declared that all processions would steer clear of

* On the 27th of October 1968.

Grosvenor Square. The Home Secretary decided not to use his powers to ban the demonstration. Despite the violent rioting in Grosvenor Square a few months earlier, he had no wish to suppress freedom of speech.

There was every indication that the organisers of the demonstration had only peaceful intentions. Nevertheless a police guard was set up around many government buildings, and wise shopkeepers on the demonstration's route boarded up their windows. 30,000 demonstrators marched in an orderly fashion from the Embankment to Trafalgar Square and created no disturbances.

But this was an opportunity to cause disruption that the subverters could not let slip. After the Trafalgar Square rally, while the demonstrators marched to Hyde Park via Downing Street, specially-drafted trouble-makers in the ranks appealed to the demonstrators to march on Grosvenor Square. Some 6,000 demonstrators responded to this incitement. They broke away from the main procession and marched on the American Embassy. Again the police acted swiftly. The militants found themselves facing a police cordon twelve deep around the Embassy building.

The master-subverters had studied the defensive tactics used by the police during the first assault upon the US Embassy earlier in the year. They believed they had devised the best method of breaking through police cordons and issued this information to their network members for circulation among the demonstrators. On four occasions, acting on a signal, the great crowd swamped forward, determined to break through the police cordon and surge up the Embassy steps. Each time they failed. Eventually, after three hours of rioting, the demonstrators were dispersed. Thirty-eight arrests were made, forty policemen were injured and some fifty demonstrators received medical attention. The students at the London School of Economics* offered their premises as an improvised casualty station, and there the injuries of an additional forty demonstrators were treated.

The only political impact of this second Grosvenor Square riot was to make the British and foreign public aware of what the authorities already knew: that the rioters were not political idealists. They were

---

* The previous day, 1,000 students had occupied the building in a sit-in strike.

unruly elements who could be easily inflamed and organised to engage in pointless but violent clashes with the police. They were pawns, senselessly propagating a political policy devised in Peking and master-minded by professional subverters.

*　　*　　*

The Vietnam war has aroused much moral heart-searching. These doubts are perhaps felt most keenly by American young people who are about to be called up. Many have given very careful consideration to the implications of the war, and have formed very strong opinions. Those young people who oppose the Vietnam War are, no doubt, sincere in their opposition; they cannot lightly be accused of being communist agitators. Nevertheless their sincere convictions are being used by astute undercover subverters for political gain.

During 1967, American students increasingly demonstrated against the Vietnam war. They strongly objected to university participation in the recruitment of students for the armed forces, and denounced university association with the Dow Chemical Company, which supplies the napalm used for bombing in Vietnam. On occasions university authorities have felt obliged to call in the police, forcibly to eject demonstrating students from university buildings that they have occupied. As a result of these incidents 'police brutality' has become associated with the Vietnam war.

In the University of Wisconsin, on the 18th of October 1967, the police used tear-gas and clubs to eject 150 students who were protesting against a recruitment campaign by the Dow Chemical Company. At Brooklyn College the following day, fifty students demonstrated against Navy agents recruiting on the premises. One student, who had been selected to provoke authority, refused to produce his identification card. The police were called in; he and another student were arrested. These two arrests were the spark that started a conflagration: 8,000 students out of 10,000 refused to attend their classes. Meanwhile, by similar means, master-subverters were inspiring resentment towards authority elsewhere, and sympathy strikes took place at Columbia University, Queen's College and Hunter College.

In Berkeley, California, several thousand students demonstrated against Vietnam. A clash occurred between students and the police, and more than a hundred were injured.

At Columbia University in April 1968 subverters encouraged a handful of gullible students to spark off a large student protest. 150 students* objected to the construction of a new gymnasium, and linked this grievance with a political denunciation of the University Consortium for conducting research for the Federal Government. The Acting Dean of Columbia University, Professor Henry S. Coleman, was for a short time made a prisoner of the militant students, but was later set free. As a counter-measure, the campus was officially declared closed that same day.

The undercover subverters worked industriously, whipped up hot-headed opinion, and by the 26th of April the number of students demonstrating had risen to 700. As a precautionary measure the police were asked to take over all the buildings not already occupied by students.

On the night of the 19th of April a violent clash became imminent between the students who had occupied the university buildings and other disgruntled students who wished to continue their studies. Fearing widespread violence and injury, Professor Kirk, the university President, called upon the police to come to the university to restore order. In the subsequent police action, 692 persons were arrested; 524 of them were Columbia students, 106 people were injured, among them fourteen policemen.

The police intervention added more fuel to the flames. During the following weeks the undercover subverters harped upon 'police brutality' and inflamed the students until they issued a strike call. Hundreds picketed the campus buildings and spasmodic clashes frequently occurred between students and police. By the 22nd of May campus arrests had reached a total of 993. On this day, Professor Kirk announced his retirement as President of Columbia University. The university authorities then asked the police to drop all outstanding charges against arrested students, and peace was negotiated with the students.

During the first half of 1968, student unrest in the United States

* The total enrolment is 27,500 students.

resulted in at least 221 major student demonstrations taking place at
101 colleges and universities. The secret Kremlin publication *The Party
Bulletin** warmly praised the American master-subverters and their
undercover networks. It congratulated them upon their 'excellent
direction of the US students throughout America, which resulted in
nationwide revolutionary actions . . .'

The continuing subverter influence in US universities was thus
encouraged until it provoked one of the most shameful incidents to
occur in a civilised country; the cold-blooded killing of innocent
students on their campus.

At Kent State University in Ohio a violent clash broke out between
students and police during the night of the 1st and 2nd of May 1970,
when students burned down a small wooden shed. Martial Law was
declared and troops of the National Guard drove the students back into
their dormitories with teargas. The Governor of Ohio banned all
meetings and assured the National Guard officers that he was in complete agreement with their action. The Governor stated the demonstration was part of 'a national revolutionary conspiracy'.

On the 4th of May between 1,500 and 2,000 students gathered in the
College grounds to demonstrate passively. The National Guard opened
fire with teargas. Some students seized teargas canisters before they
exploded and threw them back; others hurled stones. Without orders
from a superior officer and without any warning, the National Guard
opened fire with rifles. They killed four students, two of them girls,
and wounded nine others. It was later shown that these four students,
aged nineteen and twenty, were *not* participating in the demonstration
and did not hold left-wing opinions. The National Guard claimed
they had been fired upon by a sniper and had shot back in self-defence.
But no eyewitness could be found who had heard shots before the
soldiers opened fire upon the students.

These tragic deaths were the regrettable result of violent disorders.
Whenever rioting occurs, serious injury and death may result from
hot-headed action. Unfortunately, such incidents do not shock the par-
ticipants into remorseful passivity; rather, they have a contrary effect.

The Kent University killings inflamed students throughout the

* Moscow, August 1968.

nation. By the 8th of May, four hundred universities and colleges had been occupied by students, in many cases supported by the teaching staffs. These student strikes were disciplined, although occasional outbreaks of violence at some colleges resulted in police being called upon to intervene.

President Nixon received a deputation of six students from the Kent State University and assured them that the Department of Justice would make a full inquiry into the shooting. But on the 9th of May 100,000 students took part in a mass demonstration in Washington and demanded the withdrawal of all US forces from Indo-China; though the demonstration broke up peacefully, small groups of extremists later smashed shop windows, and overturned and set fire to cars.

On the 11th of May, at the University of California, a 23-year-old student soaked himself in petrol and burned himself to death as a protest against the Vietnam War.

*   *   *

Meanwhile, student riots and disorders were occurring throughout the Western world.

On the 2nd of June 1967 West German students who had been inflamed by Maoist subverters attempted to occupy the Cologne Opera House. A long and bloody street battle ensued between police and militant students; twenty policemen and twenty-four demonstrators had to receive hospital treatment, and a twenty-six-year-old student from Hanover was shot dead by a detective.

The West German federal government promptly outlawed all demonstrations. Orders were issued to the police to use any methods necessary to ensure that the ban on demonstrations was obeyed. Uneasy orderliness ensued for some months until Rudi Dutschke, a notorious political agitator who described himself as a professional revolutionary and a Marxist, was shot and wounded by a young house-painter. Afterwards the assailant barricaded himself in the basement of an unfinished building and fought a long, lone battle with the police before he was overpowered. Five days of student rioting followed the shooting, and violent clashes between militant students and the police took place in all parts of the city.

On the 12th of April 1968 student demonstrations, provoked by Moscow's and Peking's subverters, took place all over West Germany. The most violent was in West Berlin, where thousands of demonstrators marched on Berlin City Hall and on the headquarters of the American radio station. The students announced they intended to take over the Technical University of West Berlin for their revolutionary headquarters. The police beat off the attack with clubs and water-cannon. An attack was then led against the Axel Springer newspaper group.* Police surrounded the premises with barbed wire and guards were mounted upon it after the first attack was repulsed. In Munich, militant demonstrators succeeded in gaining access to an Axel Springer building; they smashed windows, furniture and equipment before the police could eject them. Throughout West Germany students prevented distribution of Springer newspapers by attacking delivery vans.

The next day† the students dedicated themselves to blocking the flow of traffic through the towns of Lübeck, Cologne, Frankfurt, Bremen, Hamburg, Duisburg, Nuremberg and many others. The 14th of April was Easter Sunday; but the West Berlin police had no holiday. 4,000 students tore up paving stones, erected barricades, used cobblestones as ammunition and provoked the police into battle.

Here is the text of a Special Division for Subversion directive, sent in code in April 1968 from Moscow to undercover master-subverters in West Germany:

HIGHLY CONFIDENTIAL! MEMORISE! THEN BURN!

Action must be taken at once to create disruptive situations that will rock the very foundations of the capitalist system. The disturbances must occur on such a large scale that they cause deep concern to the population.

Lightning strikes of key workers in important industrial centres must be encouraged. The objective is to bring the maximum of factories to a complete standstill. Such strike action must be made

* Two of the most influential Springer publications are *Die Bild Zeitung* and *Die Welt*, with a 4,000,000 circulation; both these newspapers express right-wing opinions.
† The 13th of April 1968.

known to the population. Whenever the press, radio and television maintain silence about strike action that cripples industry, the alarming news must be spread by word of mouth and by leaflets. Every industrial action not reported by the press, radio and television must be communicated immediately to Headquarters. Our Radio Centres, broadcasting news bulletins to your country, will give listeners full details of all stoppages.

Demonstrations must be instigated on every possible occasion. Demonstrations are a symptom of public discontent. News that a demonstration has taken place spreads to all parts of the country; and is often reported upon abroad. It is important that demonstrations be for popular causes: against price increases, against unemployment, etc. Demonstrations must have full public approval and sympathy.

Revolutionary action by students must be stepped up. Every effort must be made now to encourage students to demonstrate, and, if possible, to riot on the largest possible scale. Students are susceptible to an idealistic approach. They should be tackled on the lines laid down in our previous directives.

Every activist must remember that under no circumstances should the slightest suspicion be aroused that such demonstrations are in any way communist-inspired. When known Communist Party members are persuading others to take militant action, our undercover subverters must oppose this communist-inspired action. It is vitally important for them to safeguard their established undercover positions.

Informed by West German Intelligence of the root causes of the outbreaks of violence the Federal Chancellor, Dr Kiesinger, placed the facts clearly before the country. He said that student violence was

led by small but militant extreme-left forces, openly aiming at the destruction of our parliamentarian democratic order. In our democracy the representatives of any political view have the incontestable right to express and promote it; but no group may claim the right to realise their political opinion by force. We will not tolerate any violent disturbances of the legal order, regardless of their source.

The student demonstrations continued on the 16th of April, and the next day an Associated Press photographer, Klaus Frings, died as a result of the injuries he received during the rioting in Munich on the 15th. This tragic event shocked the more level-headed leaders of the Students' Union into realising that the violence was getting out of hand. The Students' Union appealed to its members, and to all demonstrators, to conduct themselves in an orderly fashion and not to give way to violence. A second victim of the Munich riots, a twenty-seven-year-old student, died on the 18th of April. At once the Students' Union decided to call off all demonstrations. The undercover-subverters did their best to encourage the students to disobey their leaders and continue rioting, but without success.

A few days later the Minister of the Interior, Dr Benda, reported that law and order had been restored. He said that a security investigation had uncovered a nation wide network of subverters that had coordinated the demonstrating and rioting. In many cases, selected troublemakers had received written orders instructing them how to resist police charges and manufacture riot weapons.

On the 30th of April Dr Benda gave Parliament a full report about the Easter disturbances. He said demonstrations had taken place *simultaneously* in twenty-seven towns. In every case the demonstrations were accompanied by rioting and acts of violence. Up to 18,000 students had been involved. 280 police officers and 296 civilians had received medical treatment for injuries, and police prosecutions were pending against 827 individuals; 87 were under eighteen years; 200 aged between nineteen and twenty-two; 246 were aged twenty-two to twenty-five; and 284 over twenty-five. Dr Benda said that although the disturbances had been serious, the State had not been endangered.

*   *   *

The students riots in Paris in the spring of 1968 were the most notable of the undercover subverters' operations, because they came close to bringing about the complete collapse of France.

The directors of the Moscow and Peking Special Divisions for Subversion had prepared their master-subverters in France long before the rioting. This is the Moscow directive, sent in code to its master-subverters in France in April 1968:

HIGHLY CONFIDENTIAL! MEMORISE! THEN BURN!

Results following our March directive are inexcusably poor. A very favourable situation exists among the French students. The action of the West German students over Easter could have been utilised for stimulating vigorous strike action by the French students.

Action must be taken *at once* by all our undercover cadres!

All support must be given to the French Party comrades. But our undercover activists must not involve themselves openly, nor damage their anti-communist reputation.

The student population must be induced to demonstrate publicly and fight vigorously for their 'rights'. Subtle undercover tactics must be adopted to ensure these demonstrations culminate in rioting and street fighting. The objective is to create a dangerous, revolutionary situation in which law and order is discredited.

Simultaneously our undercover cadres in industry, commerce, the trade unions, religious organisations and political parties, must propagate the idea that the working population should give full support to any students' strike actions.

It is imperative that all undercover activists concentrate on the realisation of these objectives during the next few weeks. A revolutionary situation is ripening in France, and if all undercover subverters play their part to the utmost a situation can develop where the existing reactionary Government is overthrown by active revolutionary action or by parliamentarian methods.

The Peking directive was very similar in its wording, though the Red Chinese Special Division for Subversion laid even more emphasis on terrorist acts playing the prime role.

Discontent had been simmering among Paris students for some time. Two hundred extreme left-wingers, describing themselves as a band of Anarchists, Maoists, Castroites and Trotskyists, formed an uneasy coalition. They staged protests, marched through the university corridors shouting out slogans and interrupted lectures and study-groups. On the 2nd of May 1968 they forcibly occupied a classroom and prevented a Professor from delivering his lecture.

The Dean of the Faculty of Letters stated:

The function of any university is to teach its students. If it is prevented from doing so, steps must be taken to rectify the position. For some weeks it has been increasingly difficult for students to pursue studies at Nanterre because of systematic agitation by small groups of students who are creating a climate of instability. On the 2nd of May many classes could not be held because of incidents deliberately created, and menaces to students, professors and university officials.

The Dean said he had decided, in agreement with the Minister of Education, to suspend studies in the Faculty of Letters at Nanterre.

On the 3rd of May the Rector of the University of Paris announced that all studies at the Sorbonne would be suspended because a small group of students had occupied the university courtyard and attempted to take possession of the lecture hall. They were protesting because the university authorities has summoned six students before a disciplinary court. The students refused to vacate the Sorbonne courtyard. The police had been called, and, using tear-gas, had forcibly evicted the students.

Not realising they were the pawns of subtle undercover subverters, an angry meeting of students resolved that militant action was the only way to achieve their demands. A street battle with the police developed in the nearby Boulevard Saint Michel, when students tore up paving stones and built them into barricades. They pulled down traffic signs to use as weapons, overturned cars to block roadways and used rocks, bottles and hand-made grenades as ammunition. The fighting lasted more than six hours. Twenty policemen were badly injured as well as an unknown number of rioting students. A total of 600 students were arrested, but most of them were released after questioning. A number of them were charged, however, and sent to prison after it had been proved that they had had clubs, iron bars, and axes.

Violence always arouses strong feelings, and a match was thrown into this explosive atmosphere by the French Students' Union. The student leaders protested against the closing of the Sorbonne and the Faculty of

Letters at Nanterre. They protested, too, against the arrest and imprisonment of students involved in the riots of the 3rd of May. They alleged
that the police had behaved in an unnecessarily brutal fashion, and they
complained of defects in the French system of higher education.

This protest took the form of an organised demonstration in the Latin
Quarter. The students' mood, was ugly, and violence was inevitable.
More than 10,000 students fought steel-helmeted French Riot Police
(CRS) in the Boulevard Saint Germain, the Rue de Rennes and the
Rue Saint Jacques. By nightfall the streets displayed scenes of devasta-
tion unknown since the war. Large areas of pavements and roads had
been stripped of their paving stones, which had been used as missiles.
Scores of buses and cars had been overturned, their tyres slashed and
the vehicles then set alight. Shop-windows were smashed, railings torn
down and private property destroyed. The riot police fought the students
with tear-gas bombs, fire-hoses and repeated baton charges. Approximately 600 students and police had to receive hospital treatment;
some 420 demonstrators were arrested.

The following day, the 7th of May, thousands of students marched
down the Champs Elysées, waving red flags and singing the *Internationale*. The police were licking their wounds. There was no violence
except when a group of militants attempted to invade the offices of
Le Figaro.★ Students and police clashed on the steps of the newspaper
building and a dozen or more students and policemen were taken to
hospital. Meanwhile other universities in Paris went on strike in response to a call for unity from the Students' Union. In the provinces,
subverter-inspired students demonstrated solidarity with Paris. They
closed down the Universities of Lyons, Marseilles, Lille, Strasbourg,
Nancy, Clermont-Ferrand, Grenoble, Toulouse, Aix-en-Provence and
elsewhere. They kept them shut for many weeks.

Paris was dominated by fanatics and violence. Lawlessness was
creating a near-revolutionary situation: the authorities became alarmed.

On the 8th of May a special Cabinet meeting was convened with
President De Gaulle present. The Cabinet recommended that the
demands of the students should be given serious consideration in order

★ This newspaper had commented unfavourably upon the student demonstrations of the previous day.

that peace might be quickly restored to the universities. But it was also agreed that public law and order *must* be maintained in all circumstances.

While Cabinet Ministers debated these problems, 20,000 students attended yet another mass meeting in the Latin Quarter. A strong cordon of police was quickly thrown up around the Sorbonne to prevent the students gaining access to it. However, the Paris Prefect of Police told the students, via a public address system, that he had orders not to interfere with them unless the police were attacked, or in the event of students deliberately embarking upon destructive disorder.

An uneasy peace endured throughout Paris on the 9th of May. Then reports filtered through to the authorities from their agents that the students planned to occupy the Sorbonne, while students in other university towns would mount supporting protest demonstrations. The cordon of police around the university was redoubled.

In Paris the Students' Union announced that another monster demonstration would march through the already devastated Latin Quarter the following day. The student leaders stated that the objective of the demonstration was to demand the release of all students who had been arrested and were still in custody.

The demonstration began at 6.30 in the evening, and almost at once it developed into rioting that lasted until the following day. The students built more than sixty barricades out of uprooted paving-stones, the steel shutters from shops and the wrecks of burnt-out cars and trucks. To clear the streets, the police were obliged to storm the barricades, after softening up the defenders with tear-gas grenades. Four students and eighteen officers were seriously injured; 345 others had to receive hospital treatment. A total of 188 cars were damaged or destroyed—the Rue de Lussac alone was littered with the wreckage of some forty burnt-out vehicles.

'It might have been the days of the Paris Commune,' was the way one observer described the fighting.

Red flags fluttered on the barricades and were enveloped in dense clouds of smoke; from time to time red signal flares illuminated the dark sky, flames and smoke billowed from burning cars and loud explosions punctuated the angry and excited shouting. It all had the terrifying reality of an historical reconstruction. Some brave student occasionally dashed across the street to throw a fire-bomb, or drove yet another car through the fighting to reinforce the barricades. The police fought with trained precision. They demolished the barricades one by one and methodically mopped up the defendants. These boys and girls may not have known what they were fighting for. But they certainly fought with the energy of despair . . .

The following day the Paris Prefect of Police announced that the riot police, although anxious to avoid being involved in street-fighting, had finally been provoked to action by the students guerrilla warfare which had been directed against them.

The Government held out an olive branch. It announced that the Sorbonne would be opened the following day. This meant that academic studies could be resumed and students could sit for their exams. A special Court of Appeal would consider granting an amnesty to all arrested students.

But that same day, the two largest trade unions in France, the CGT and the CFDT, called upon their members to come out on a twenty-four-hour general strike in support of the students. The undercover subverters were coordinating their efforts. And meanwhile, in Strasbourg and in Lyons, demonstrating students had forcibly occupied their university buildings.

The general strike of the 13th of May caused a total shut-down of Paris. Electricity, gas, postal services, public transport, and industry were all affected. Only a few airliners maintained their scheduled flights from Orly and Le Bourget. At the same time strikes and mass-demonstrations took place in the provinces, crippling the entire country. Dockers struck at the ports, and the car ferry service from Le Havre to Southampton was closed down.

In Paris, a monster demonstration, estimated at 200,000 strong, marched for four hours across the capital, from the Place de la République, through the Latin Quarter, to the Place Denfert-Rochereaux. Students and trade unionists marched shoulder to shoulder in this procession; but apart from minor skirmishes there was no violence.

In the provinces, students and workers supported the Paris strikers with their own demonstrations, open-air rallies and public meetings.

That same day, all the students and other demonstrators who had been arrested for rioting were released. Among them were students who had already been convicted and sentenced to imprisonment. Also that same day, the heads of the Paris universities announced they would set up a commission which would represent both teachers and students, to study the problems of university life. Whatever the original grievances of the students, the authorities were falling over themselves to settle them quickly and quietly.

Authority had yielded. Students and lecturers together could thrash out the problems of university life. The rioting students had been forgiven and their punishment was rescinded. The police guards were withdrawn from universities.

But the olive branch was spurned.

On the 14th of May the Sorbonne was occupied by a small group of militant students who flew from its roof the red and black flags symbolising communism and anarchism.

Neither the university authorities nor the police resisted this occupation. France's Prime Minister told the nation that the Rector of the university and several professors had called for police protection only when they found themselves surrounded by a group of angry students armed with clubs.

Urged on by subverters who called authority's appeal to reason a 'students' victory', students all over France forcibly occupied their universities during the following two days. They set up Students' Revolutionary Action Committees and declared themselves independent of the authority of the State.

In Paris, one of the capital's three National Theatres was taken over by 3,000 students at the end of a performance. The students proclaimed from the stage that they rejected 'consumer culture'. Red and black flags were flown from the building and a large placard in the foyer announced the theatre was closed to 'bourgeois audiences'; it ceased to be a theatre and was converted into a 'Centre of Cultural Exchanges for contact between the workers and students, and for uninterrupted meetings'.

Meanwhile the students in the Sorbonne passed a resolution announcing the abolition of all traditional examinations. Simultaneously, throughout the country, workers occupied many of France's biggest factories, including the nationalised Renault car factories. The workers proclaimed strikes of unlimited duration, demanded a forty-hour week, a higher basic wage and better social facilities. A total of 60,000 workers were out on strike at the Renault car factories alone and the red and black flags flew over their roofs. At Nantes, the Sud Aviation plant was taken over by 2,000 workers.

When the French Prime Minister, M. Pompidou, spoke to the nation on television on the evening of the 16th of May, he could have been forgiven for his air of bewilderment. In the interests of preserving peace, law and order he was ready to make almost any concessions demanded. What more could the students and strikers want? The Prime Minister appealed to the nation:

> I have given proof of my desire for appeasement. With the agreement of the President of the Republic, who will address you in a few days, I have restored the university of Paris to its teachers and students. I have held out my hand to them for the broadest and most constructive cooperation.
>
> I have freed the arrested demonstrators. I have announced a total amnesty. My appeals have gone entirely unheeded. Groups of hotheads . . . propose to make the disorder general, with the express aim of destroying the nation, and the very foundations of our free society.
>
> The government has a duty to defend the republic. I will defend it. I address myself to you with calmness, but with gravity. Students, do not follow the provocateurs who declared themselves unconcerned with three quarters of you. Listen to the voice of reason. We are ready to hear all your legitimate demands.
>
> Frenchmen, Frenchwomen. It is up to you to show, by your calmness and by your resolution—whatever your political preferences may be, whatever your social demands may be—that you reject anarchy. The government will do its duty.
>
> It asks you to help.

The Prime Minister's appeal went unheeded. The strikes spread. All over France more and more large factories were taken over by workers, hot-headedly following the lead given by undercover subverters. The Berliet heavy-vehicle plant in Lyons was occupied by strikers; so were the synthetic textile industries in Lyons and Besançon, the shipyards in Nantes, Le Havre and Marseilles and the armament factory in Bayonne. Rail transport came to a standstill when railwaymen and locomotive drivers struck; air traffic was reduced by 75 per cent. By the 18th of May half a million workers were on strike and had occupied more than a hundred factories.

France was almost at a standstill.

This revolutionary situation had been independently manipulated by the Soviet and Red Chinese Special Division for Subversion through their master-subverters' undercover networks. M. Waldeck Rochet, the Secretary-General of the French Communist Party, now cleared the decks for action. The Party's newspaper *L'Humanité*'s headlines announced that the French Communist Party demanded a Popular Front Government. It stated that the Communist Party was 'ready to assume all its responsibilities'. The newspaper announcement terminated its demand with the coy suggestion: 'Why not call for the immediate overthrow of the Government? It is evident that conditions are ripening for its eventual overthrow!'

By the 19th of May more than two million workers were on strike and 120 factories were occupied. Paris was paralysed without the Metro, buses and other public transport services. The airports were deserted and all the power-plants were in the hands of the employees. To add unpleasantness to an uncomfortable situation, the dustmen had contributed their own special brand of brotherly solidarity; the streets were full of great piles of uncollected evil-smelling garbage.

In the provinces, 8,000 shipyard workers took over the Pehoet Naval Yards at Saint Nazaire; 4,500 workers brought the Dunlop works to a standstill at Mont Lucion, while coal mines were taken over by the workers in the Nord and Pas-de-Calais area. Every large railway station in the country was picketed by strikers, and in Cannes the annual Film Festival had to be abandoned because the technicians came out on strike. The film directors backed them by refusing to permit their films to be screened.

By the 20th of May France was totally isolated from the outside world. Her economic life was paralysed. More than six million workers were on strike and all airports and railways were at a complete standstill. Only the Port of Bordeaux was still operating. The taxi drivers, the last remaining form of public transport, now also came out on strike. The city's uncollected garbage formed stinking ten-foot high walls that lined the streets. By agreement with its staff, the State radio network continued broadcasting recorded music, interspersed with news bulletins, but there were no other programmes.

On the 21st of May the National Assembly debated a vote of censure against the government. The number of strikers had risen to more than eight million. Bank employees were striking, civil servants at the Ministry of Finance and other Government departments had ceased to work, and all stocks and shares dealings were suspended on the Bourse. Even the girls at the Folies Bergères were on strike; 300 dancers, singers, dressers and stage hands had taken over the famous theatre and occupied it.

The Secretary-General of the French Communist Party spoke in the National Assembly and called for the end of the Gaullist régime, and for a Popular Front Government.

The destiny of France trembled in the balance.

A vote of censure moved in the National Assembly by the Communist Party failed to bring down the government by a hair's-breadth. The combined Opposition vote of 223* failed to gain its objective by just eleven votes. The Communist Party's bid to gain the balance of power in the National Assembly had come dangerously close to success.

On the 23rd of May France reached deadlock. But the government was as strong as ever. It had withstood a nationwide plot by Moscow and Peking to unseat it. The army was solidly behind it; the country was in turmoil but it was politically strong. A carefully engineered revolutionary situation had been coaxed along to a climax of very noisy fireworks, but there was no final Big Bang. The Communist Party's bid for political power proved to be a very damp squib.

On the 24th of May, President de Gaulle spoke to the nation. He said that in June he would hold a referendum. He planned to reform the nation's economic, social and educational structure. The reform

* Including 73 Communist Party votes.

would include the reorganisation of the universities, modernisation of the nation's economic structure, improvement of working conditions and workers' participation, in the widest sense, in the running of their factories. Students would share in the organisation of their universities. The French nation would be asked to vote simply 'Yes' or 'No'.

These had been days of great excitement, and of great inconvenience. Now President de Gaulle was offering the people everything they demanded. Many people were wondering what the disturbances had been about. The President's honest and sincere words to the nation had undeniable impact. Authority was prepared to grant all reasonable demands.

But Moscow's and Peking's undercover subverters wished to drown the voice of reason and appeasement. Within half an hour of President de Gaulle's speech, more violent disorders erupted all over Paris. In the Latin Quarter, the Place de la Bastille and the Gare de Lyons, students erected barricades of sawn-down trees, mountains of garbage and torn-up flagstones. The riot police went into action again, with steel helmets pulled down low to protect their faces from flying stones, their riot clubs swinging purposefully. Tear-gas rolled like smoke over the battle-fields. Casualties were so high the students were obliged to organise their own emergency hospital service. Hundreds of students, armed with axe-handles, clubs and iron bars, stormed into the Paris Stock Exchange, pulled down the quotation boards, smashed the windows and set the entrance hall on fire. A total of 10,000 students were involved in this attack.

This violence was in marked contrast to two other demonstrations that had taken place that day, organised by the CGT. In the first, a total of 100,000 strikers had marched from the Place de la Bastille to the Boulevard Haussmann and then quietly dispersed. The second demonstration had begun at the Citroen works in the south-western suburbs, and ended at the Gare d'Austerlitz. This, too, dispersed without clashing with the police.

By the following day, the number of workers on strike in France had reached ten million. But now began a rapid cooling-off of militancy. The undercover subverters did their utmost to foment the revolutionary spirit, but de Gaulle's plain speaking had taken the steam out of a revolt that had no underlying cause.

The trade unions and the Employers' Federation accepted the Prime Minister's invitation to peace talks. On the 27th of May they reached a tentative agreement.On the 28th the strikers began to return to work. Two days later, de Gaulle announced the dissolution of the National Assembly in preparation for a general election. On the 31st of May M. Pompidou formed a new Cabinet.

During the first week of June 1968 there was a general resumption of work, although demonstrators still marched and clashed with the police. At the Peugeot car factory in Eastern France, a young worker was shot dead by riot police.

De Gaulle bluntly told the nation on television that the freedom of France was threatened by a totalitarian communist dictatorship. He sounded a grim warning:

> Elections will take place unless an attempt is made to gag the French people, preventing them from expressing themselves by the same methods which are used to prevent the students from studying, the teachers from teaching, and the workers from working. These methods are intimidation, deception and tyranny, exercised by groups long organised for this purpose, by a party which is a totalitarian enterprise.

Throughout the affair President de Gaulle and Prime Minister Pompidou had respected the French Constitution. There had been movements of French troops around the capital, including concentrations of tank units which were ready for any emergency; de Gaulle had even arranged to call upon French troops stationed in West Germany. But these were purely precautionary measures. The political scene had seemed dangerous, but political events never got out of hand.

The students were more easily influenced by undercover subverters than the workers, and student disorders continued. There were two nights of violent rioting in the Latin Quarter on the 11th and the 13th of June, resulting in 72 policemen being injured, and 194 demonstrators; 72 barricades were erected, 75 cars were damaged and burned out, and 10 police vans were wrecked. Five police stations were attacked, 25 trees were cut down and 24 shop windows smashed. The Minister of the Interior announced the same day that 30 foreigners had been arrested during the students' riots. He said: 'These professional trouble-makers, imported from abroad for the occasion, have been deported.'

The Sorbonne continued to be occupied by militant students for a total of five weeks, and then, on the 16th of June, the 200 students in occupation agreed to leave the university, after an afternoon of negotiations with police officers. The students' takeover of universities throughout France finally ended on the 1st of July 1968.

The events of the spring of 1968 were a grim warning to the French government, and to all other governments of the Western democracies.

* * *

During the summer and autumn of 1968, Mexico City suffered the worst public disorders it had known in fifty years. A four-month strike by 150,000 university students in the capital became a students' revolt that violently disrupted academic life, and resulted in bloody clashes between the students and the armed forces.

As in America, France, Japan and other countries that have suffered serious student rioting, the basic cause of the outbreak in Mexico was obscure. One version was that it began on the 23rd of July as a result of a trivial quarrel over a girl between students of two different universities. This led to a fight in which several hundred students were involved. Within a week students were overturning buses and cars to build street barricades, and repelling government troops that had been brought in to assist the riot police. On the 30th of July a large-scale battle took place in the centre of Mexico City, in which the students fought against troops, armoured cars and tanks.

By that time, every educational institute and university building in Mexico City had been closed down by the students. When troops used a bazooka to smash down the doors of a high school which students were occupying, resentment against the army became widespread. The students formed a National Strike Committee which made the following six demands of the Government:

1. A free pardon for all political prisoners in Mexico.
2. The abrogation of both sections of the Penal Code that punishes acts of subversion and public disorder.

3. The disbandment of the riot police.
4. The dismissal of the police chief of Mexico City and his deputy.
5. Compensation for the victims of the security forces' aggression.
6. An investigation to determine the official responsibility for the aggression.

The Mexican Government and other independent observers were aware that these disturbances were due to 'the communist professional subverters who have infiltrated and largely dominated the student movement'. A neutral observer described conditions on the 8th of September as follows:

> The Auditorium of the School of Philosophy and Letters has been renamed Auditorium Ernesto Che Guevara, and classroom doors have been painted with such names as Lenin Room or Ho Chi Minh Room. Schools all over the city have taken on a revolutionary look, the students manning them twenty-four hours a day against intrusion by Government forces. The strike committee has moved its meeting place, and its members are reluctant to have their pictures taken for fear of reprisals. Every political student organisation is involved: Moscow Communists, Mao Communists, Castro Communists and Trotsky Communists . . . From almost all students come expressions declaring their great lack of respect for governing officials; the Institutional Revolutionary Party, which has ruled under various names for almost forty years, and all other political groups . . . The bulk of the student body come from the middle and upper classes, the peasant and industrial working classes rarely being represented.

After almost two months of non-stop student disturbances the Mexican army finally seized control of the National University on the 18th of September. The campus of the university had been used as the headquarters of the Students' Strike Movement. It was from this Campus that the Students' Brigade had set off daily for the city to seek support from the population.

The Olympic Games were due to begin on the 12th of October, and the Mexican government was concerned to re-establish public order so that the Games would not be disrupted. From the 21st to the 22nd of September many battles were waged between the Police and students

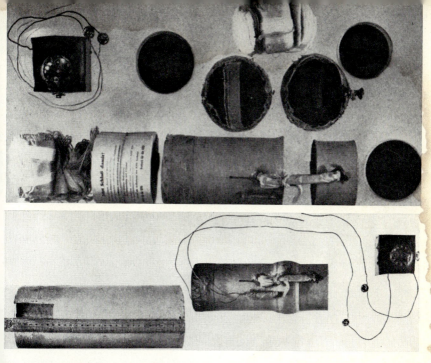

Above, home-made incendiary devices, bombs and rockets manufactured by Moscow and Peking-directed subverters, and widely used by terrorists in Northern Ireland, France, Germany, Italy, Japan, the USA and many other countries of the Western world. Below, containers for secretly passing information and orders between master-subverters and their undercover network agents.

Above, Ernesto Che Guevara, with his comrade and lover, 'Tania'. Here they are on their 'honeymoon', but 8 years later, in 1967, she betrayed him to Bolivian troops because he had not toed Moscow's party line. Below, master-subverter Richard Cooper—he operated in Great Britain, but Moscow pulled the strings.

Communist student leader Daniel Cohn-Bendit (left) talks with German customs officers at Saarbrücken before re-entering France—from which he had been banned for his role in the 1968 student riots.

Leila Khaled—perhaps the best-known skyjacker. She took over a TWA jetliner in August 1969 but failed to hijack an El-Al plane in September 1970.

Flight		from	last stop	due at	expected	landed	information
BE	915	DUBLIN			11:20		CANCELLED
BE	505	AMSTERDAM			11:25		CANCELLED
BE	627	DUSSELDORF			11:50		CANCELLED
BE	3021	JERSEY			12:00		CANCELLED
BE	603	FRANKFURT			12:10		CANCELLED
BE	5027	GLASGOW			12:20		CANCELLED
BE	647	STUTTGART			12:20		CANCELLED
BE	5377	EDINBURGH			12:25		CANCELLED
BE	009	PARIS/ORLY			12:25		CANCELLED
BE	427	ATHENS	ROME		12:30		CANCELLED
BE	643	MUNICH			12:40		CANCELLED
BE	463	NICOSIA			12:45		CANCELLED
CS	4551	ISLE OF MAN	LIVERPOOL		12:45		

Further information obtainable at appropriate airline desk

Flight arrivals

Right, top and 2nd pictures: all BEA flights were grounded as a result of a walk-out by 2,000 maintenance engineers. The blank flight-announcement boards and the deserted Trident jets tell the story. The cost of the strike to BEA: £250,000 a day.

3rd picture: piles of rubbish in London as the six-week-old 'Dirty Job Strike' continues.

4th: London's Royal Albert Docks during the national Dock Strike. 47,000 dockers at all the British seaports stopped work to back an 80% pay demand.

5th: the national Postmen's Strike in Britain brought postal services to a complete standstill when the 230,000-strong Union of Post Office Workers called out their members. Millions of letters and parcels, like these at London's Mount Pleasant main sorting office, missed the last post.

Crash-helmeted police face an angry mob in Londonderry's Catholic Bogside area—N. Ireland's most notorious trouble spot. Police used tear-gas, and
80 policemen and 120 civilians were taken to hospital.

Top, fighting at San Francisco State College between militant students and police; dozens were injured on both sides. Bottom, anti-Vietnam War demonstrators are held back by police as they besiege the American Embassy in London. 8 policemen and some 20 demonstrators were injured.

Jack Dash (left), leader of the London dock strikers, successfully urges the dockers at the Royal Group of Docks in East London to continue the stoppage

in numerous districts of the capital. Tear-gas and petrol bombs were used, and hundreds of police and students seriously injured. Some reports put the death toll as high as fifteen for these two days. But by the 30th of September the rioting had died down and the 1,300 troops that occupied the National University campus were withdrawn, together with their armoured personnel carriers and tanks.

But peace did not prevail for long. The combined forces of undercover subverters made an all-out effort to rekindle the revolutionary spirit, and on the 2nd of October severe fighting broke out again, with the appearance of a full-scale Civil War.

Fighting broke out when many thousands of students were marching through a working-class suburb. Soon the riot police were reinforced by some 1,000 troops. They were obliged to use rifle and machine-gun fire against marksmen sniping from the windows and rooftops of apartment buildings. The Plaza of the Three Cultures became a battlefield. This one night of bloodshed is known to Mexico as 'The Night of Sorrow'. It produced a death toll of 28, with more than 200 injured.* Many of those killed and wounded were civilians, and among them were women and children who had been trapped in the fighting.

On the 8th of October, with the Olympic Games due to open in four days, an agreement was reached between representatives of the Government and the students. The students gave assurances there would be no disorders during the Olympic Games, and the Government made concessions to the students' demands.

*   *   *

In November 1968 the students of West Pakistan, incited by Red Chinese master-subverters, agitated for educational reform. A wave of rioting spread throughout West Pakistan. In December it contaminated East Pakistan.

The rioting and disorder was so grave that a state of emergency was declared. To appease the students, the Pakistani President released

* These are the official Mexican Government figures. The *New York Times* Correspondent in Mexico City has thrown doubt on these official figures. He has stated that 'it is virtually certain that at least 49 persons were killed and more than 500 injured'.

E

political prisoners and announced that he would not seek re-election as a President.

*   *   *

The Ivory Coast also suffered a serious student strike. The students occupied the university and clashed with the army. The Abidjan Government discovered that the Soviet Embassy's undercover subverters had incited this student unrest. As a reprisal, the Soviet diplomats were expelled from the Ivory Coast, and diplomatic relations between Abidjan and Moscow were severed. Subsequently, twenty-six foreign students who had been proved to have taken an active part in the student disturbances were deported.

*   *   *

In the Congo, student strikes, demonstrations and protests were as vigorous and as violent as elsewhere in the Western world.

In June 1969 six students were killed and twelve were wounded when demonstrating students clashed with the army. Four soldiers and two policemen were seriously injured, and two army officers disappeared. Evidence was gathered which established that Peking-directed undercover subverters had instigated the riots. An official radio report stated:

> Students, manipulated by political troublemakers, launched a wildcat strike, and attacked the forces of order that were trying to restrict them to their campus with Molotov cocktails. This provocation resulted in violent disturbances. It is now known that foreigners were involved in this affair and encouraged the students to violence.

Subsequent to this an investigation was opened to discover who, and by what means, the Molotov cocktails, Mao Tse-tung propaganda and instructions about street fighting, were introduced into Lovanium University. Conclusive evidence about 'foreign intervention' was established, and as a consequence five students were sentenced to twenty-five years' imprisonment for 'plotting against the security of the State' and another twenty-five students received sentences varying from three months' to ten years' imprisonment.

*   *   *

During 1969 at least sixty-nine Japanese universities were taken over and occupied by rioting students, directed by Red Chinese master-subverters. There was serious disruption of all academic studies, and most of the country's leading educational institutions were immobilised for many months. Whenever the police were called in to restore law and order, there was rioting and battles between the police and students grew more and more violent.

Although the students claimed that their protests were caused by overcrowding and lack of facilities in the universities, their placards, slogans and banners made no mention of these grievances. Instead, the students campaigned against the security treaty that the USA was about to sign with Japan. Any peace pact between Tokyo and Washington would be unpalatable both to Moscow and Peking. The year-long rioting that the Japanese students pursued therefore propagated the political policy of Soviet Russia and Red China.

*   *   *

When violent student disturbances broke out in Egypt, they were planned and organised by Red Chinese master-subverters. Rioting resulted in the closure of all the universities and colleges in Alexandria and Mansoura.

On the 21st of November 1969 twelve people were killed and forty-three wounded in Mansoura during street-fighting between riot police and demonstrating students. Two days later even more violent rioting took place in Alexandria, when students staged a sit-in strike at their university.

Thousands of students were involved. Cars and buses were set alight; students wrecked public property and road signs, smashed windows and burned buildings. Strong forces of police retaliated, using truncheons, tear-gas and water-cannon. The death-toll in Alexandria was sixteen, and more than a hundred people were wounded.

*   *   *

Carefully planned disruptive tactics which exploit several molehill grievances simultaneously, and build them into mountains of violent rioting, can cause grave political consequences. But the directors of the Special Division for Subversion considered the 'spectacular' student riots in America, Britain, France, Germany and elsewhere a dress-rehearsal for more decisive action in the future.

One day, another revolutionary situation will be engineered in the countries of the Western world. The enemy is always within.

12

Black Power and the Subverters

While some of Moscow's and Peking's master-subverters, and their undercover networks, concentrated upon student riots, others made racial issues their target.

'Wherever a seed of grievance takes root, disruption by demonstrations and riots may later be reaped,' stated a directive sent in February 1967 by Moscow's Special Division for Subversion to its master-subverters in the USA. 'Genuine grievances must be converted by our undercover cadres into urgent problems burning for settlement . . .'

The USA has planted the seeds of many grievances; now they are reaping the sad harvest of their past injustices.

Nobody can dispute that colour discrimination in America has underprivileged a large percentage of her population. The US government does its best to eradicate this discrimination, but it is not easy to alter attitudes that have endured for centuries. In time America's negro population may integrate with the white, but meanwhile, the resentful and impatient coloured citizens of the United States justly object to social and economic discrimination. This resentment is continuously stoked-up by subverters' agitation.

It is asserted by some American politicians and sociologists that colour discrimination will disappear within two generations. But those who live today are determined to live. The resistance shown by some organised groups of white Americans towards racial integration has aroused serious doubt that the future will be different. Many coloured Americans believe that it will not change at all without political agitation.

These underprivileged Americans are deprived of good education, are impoverished and are unable to gain recognition for their ability, even when it is superior to that of white people. They have a genuine grievance. Stimulated by master-subverters they can become ripe for revolt. Their smouldering resentment against society and their sense of injustice can be inflamed and channelled into violent, bloody action.

America's racial problem cannot be solved simply by passing laws. The true obstacle to integration is human emotional prejudice. This cannot be turned off like a tap. Only the growth of new generations can breed it out.

The racial problem in the United States *cannot* be solved quickly. It will endure for many years. It will provide Moscow's and Peking's subverters with a deadly weapon for a long time.

The negroes have campaigned for justice and equality. Their Civil Rights demonstrations were law-abiding and orderly. But, regrettably, white violence was sometimes organised against them. When this happened, the police favoured the attackers, and victimised the defenders.

When Dr Martin Luther King and 250 marchers visited Philadelphia on the 21st of June 1967, to commemorate the murder of three negroes who had been killed in the neighbourhood in 1964, they were attacked and stoned by a large mob of white people. The police swiftly vanished. Later that same day, a cavalcade of cars raced through the negro quarter of the town with guns blazing. The Civil Rights Headquarters were riddled with bullets and bystanders were obliged to drop to the ground and take cover. Again there was no police intervention. But the following day, when the negro marchers were pitching a tent in the grounds of a school, they were dispersed by State Highway Police, using rifle-butts, clubs and tear-gas in a manner intended to beat up the negroes rather than maintain law and order.

This was just one of many similar incidents that provided undercover subverters with the arguments to inflame passions to explosiveness. Referring to this incident, the Chairman of the Students' Non-violent Coordinating Committee coined the phrase Black Power.

He said: 'We need power to stop the kind of brutality that occurred the night before last. We need Black Power to get out of the slums. But there is no intention of using it to lead us to black supremacy.'

Dr Martin Luther King, a peace-loving man whose influence over his followers restrained them from violence, was uneasy about the reference to Black Power. He said in an interview later: 'Black supremacy would be equally as evil as white supremacy.' But the undercover subverters persuaded some easily-led negro youths to group themselves into a Coloured Freedom Fighters Force. The subverters' exploitation of a genuine grievance found fertile soil. The Coloured Freedom Fighters movement grew swiftly. The director of the Congress of Racial Equality told a convention on the 4th of July:

'To become total citizens of this society, six basic ingredients are needed: political power; economic power; an improved self-image of the black man; young militant leadership; the enforcement of federal laws; the abolition of police cruelty; and the development of the black consumer block.' He continued: 'As long as the white man has all the power and money, nothing will happen because we have nothing. The only way to achieve a meaningful change is to take power . . .'

*   *   *

Racial riots in the US during the summer of 1967 were more widespread and violent than at any other time in its history. They began in April with disturbances in the negro universities in the southern states; they spread to the northern cities and towns by June. They reached a climax in July with major riots in Detroit and many other cities.

These riots, instigated by master-subverters, were extremely destructive. Looting and arson were carried out under the covering fire of Red Chinese-trained snipers. Most riots functioned like an organised military manoeuvre, planned with careful foresight.

*   *   *

Half of the 400,000 population of Newark, New Jersey, are negroes. Rioting started there on the 12th of July 1967 when a mob armed with bottles and rocks went to the aid of a negro taxi driver who had been arrested.

The rioting spread, taking on an almost identical pattern to the rioting in Detroit.

On the 14th of July the Governor declared the city to be 'in criminal insurrection'. On his orders, 375 State Troopers arrived in the city, and 3,000 National Guards. A state of emergency was declared and a curfew imposed. Although National Guardsmen with fixed bayonets moved into the area, rioting and roof-top sniping continued until the 17th of July. By that time the city had been declared a disaster area. Food supplies had to be brought into the devastated section of Newark by the authorities, and distributed by volunteers.

In those five days of rioting, 26 people were killed and 1,200 injured; more than 1,600 people were arrested and the damage caused was estimated at 47 million dollars. Rooftop snipers were responsible for the deaths of policemen and firemen, and for wounding many citizens.

*   *   *

Detroit suffered most from racial riots in 1967.

Detroit is the fifth largest city in the United States, with a population of nearly $1\frac{1}{2}$ million—one third of them negroes. It is one of the most enlightened cities on racial policy. Its large-scale housing projects are integrated. The discriminating arrest and humiliating treatment of negroes by arresting police officers has been stamped out. Negroes have been appointed to high civic offices; negroes earn high salaries and wages in the car factories and enjoy equality with the whites. Here, more than anywhere else in the USA, it is evident that racial discrimination is vanishing, albeit slowly.

The Detroit riots began in the early morning of the 23rd of July 1967, when police raided an illicit drinking den and arrested seventy-three people. A crowd gathered, among them many negroes. They impeded the police. A brawl developed, and became a riot.

The news spread like wildfire. Urged on by ever-active subverters coloured people poured out from their homes to join the rioting. Vandalism was rampant, shop windows were broken, looters invaded private property and incendiary gangs fired buildings. While trying to restore law and order, the police found themselves fired upon by rooftop snipers.

The rioting and looting continued all through the day. 1,000 National Guards were ordered into the city to help the police. To no avail. The rioting spread to every sector of the city.

During the first two days of the rioting more than 1,000 shops and stores were ransacked and more than 300 fires were started, including entire blocks. A curfew was imposed, but ignored. After a helicopter flight across the city, the Governor of Michigan said, 'It looks like a city that's been bombed.' He declared a state of emergency. 8,000 National Guards were mobilised to assist the city's 4,000 police. Rooftop sniping continued and police were ordered to return the fire.

During the evening of the 24th of July, the Governor asked the Attorney General to send in 5,000 federal troops. These troops were flown to Detroit on President Johnson's orders. They moved slowly into the city that same night while steady fire from rooftops was directed indiscriminately against firemen, police, troops and tanks.

The following day, the 25th of July, the troops used helicopters to fly low over the city and flush out the rooftop marksmen. In one area of the city the sniping was so intense that all policemen and firemen were withdrawn, and armoured troop carriers were moved in to sweep the rooftops with machine-gun fire.

By the 27th of July, Detroit had been brought under control, except for isolated pockets of sniping. Thirty-four people were killed in these riots and over 1,500 injured. 5,000 people were arrested, about 10 per cent of them were white. A total of 1,110 buildings were set on fire, and the damage was estimated at 200 million dollars. The number of rooftop snipers was estimated to be about 100; *a high percentage of them were white.*

*   *   *

Rioting took place in so many American cities that on the 27th of July 1967 President Johnson appointed a Special Advisory Commission on Civil Disorders. Its mission was to investigate the origin of riots and to recommend measures to prevent and contain riots in the future. A very significant Bill was unanimously passed by the Senate on the 30th of August; it made it an offence for anyone to cross a State border, or to use the mail or any other facilities of inter-State commerce, with the intention of inciting rioting and violence.

The report of the Commission was long and thorough. It scrutinised hundreds of eyewitness statements and reports from people in all walks of life. It was supplied with thousands of documents by the FBI and the police. It contained this significant paragraph:

'Specifically, the Commission has found no evidence that all or any of the disorder, or the incidents that led to them, were planned or directed by any organisation or group, international, national or local.'

Is it surprising that the Commission has found no evidence that undercover subverters provoked these riots? Undercover subverters take little active part in rioting if it can be avoided. Their task is only to promote violence. But even if undercover subverters are directly involved in rioting and are arrested, they do not confess their role in spreading violence and disorder. The Commission realised this. Although it possessed no physical evidence, it added two more paragraphs of great significance to its report:

> Militant organisations, local and national, and individual agitators who repeatedly forecast and called for violence, were active in the spring and summer of 1967. We believe that they sought to encourage violence and that they helped to create an atmosphere that contributed to the outbreak of disorder.
>
> We recognise that the continuation of disorders and the polarisation of the races would provide fertile ground for organised exploitation in the future.

*   *   *

The rioting in New York on the 30th of July 1967 seemed to start spontaneously, when a group of negro youths hurled bricks and bottles at shops and buildings. The youths were soon joined by adults who looted the shop windows and started fires in them. The police and fire brigades quickly moved in.

Usually a show of authority is enough to subdue a riot. But on this occasion rooftop snipers' shots rang out, Molotov cocktails were hurled and the riot swiftly developed into organised guerrilla warfare.

A survey of negro public opinion later showed that 48 per cent believed the riot helped the negro cause. It concluded that a significant number of negroes are emotionally ready for violence as a solution to the problems of segregation, exploitation and subordination.

*   *   *

Dr Martin Luther King, the negro Civil Rights leader, was an apostle of non-violence. He was revered by America's negroes and his influence over them was enormous. But he was an obstacle to the undercover subverters who wished to see political action expressed in violent rioting and guerrilla warfare. Dr King was shot dead on the 4th of April 1968; he was cold-bloodedly murdered on orders from Moscow's Special Division for Subversion.

The negro Civil Rights leader arrived in Memphis to lead a march of the city's 1,300 garbage collectors, most of them negroes, who had been out on strike since the 12th of February. He took a room in the Lorraine Hotel on Mulberry Street. At 6.00 p.m. he went out on to the balcony of his room and leaned over the railing to chat with a friend in the parking lot below. A shot was fired and Dr King fell with a bullet wound in the neck and lower jaw. He was rushed to hospital but was dead on arrival. The Man of Peace had been eliminated. The obstacle to violence was removed. Black Power, incited by Moscow's undercover subverters, could now adopt a more militant and violent policy.

On President Johnson's express orders an intensive search was begun for Dr King's murderer. In due course he was arrested. On the 17th of April the FBI stated:

'The arrested man, one Eric Starvo Galt, together with an individual alleged to be his brother, entered into a conspiracy to kill Dr Martin Luther King; in furtherance of this conspiracy, Galt purchased a rifle in Birmingham, Alabama, in March 1968.'

Subsquently the FBI reported that 'Galt' was one of many names used by James Earl Ray, a confirmed criminal. Ray had been a drifter since leaving school, and at the age of twenty-one was arrested for burglary. His last crime had been armed robbery, which earned him a twenty-year prison sentence, but he had escaped from the penitentiary in 1967.

He had booked a room in a boarding house facing the hotel balcony on which Dr King was killed. He specifically asked for this room and paid cash in advance. The lethal bullet had been fired by a 30.06 calibre rifle fitted with a telescopic sight.

Ray had had many jobs, among them cook, merchant seaman and bartender. He'd been discharged from the US Army as inept and lacking adaptability. He had forged postal orders and robbed and lived under half a dozen aliases. He was a man who sought easy pickings, and somewhere he had found them. For months prior to murdering Dr King, while on the run from prison, he'd possessed ample funds. He'd spent about $4,500 in a few short weeks in Birmingham, Alabama, in the autumn of the previous year. The FBI could not trace the alleged 'brother' who had conspired with him to kill Dr King.

Ray had no political convictions. He had no motive in murdering Dr King, except financial gain. Secret reports in Kremlin files* confirm, however, that Russian undercover subverters in the United States employ professional gangsters to eliminate influential men who are political obstacles. And a directive from Moscow's Special Division for Subversion, sent in April 1968 to its master-subverters in America, stated:

> The assassination of the Negro leader Dr King by a known white American hoodlum was a well-prepared and organised action which must be turned to advantage by fomenting racial riots throughout the USA. The lessons from previous American racial riots must be remembered. The tempers of the negroes must be aroused by reiterating that a *white* man murdered a *black* man. Negro communities everywhere must be encouraged, and assisted, to riot for Black Power . . .

The murder of Dr Martin Luther King was followed by outbreaks of racial violence all over the United States. 110 cities were involved; thirty-nine people were killed; more than 2,500 injured and some 14,000 arrests took place. More than 2,000 fires were started, and the restoration of law and order required 45,000 National Guardsmen and 21,000 federal troops. Thousands more stood by ready.

The road had been opened for Black Power to show its true strength —assisted by Moscow's undercover subverters.

*   *   *

From the 18th of July 1968 street rioting paralysed the city of Cleveland for five days. Over a hundred buildings were burned down and four negroes were shot dead.

Simultaneously with this episode, there was rioting in Brooklyn,

*See pages 32, 33

New York. The negro rioters used firearms, looted shops and burned property. A negro boy was shot dead and seventeen other people were wounded.

Five weeks later, in Atlanta, Georgia, there was violent rioting, looting and arson. Two negroes received gunshot wounds, one of them died; a policeman was also shot and wounded.

Two weeks after this, San Francisco suffered the worst racial riots in history. They began when a white policeman shot and killed a negro youth who was fleeing from a stolen car. The subsequent damage from looting and arson was estimated at a quarter of a million dollars; 362 people were arrested.

* * *

The Ku Klux Klan and other groups of white people in the southern American states hold the lives of coloured people in contempt. 'Shooting a nigger' is considered by many not to be a social crime. A great many negroes have been shot, and the judges and juries—if the incident ever gets to the Courts—very often failed to find the accused guilty.

After the Governor of Alabama had illegally revoked the new (1968) law of non-segregation in schools, a mob of white people armed with axe-handles, chains and lead pipes, attacked the negro children attempting to enter the newly-integrated schools. Many children were badly hurt. One boy of twelve had his leg broken. The police stood by, laughing. This caused such an outburst of public indignation that the US Department of Justice was forced to intervene, and unwilling State Troopers finally found themselves obliged to protect the negro children.

It is not surprising that negroes react strongly and violently to such blatant injustice; nor is it surprising that Moscow and Peking subverters can make so much capital from these incidents. The expert handling of resentful negroes by Russian and Red Chinese subverters during the last few years has channelled resentment into organised rioting of such violence that it has often come close to minor revolution.

* * *

The directors of Peking's Special Division for Subversion resented the notable success that Moscow's master-subverters and their networks had achieved with racial riots in the United States. Coded directives were flashed from Peking to its master-subverters, ordering them to 'stage an all-out effort to revolutionise America's negro population and incite and organise demonstrations, looting, arson, bomb explosions, sniping and all forms of guerrilla warfare wherever negroes live'.

The Red Chinese master-subverters inspired their networks to greater efforts, and this small army of skilled operatives began to condition the negro population to declare war against the whites.

The Chicago Riots were an American equivalent to the West German students' revolts, London's Grosvenor Square riots and France's nationwide strikes. They became a grave threat to law and order. Demonstrators from as far away as New York and California established a base in Lincoln Park in Chicago. They numbered about 10,000. Among them were hundreds of hippies wearing long hair and love-beads; most were unwashed and unprepossessing; they made love in the open and ignored all the rules of conventional society. These demonstrators were students, yippies, youngsters working for a political candidate, professional people of widely conflicting political views, anarchists, motorcycle gangs, young thugs, and, inevitably, the undercover subverters. This motley crowd subjected the Chicago police to continual provocation both by word and by deed. They called the police obscene names and pelted them with rocks, sticks, bottles, tiles and even human excrement. Some of these actions were spontaneous but many were planned. The police were repeatedly taunted with threats that the demonstrators would disrupt the city and take it over. This provocation finally resulted in the police retaliating with physical violence. Fundamental police training was ignored and those superior officers who happened to be on the scene were unable to control their men.

The majority of the demonstrators intended to join the major protest demonstration against the Democratic National Convention. They did not plan to disrupt the proceedings of the Convention, they did not plan aggressive action, or physical provocation against the authorities; they did not intend to stage an assault against any person, institution or place of business. But despite their peaceful intentions they could not prevent young hotheads being inflamed by vicious police action and turning a peaceful demonstration into a riot.

During the night of the 27th of August 1968 the police made a number of calculated attacks upon the demonstrators, on the pretext of wishing to break up an all-night vigil of prayers in Lincoln Park. Early on in the morning of the 28th, orders were given to the police to clear Lincoln Park. The exercise was carried out with considerable violence.

The demonstrators were taken by surprise and forced out into the surrounding streets. They retaliated with stones and bottles, which they hurled at police cars. The police fired rifle shots into the air. Soon the police were joined by 1,400 National Guards. Some 2,500 demonstrators who had taken up positions in front of the Hilton Hotel were cleared away into neighbouring streets. The hotel lobby was filled with fumes from the tear-gas canisters fired by National Guardsmen. Violent rioting continued long into the night; 267 were arrested and 700 injured. The police casualties were seven.

The Chicago Riots were considered of such importance that Washington appointed a Special Commission* to examine objectively all the circumstances. The Commission's unbiased report, based on eyewitness reports and official data, made it clear that police brutality was rampant:

On the part of the police there was enough wild club-swinging, enough cries of hatred, enough unrestrained beating to make the conclusion inescapable that individual policemen, and lots of them, committed violent acts, far in excess of that needed for crowd-dispersal, or arrests. To read dispassionately the hundreds of statements describing at first hand the events in Chicago is to become convinced at the presence of what can only be called a police riot.

The Committee added: 'The extremely obscene language used by demonstrators and police alike was a contributory factor to the violence described in our reports; its frequency and intensity were such that it

* This official American analysis of the Chicago Riots was undertaken by a study team of 212 members. They recorded 1,410 eyewitness statements, reviewed 2,102 other statements provided by the Federal Bureau of Investigation, studied 180 hours of motion picture films, 12,000 still photographs, and thousands of newspaper accounts. The conclusions drawn by the Commission were summarised in 233 printed pages.

was omitted from the report and would inevitably understate the effect it had.'

One important directive that the Special Division for Subversion issued to master-subverters states that the police shall be provoked. Policemen are human beings and can be angered; if provoked to club-swinging, they can provoke retaliating anger in their victims. Then the barricades are built and stones and bottles begin to fly. Any subverter who infiltrates a crowd of protesters, and shouts insults at police officers until they respond with swinging batons, sparks off a violence that can spread swiftly. One single act of provocation can cause many days of violent street-fighting between the police and the public.

*   *   *

After the Chicago Riots any small grievance would spark off violence that was remarkable for the speed with which it spread.

Black Power found expression through many negro organisations. The most militant was the Black Panther Party. The Black Panthers, assisted by Red China's master-subverters and their networks, trained armed patrols 'to protect negroes from police brutalities'. Their emblem, the Panther, was chosen because the panther does not attack, but if subjected to attack, will fight to the death.

The Black Panthers possessed arms and used them. They made their own judgement as to whether negroes had been unjustly attacked by whites, and took violent revenge. The Panthers were ruthless, illegal and dangerous. They were armed guerrillas. All over America, they fought gun battles with the police, killing many of them. The police retaliated, determined to stamp out this small but desperate gang of outlaws. The Black Panthers steadily lost their leadership in battle. Eventually, most of the party leaders were in prison, had fled into exile, or had been shot by the police.

*   *   *

But gangs of gunmen who tried to impose their own justice upon the community like lynchers were not the only problem of violence confronting the US Government. During the second half of 1969 and the first six months of 1970 a wave of bomb outrages afflicted the United

States. President Nixon was forced to urge the death penalty for instigators of bombings when lives were lost.

New York was hit particularly grievously. When the Marine
Midland building in Broadway was blown up, nineteen people were
seriously injured. A federal office was destroyed. The bombing of
Macy's department store activated the sprinkler system, greatly
aggravating the damage.

In one day, bombs exploded in the General Motors building on Fifth
Avenue; in the sixty-storey Chase Manhattan Bank building; and in
the Radio Corporation of America building in the Rockefeller Centre.

In each instance, telephone warnings were given beforehand so that
staff could be evacuated from the buildings before the explosions took
place.

The telephone warnings of bomb outrages served a double purpose.
They saved lives. But for every genuine warning received there were
a hundred false ones. Hundreds of businesses and factories were brought
to a standstill while staffs were evacuated, and thousands of working
hours were lost while police and bomb-disposal units searched futilely
for explosives. So the false warnings had an effect just as the true ones
did.

The University of Wisconsin's Army Mathematics Research Centre
was wrecked by an explosion that killed a scientist and caused five
million dollars of damage. There were four suspects, all under the age
of twenty-two. They disappeared after the incident. The FBI have no
records that these four young people had any political associations. But
a secret Kremlin publication* credits them with 'having carried out
important destructive work as activists in their undercover subverter
network'.

Greenwich Village was torn apart by a series of explosions and swept
by fire when a four-storey building used as a 'bomb factory' blew up.
Police found sixty sticks of dynamite, and fuses and caps among the
ruins. One of the bodies recovered was identified as Theodore Golt, a
Columbia University graduate who had been one of the student revolt
leaders at that university. A number of other bodies were found, but
so mutilated that they could not be identified.

* The *Party Bulletin*, Moscow, September 1970.

Six days later, bombs exploded in the Mobil Oil Company, the International Business Machines Company and the General Telephone and Electronics Company. Great damage was caused to these three Manhattan skyscrapers. Once again telephone warnings were received in time for the staffs to be evacuated.

United Press International received a letter from a Bombing Squad. They signed themselves 'Revolutionary Force 9'. One paragraph of the letter read:

'In death-directed America there is only one way to a life of love and freedom: To attack and destroy the forces of death and exploitation, and to build a just society—Revolution!'

Similar bombings occurred in San Francisco, Chicago, Buffalo, Detroit, Pittsburgh, Seattle, Denver, Cleveland, Tucson and other American cities. The bomb targets were usually government offices, military training centres and police stations.

'The home-made bomb is rapidly taking over from the revolver and rifle as a violent instrument of political change . . .,' an observer commented.

From what little is known, the new Anarchists appear to be white more than black—young people with relatively affluent backgrounds, who have served an apprenticeship in an extremist organisation, and, as likely as not, are female. They receive their armament instructions from bombing manuals—some of them official army handbooks—published and circulated by the Revolutionary Left . . . Gunpowder can be bought legally in many states, and dynamite can be obtained just as easily. Both are being discovered with alarming frequency in police investigations.

A violent explosion occurred in an East Side tenement house on the 28th of March 1970. It was the 'bomb factory' of a militant negro organisation.

Among the ruins of this six-storey building the police found live bombs, a large store of chemicals for the manufacture of explosives, combustible gasoline and armaments. They also discovered a large quantity of propaganda leaflets, among them Black Panther publications. Subsequent police investigations of other bomb incidents showed that the perpetrators were black and white men and women.*

Fear became widespread throughout the country, and President Nixon told Congress:

'Schools and public buildings have had to be evacuated; considerable property has been destroyed; lives have been lost. Clearly, many of these bombings have been the work of political fanatics, many of them young criminals posturing as romantic revolutionaries. They must be dealt with as the potential murderers they are.'

In New York City alone the police reported in 1969 ninety-three explosions; nineteen unexploded devices discovered and 3,191 telephone warnings of bomb explosions.

A great nation was terrorised by a handful of ruthless men and women master-subverters. There is almost no defence against terrorists. What defence can there be against individuals who pose as honest citizens, while secretly planning to disrupt and, perhaps, destroy their neighbours' lives—and for no apparent purpose?

Most disturbing of all for the American authorities in the last few years has been the increasing tendency of demonstrating and rioting to escalate to extremes of violence. Organised and peaceful demonstrations dissolve into rioting and vandalism which blends into guerrilla warfare. These are the same terrorist tactics that were practised by Mao Tse-tung in China and Che Guevara in South America.

This terrorist activity is not a spontaneous outbreak of resentment by isolated groups of individuals. It is guerrilla warfare, waged by Peking's and Moscow's master-subverters. They incite and direct the world-wide sabotage of freedom, and of human rights. The CIA and the FBI have proof that the negro riots and the Bomb Squads were organised by subverters in the employ of Peking and Moscow.

* These publications propagated a revolutionary socialist ideology based upon the violent-action philosophy of Mao Tse-tung, Che Guevara and Régis Debray. The Black Panthers are a negro organisation but they are prepared to cooperate with white radicals to achieve a common objective.

13

The Wide Scope of Organised Terrorism

Newspapers have limited type-space; radio and television have limited time. Moreover, the public has no wish to devote too much of its leisure to learning all the details of international news. So 'happenings' in the world are encapsulated, in print and in broadcasts, for rapid digestion. Only a fraction of what occurs all over the globe is reported; few people can know more than a very little of what is happening to the rest of the world. This is why the enormous scope of worldwide terrorist activity is not easily recognised. Nevertheless Moscow's and Peking's master-subverters and their fifth-column networks are ceaselessly spreading discontent, aggressiveness and violence to even the remote corners of the world.

* * *

In Burma, during the summer of 1967, and after some months of violent terrorist activity including the daily derailment of trains and the ambushing of troops, Peking-directed guerrillas launched a powerful attack on the town of Gyobingauk, about a hundred miles north of Rangoon.

On the 13th of May 1967 Gyobingauk was attacked by more then 200 terrorists, who assumed control of the town for many days. They drove out all the inhabitants and systematically burned down the town hall and all other public buildings. They created damage estimated at more than £800,000.

The guerrillas were activated and directed by a Red Chinese master-subverter known by the alias of Than Yin. There was a political motive behind this attack. It coincided with the increasingly warlike attitude adopted by the Peking government towards the Burmese government.

This small guerrilla war weakened Burma's bargaining power at a moment of political stress.

In 1967, and during the early months of 1968, the Far East was the scene of many such violent disorders.

Frequent armed clashes took place in Central and East Java, and in West Borneo, between the loyal army and Peking-directed terrorist guerrillas. Almost weekly there were grave incidents which never reached the newspaper headlines. The following report describes a typical incident:

Two soldiers and eighty terrorists were killed in a nine-hour battle. The terrorist guerrillas attacked a military post at Blora, Central Java, under the leadership of a 'Mystic' who claimed that his magical powers made him bulletproof. He was not a mystic but a Red Chinese subversion leader, and he was killed in the fighting. Later, troops destroyed the 'Mystic's' shrine. In the cave which was used for clandestine guerrilla meetings, 1,500 of his terrorist followers were arrested and a large store of weapons was seized.

A week after this incident, armed terrorist guerrillas under the direction of Red Chinese subversion leaders, raided an Air Force ammunition depot at Surabaya and blew it up.

Such terrorist activity is directed by Peking's master-subverters with military discipline and precision. These terrorists can correctly be described as Red China's underground army in Indonesia and Java.

Lieutenant-Colonel Pratomo, who was an officer of the Silliwangi Division, confirmed this in greater detail. He went into hiding after the 1965 *coup d'état* but was arrested in April 1968. Under interrogation he divulged a great deal of useful and sensational information about Peking's undercover subverters' activities in Indonesia.

Indonesia seethes with political unrest, organised and directed by Peking's master-subverters. On the 12th of December 1968 the Indonesian Government officially stated that 80,000 communists were imprisoned. But an estimated 120,000 hard-core communist under-cover subverters were still at liberty and conducting terrorist guerrilla actions.

*   *   *

In the autumn of 1968, in Mozambique, the Portuguese armed forces were involved in a bitter, bloody battle with Moscow-directed guerrillas calling themselves Freedom Fighters. These had been organised by master-subverters who also supplied the necessary arms and ammunition, manufactured behind the Iron Curtain.

Previously terrorism in Mozambique had been confined to about five per cent of the territory and had affected only three and a half per cent of the population. But after the undercover-subverters had concentrated on recruiting and training terrorists, there were approximately 3,000 guerrillas among the Macombas* and another 3,000 being trained in Tanzania.

Only ruthless, disciplined military action by the Portuguese Army, combined with an excellent counter-intelligence service, gave the Portuguese Military Authorities complete control over the situation in Mozambique.

*   *   *

On the 13th of March 1969 rioting again broke out in West and East Pakistan. The militant action of agricultural workers in rural areas was prompted and directed by Red Chinese master-subverters and flared up into a 'Peasants' Revolt'.

Supporters of the existing régime were murdered by terrorist gangs, martial law was proclaimed and order was restored only with the greatest difficulty. At a parliamentary session, the Pakistani President informed the House that rifles and other weapons were being smuggled into East Pakistan and distributed to villagers. Documentary evidence seized later established that Peking's master-subverters had planned, organised and directed this 'Peasants' Revolt'.

*   *   *

On the 14th of May 1969 The National Revolutionary Council of Guinea set up a Court to try fourteen men who were accused of plotting to overthrow the Government. During the proceedings it was revealed that on the 19th February 1968 a secret camp had been discovered in a neighbouring African country, from where armed men—recruited,

---

* A tribe living on the Tanzanian border.

trained and equipped by Moscow's master-subverters—infiltrated into Guinea.

This camp was established by the self-styled National Liberation Front of Guinea which was directed by Russian guerrilla warfare experts. It was equipped to train 500 recruits at a time in jungle combat, sabotage and terrorist warfare.

*   *   *

Malaysia, like most other countries in the Far East, has continuously suffered its share of rioting and violence.

The general elections in West Malaysia in May 1969 resulted in a return to power of the ruling Alliance Party. Peking's master-subverters made an all-out effort to incite the masses to take militant action. The following day violent rioting broke out in Kuala Lumpur. It continued until the 15th of May, when a state of emergency was proclaimed.

The civil and riot police were quite powerless to prevent the rapid spread of violence. Chinese groups in various parts of the city simultaneously formed gangs, erected barricades and brought out weapons. The ensuing terrorist activity followed the pattern of that of the Western world. Blocks of apartment houses, businesses and shops were burned down; public transport and private vehicles were overturned and set on fire. The hospitals filled to overflowing with dead and wounded as home-made bombs exploded and stones and bottles flew through the air. Rooftop snipers maintained the civilians' nervous tension at breaking point as victims were killed or wounded indiscriminately.

When the troops marched in to restore law and order, they found themselves at war with many roving groups of Chinese and Malayans, each as many as several hundred strong.

The rioting was not suppressed until the 21st of May. 10,000 homeless people had to be removed from the devastated area of the city and be fed and given shelter by the Red Cross. During the rioting, one hospital alone reported 57 corpses and 190 casualties.

*   *   *

In Ceylon, the strict censorship imposed by the government has failed to prevent knowledge of its thirty internment camps from leaking to the outside world. Following the abortive attempt by Guevarist guerrillas to seize power, the government, deeply disturbed, has enacted Emergency Powers which enable the police and armed forces to arrest anyone on suspicion, 'dead or alive'. It is estimated that 14,000 suspected terrorists are being detained and interrogated, and 1,500 are reported to be ready for trial, accused of treason, terrorist acts and possession of arms.

*   *   *

The Brazzaville Government of the Congo has also discovered plots against the State and suffered terrorist activity. It has established that Russian-controlled master-subverters trained Special Commandos in a neighbouring country. 'The arms, ammunition and uniforms that have been seized have been proved to be supplied by East-European countries,' a government statement disclosed.

*   *   *

In Itnzaingo, a small border town between the Argentine and Paraguay, the Paraguayan Consul was kidnapped by Peking-controlled guerrillas calling themselves The Argentine Liberation Front. They threatened that unless imprisoned members of the ALF were released, the Paraguayan Consul would be executed.

The Argentine government refused to treat with the kidnappers. Five days after his capture the Paraguayan Consul was released in a suburb of Buenos Aires 'for humanitarian reasons'.

*   *   *

In Canada, on the 29th of September 1969, ten sticks of dynamite exploded in the home of M. Jean Drapeau, the Mayor of Montreal. This was the ninety-eighth bomb explosion in Montreal in less than two years.

The scale of bombing outrages in Canada can be judged from the few that are mentioned below:

31st of December 1968: The City Hall and the Federal Manpower Building were seriously damaged by explosions.

21st of January 1969: Two policemen were injured by an explosion at the headquarters of the Canadian Federation of Independent Associations.

13th of February 1969: A number of people were treated at hospital after an explosion at the Montreal and Canadian Stock Exchange.

28th of April 1969: M. Savageau, a member of the Quebec National Assembly, narrowly escaped injury when a petrol bomb was flung through the window of his home.

2nd of May 1969: An office building and an apartment block under construction were seriously damaged by bomb explosions.

7th of July 1969: In the northern part of the city, five explosions seriously damaged the work on four new construction projects.

9th of August 1969: The Federal Revenue Building was greatly damaged by an explosion reported by the police to be the most powerful they had yet encountered.

15th of August 1969: Dynamite almost completely wrecked an office of the Confederation of National Trade Unions. Incendiary bombs thrown into a department store caused widespread damage and injured a guard.

As in New York, before any of these bombs exploded telephone messages warned that the explosions were due to take place. These warnings saved lives; but there were several dozen false 'warnings' every day. During the course of the year the security measures taken after bomb-warnings resulted in hundreds of thousands of lost man-power hours. Long-scale industrial disruption was unavoidable.

*   *   *

South Africa is scorned by the Western democracies because of its official policy of discrimination against coloured people. It has held many trials of accused terrorists. Because South Africa legally condemns racial integration, the West has lost confidence in South Africa's legal system, and the justice exercised by its judges and courts. Nevertheless it does not follow that *all* the accusations levelled against terrorists by South African prosecutors are false ones.

The coloured population of South Africa bitterly resents the Pretoria government's oppression of the non-whites. These underprivileged people are ripe for subverters' agitation; they are fertile soil for the seeding of grievances, the fanning of the flames of resentment, and the explosion of mob hatred and violence. A South African police report of the 30th of May 1969 referred to subversive activities within the country between the 1st of July 1967 and the 30th of June 1968, and added:

'Throughout the country, many men and women have been sentenced to death for conspiring against the State; many others were imprisoned.'

A typical case report reads:

In the Pietermaritzburg Supreme Court on the 26th of March 1969, ten African men and women received prison sentences of from five to twenty years for having contravened the Terrorism Act of 1967, and The Suppression of Communism Act; and of having plotted to ferment discontent, violent revolution and open warfare in South Africa, involving collusion with foreign communist-led groups.

The report revealed that many of the accused terrorists had undergone special military training, and had established bases outside the country from which guerrilla attacks on South Africa could be launched.

The South African government and courts officially recognise that a network of undercover subverters, agitators and saboteurs, is working to destroy the State from within. This organisation has been given a name by the South African authorities. They call it communism.

*   *   *

Latin-American countries are notorious for the instability of their political régimes. They are mostly dictatorships, and armed revolts occur regularly. The changes of régimes usually result from military coups, accomplished after a few days of sporadic fighting between loyal and rebel troops.

In recent years the trend has changed. Moscow- and Peking-directed communists, independent national communist factions, anarchists, Trotskyites and other revolutionaries, working behind the scenes, have brought about this change. The threat to the governments of South America no longer comes from the legendary disgruntled general who has plotted with other ambitious generals to whom he has promised the Big Plums in the new régime. Instead, the threat now comes from communist-organised terrorists and trained guerrilla armies.

Dr Fidel Castro has established in Cuba his own personal brand of communism. It is unlike the rigid party policies practised by Moscow and Peking. Castro has proclaimed to the world that 'Cuba is ready to prove its solidarity with all the revolutionary movements in South America by actively supporting them'.

Cuba has given very solid assistance to South American revolutionaries, but Castro has acted independently of the Soviet Russian and Red Chinese governments, much to those countries' stern disapproval. Moscow and Peking are competing to mastermind Latin-American terrorist activity, and they both bitterly resent Castro's intrusion upon their ambitions.

The extent of terrorist activity and guerilla warfare waged ceaselessly within the vast South American continent, is illustrated by the experience of just one Latin-American terrorist—Che Guevara. Guevara was a Marx-inspired revolutionary killer, whose Christ-like appearance as he lay dead made a romantic impact upon young political idealists, who have glorified him into a revolutionary hero and an inspired political philosopher. But there are dozens of other guerrilla leaders operating in South America who have successfully concealed their true identity and avoided publicity.

Originally, Che Guevara was a Moscow-directed undercover subverter. But he was a very egotistical individual, so he eventually rejected Moscow's control and pursued his own revolutionary policy. The Kremlin itself directed that he must be 'rubbed out' as soon as it realised Che had become a dangerous threat to Russia's policy in South America. He was betrayed by a woman who had once been his comrade and lover—Laura Martinez.

Laura Martinez was born in Buenos Aires and christened Haides Bunke. She was the daughter of a German communist immigrant father and a Polish mother. In 1952, at the age of fifteen, Laura was taken by her parents to East Germany, where she attended a grammar school in Stalinstadt. She joined the Communist Youth League and studied at Humboldt University in East Berlin from 1957 to 1959. In 1958 she was recruited by the East German Foreign Intelligence Department and trained for undercover subverter work in Latin-America. She first met Che Guevara when he visited East Berlin to negotiate a large credit for Dr Fidel Castro's Government through the Cuban National Bank, of which he was President. In 1961 Laura was recruited for the Soviet Secret Service. That same year she was sent to Cuba with the specific task of assisting Che Guevara with his revolutionary work in South America. She enrolled at the University of Havana, cemented her relationship with Che, and with his assistance found work in the Ministry of Education and a position of rank in the Cuban Women's Militia.

Later, Laura was ordered to go to Bolivia. She travelled on a forged Argentinian passport which gave her name as Laura Bauer. Her 'cover' was that she was a language teacher. She did, indeed, teach the children of a man who became the chief of the Presidential Press Office in La Paz. Laura, indeed, participated in his glory, and was promoted to a secretarial post in his department. She also enrolled as a student at the Andrea University in La Paz.

In 1966 Laura obtained Bolivian nationality by a marriage of convenience to Antonio Martinez. The marriage did not last long; in 1967 they were divorced. Now of undisputed Bolivian nationality, Laura travelled widely through the country, ostensibly recording Indian dialects, but in fact acting as a contact for Che Guevara, who was marshalling a guerrilla army. She passed on all Che's thoughts, plans and movements to Soviet Intelligence officers.

Laura was intimately involved with Che Guevara. She assisted him to put his revolutionary plans into effect in Bolivia. While in La Paz, she helped him establish his guerrilla bases in the Oriente mountain region. As a Kremlin-accredited agent, she could count upon the full cooperation of the Moscow-loyal Bolivian Communist Party executive. The first guerrilla base camp set up was in an abandoned cattle ranch at Mancahuaca, close by the oil town of Caniri, and it was established with the cooperation of the Bolivian Communist Party. All of Laura's communications were made under the code-name of 'Tania'.

Che Guevara had left Cuba in October 1966, disguised and carrying two passports, one of them Uruguayan. He reached La Paz on the 5th of November, having travelled a roundabout route via Prague, Frankfurt, Zurich and Dakar. He met 'Tania', who provided him with forged documents. These proved Che to be a sociologist engaged on rural research for an American organisation. This 'cover' enabled him to reach Guerrilla Base One without difficulty. There he was joined by other Cuban terrorists who had travelled by equally roundabout routes.

Guevara was an idealist. He'd played a leading role in Castro's revolution; power, position and fortune were available to him in Cuba, but he had spurned material prizes. He had dedicated himself to 'inspiring the downtrodden workers of Latin-American countries to rise in revolt against their tyrannical masters'. Bolivia is a vast country of great potential wealth but with a large, impoverished population. Che, and Moscow, believed Bolivia was ripe for revolt.

Under the code-name of 'Ramon', Che supervised the construction of underground arms dumps, subterranean tunnels and hideaways. He even built a well-equipped underground field-hospital. Many base-camps were constructed, and military training centres were set up for drilling recruits for the guerrilla army. Che won world fame as a bearded, cigar-smoking guerrilla leader.

His constant harassing of the Bolivian troops finally forced the Bolivian Army Command to train and equip a special force of 800 men who specialised in jungle fighting. Its instructors were US veterans of Korea, the Congo and Vietnam. Despite this innovation Che Guevara's guerrillas operated with considerable success and inflicted heavy casualties whenever clashes took place with the army. Che even found time to engage in side-issues, such as demanding 100,000 dollars protection money from the Gulf Oil Camp.

Che Guevara's guerrillas also fought on the political front. They distributed Castro-supplied propaganda* and held subversive lectures for simple peasants. This was very effective. The primitive Bolivian

* In opposition to Moscow's and Peking's party policy.

tin-miners, and the hot-headed students, as well as considerable numbers of peasants, supported the guerrillas so openly that the La Paz government finally felt it necessary to declare a state of siege in the mining area.* Fighting broke out between government troops and the tin-miners who had declared their region a Free Territory.

Che Guevara's guerrilla units were greatly outnumbered by Bolivian troops and handicapped by lack of freedom of movement. They had difficulty in obtaining supplies of food, clothing and medical equipment. They depended upon their secret bases. So they were dealt a mortal blow when a Moscow-directed undercover subverter, on orders from the Special Division for Subversion, betrayed Che Guevara's secret guerrilla bases to the Bolivian Government.

The betrayal deprived the terrorists of their storehouses, hideways and field-hospitals. The loosely scattered groups of guerrillas tried to subsist until they could renew contact with each other, in order to plan new guerrilla strategy. But meanwhile, informed of all details of the guerrillas' desperate plight by the Moscow-directed traitor, the Bolivian troops hunted them down and cut them to pieces.

On the 7th of October 1967 Che Guevara's guerrillas were reduced to scattered groups of terrorists, without bases from which to draw upon supplies and without leadership.

At 6 o'clock in the morning of the 8th of October, Bolivian troops saw in the moonlight a single file of guerrilla stragglers picking their way along a ravine. They opened fire. One man tried to assist another who was wounded in the leg and throat. He hoisted the wounded man upon his back and carried him to the top of the hill. There he attempted to render first aid. The Bolivian troops advanced and called upon the man to surrender. He snatched up his rifle, but before he could level it, he was struck by bullets.

'Stop, stop!' his wounded companion shouted. 'Don't kill me. I am Che Guevara. I am more valuable to you alive than dead.'

The wounded man was taken prisoner but died later that day of his wounds. Moscow had ensured that any successful revolt in Bolivia would *not* be controlled by Dr Fidel Castro.

Positive identification of Che Guevara's corpse was made by compar-

* On the 6th of June 1967.

ing his fingerprints with those upon his original Argentine passport application.

Che Guevara's admirers and supporters refused to believe that their hero had died. But Dr Fidel Castro announced on the 15th of October 1967 that he was convinced that Che Guevara was dead. He added that the guerrilla leader had been 'murdered' by the Bolivian Army. He announced thirty days of official mourning for the terrorist leader.

The official statements issued by the Bolivian Government about the death of Che Guevara, the conflicting accounts of how he died, and how his body was disposed of, gave rise to world-wide speculation. It contributed to the growth of the romantic myth that is already becoming accepted as truth, that Che Guevara was a great visionary.

'Tania', as Laura Martinez was known to the guerrillas, was reported to have been killed before Che Guevara. No proof of this has ever been demonstrated. But Soviet sources claim that she returned quietly to Moscow. The same source confirms that 'Tania', or another Soviet undercover subverter, deliberately betrayed Che Guevara's guerrilla bases to the La Paz Government. Certainly Dr Fidel Castro of Cuba had no doubts about Moscow's enmity towards Che Guevara, and openly accused the Soviet-loyal Bolivian Communist Party of obstructing Che Guevara's guerrilla activities because Moscow and Peking had condemned activities which deviated from their own party policies.

*   *   *

The fomenting of revolt in Latin America never ceases. The inciting of poverty-stricken peasant Indians to revolt against their governments and to practise terrorism and guerrilla warfare, is gaining momentum. But the men who will control and benefit from this coming revolution are in Moscow and Peking.

14

The Enemy Within

Between 1965 and 1967 Mao Tse-tung's master-subverters and their undercover networks concentrated on strikes, demonstrations, riots and terrorist acts of every description. But when success after success had been scored, proving the efficiency of the subverter networks, Peking decided to increase the pressure. The Red Chinese Special Division for Subversion issued a coded directive to all master-subverters telling them to expect smuggled deliveries of large quantities of drugs of all descriptions. They were ordered to 'seize every opportunity to spread drug addiction'.

Peking's orders were carried out with customary determination and ruthlessness, and in due course, Soviet 'Control Agents' reported to Moscow that Red Chinese subverter networks were actively engaged in smuggling drugs into the Western democracies and encouraging drug addiction. The Kremlin called for a special Inner Circle conference at which the directors of the Special Division for Subversion were present. Great concern was expressed about Red China's latest moves to steal the political and economic initiative from the Soviet Union, and about the spread and success of Mao Tse-tung's subverter networks.

This Kremlin conference lasted two days and made far-reaching decisions. A directive was drawn up and transmitted in code to all Soviet master-subverters throughout the Free World. This secret (February 1968) directive repeated orders given in previous directives to master-subverters. It insisted upon:

Intensified activity on the part of all master-subverters, and the stepping up of recruitment of network subverters and undercover hard-core agitators, who will enlist in trade unions, religious movements, sports organisations and diverse political parties. Undercover hard-core agitators are to infiltrate deeply into all spheres of social, political and physical activity within the Western world.

The same directive demanded that militant action must be exercised to a maximum, and called for:

More grievance strikes, more wildcat strikes, and more trade union obstruction to the smooth working of industry; more racial riots, and more sabotage to industrial plants.

It emphasised that industrial chaos causes economic collapse, and exhaustively described the best ways to organise demonstrations, riots and sabotage, to obtain the greatest publicity about incidents that embarrass governments, and to arouse widespread resentment towards authority. Finally, the directive gave long and detailed orders about:

The best methods to introduce drugs into the class-struggle as a means of destroying and overthrowing the capitalist system.

Unwilling to concede the initiative to Peking, Moscow had adopted Red China's plan of corrupting the peoples of the Western democracies by spreading dangerous drugs amongst its population.

Bacteriological warfare, or the spreading of deadly germs and viruses within the countries of the free world could destroy more swiftly. But contagious diseases, such as cholera, or bubonic plague, are uncontrollable and can spread to all the corners of the world. The Russians and Chinese, as well as the Europeans and Americans, could fall victims to the indiscriminating death spread by disease-germs and viruses.

Narcotics, however, are insidious and act slowly. It takes a full generation before their influence can corrupt and endanger a healthy nation. Drug addiction is not contagious and can be prevented from spreading from one country to another. Narcotics can be controlled by border guards and customs officials; and drug pushers can be tracked down swiftly by political police, aided by informers.

Moscow's Special Division for Subversion gave practical and precise orders to its master-subverters. Refined drugs would be smuggled into the country of their operations, They must prepare caches suitable for the storage of large quantities of *all* types of processed rugs. They were to prepare dead-drops where drugs could be deposited for collection by distributing agents. All existing methods of drug-pushing were to be contacted and utilised to the maximum. The widespread recruitment of drug-pushers was to be encouraged by providing high profits for the operators. Give-away prices were to be asked for the processed drugs. 'Pushers must find they can make small fortunes, and increase them by employing many new assistants and enlarging their clientele.'

The subverters developed a four-stage working system:

1. Identifying and contacting the professional distributors of drugs.
2. Selling these distributors drugs at ridiculously low prices.
3. Keeping the professional distributors under surveillance, and learning the identities of their pushers.
4. Making contact with the pushers through undercover network subverters, and offering them drugs so cheaply they are encouraged to appoint their own pusher-agents and enlarge their clientele.

* * *

Since Peking and Moscow embarked upon this giant-scale drug-peddling, both Red China and Soviet Russia have intensified their drug-plant growings, and drug-processing, within their own countries. They have also set up undercover drug-buying agencies. These agencies masquerade as legitimate business houses, but purchase large quantities of unprocessed drugs from Africa, India and other drug-plant growing countries. Reluctant peasants have been encouraged to grow illegal crops by an initial loan that richly capitalised the venture and insured them against any possible loss. Both Peking and Moscow have spent enormous sums of money to stimulate drug production.

Red China and Soviet Russia next founded new undercover departments that studied Western methods of contraband detection, and devised elaborate methods to escape that detection. A few pounds of drugs can always be smuggled in the diplomatic bag, but that is trivial. The world-wide network of drug-smuggling that Peking and Moscow have created handles enormous quantities of processed and unprocessed drugs. An army of smugglers is required to keep it moving. So many new methods of smuggling have had to be invented. And as soon as they are discovered by narcotics detection agents or Customs investigators, they are substituted by yet other and even more improved methods of contraband.

Customs officials and narcotics detection squads are powerless to cope with the avalanche of drugs flowing into the countries of the free world. Peking and Moscow, unlike professional drug-smugglers, are quite undeterred by the financial loss if consignments are intercepted and seized, so long as a good deal slips through. Despite all Western vigilance and precautions, enormous quantities of drugs filter through into the countries of the free world every day, and are pushed on to do their deadly work.

*   *   *

The methods by which a powerful government can smuggle goods are vastly superior to any adopted by experienced professional smugglers.

One very efficient smuggling method used repeatedly upon the long US coastline illustrates this.

The supply vessel fixes a rendezvous outside territorial waters with an American sea-going yacht. The supply vessel transfers to the yacht a large cargo of drugs, carefully packed and waterproofed. The yacht returns to port with its illegal cargo on board. If it is approached by a Customs or Coastguard vessel while sailing to port, the entire cargo of drugs is dumped overboard; the cargo has been weighted in anticipation of such an emergency. In such an event the yacht returns later with frogmen aboard to recoup the cargo. But, if all goes well, when the yacht draws close into shore, it drops its cargo of drugs (no longer weighted) and frogmen swim into land under cover of darkness, towing lines of floating, waterproofed packages of drugs.

Britain has been 'privileged' to experience one of the most remarkable systems of smuggling practised anywhere in the world. The supply vessels would approach to the fringe of British territorial waters. Specially constructed radio-controlled model aircraft, heavily laden with drugs, were then launched from these vessels and radio-directed to selected sites on the British coast, where undercover network agents were waiting. The cargoes of drugs were unloaded and the model aircraft returned to base to make more flights.* These model aircraft could not carry more than a few pounds of cargo on each flight; but

---

* These radio-controlled model aircraft escaped detection because, flying low, they were not picked up on aircraft-detection radar screens.

drugs are as dangerous as explosives, and a few pounds of either are immensely destructive.

West German Security Officers have been noticing that too many foreign private aeroplanes seemed to get off course and strayed over the border into the Federal West German Republic. They discovered that these small private planes are piloted by navigational experts who can pinpoint a dropping zone for large packages of drugs. Waiting undercover agents of the West German Red fifth column scoop up these packages and disappear into the night as the 'lost' aeroplanes turn back into East Germany.

The long, rugged coastline of Norway provides unlimited opportunities for smugglers to land drugs without detection. But the fjords are policed by patrol vessels that challenge all suspicious craft and prevent large-scale professional smugglers from operating. However the fjords can easily be penetrated by submarines, of which the Soviet Union has plenty; modern radar instruments assist them to avoid detection. The Norwegian authorities have discovered large caches of drugs awaiting collection and distribution in remote areas of the fjords. They know that these could only have been smuggled into Norway by the use of submarines.

Cargo boats are the most commonly used vessels for drug-smuggling. The drugs are dropped overboard in water-proofed packing and submerged by weights. Later on they are retrieved by frogmen aboard smaller craft. Smuggling on this large scale requires costly organisation, far beyond the means of professional smuggling-rings or individual operators.

Contraband activity constantly violates the laws of all the countries of the Western world—from Britain to Scandinavia, the Channel coast of France, Germany, Holland and Belgium, and the Mediterranean coast of France, Greece, Italy and Spain. These giant-scale operations can only be mounted by a task force that has all the resources of a government behind it.

Peking's and Moscow's professional master-subverters work ceaselessly to destroy the Western way of life. By stimulating drug-addiction among schoolchildren and youngsters the Red fifth columns are coming perilously close to achieving their target. Only the future will show if our younger generation can withstand the moral corruption spread by the communist East.

* * *

It is significant that while medical, legal and social campaigning has decreased the smoking of tobacco, other and more dangerous drugs have grown in popularity.

In recent years all nations have multiplied their efforts to prevent the smuggling and illegal distribution of narcotics. But they are fighting a losing battle. Habit-forming drugs, which were almost unobtainable a few years ago, are now readily available to anyone who exercises a little ingenuity.

The governments of the Western world are deeply disturbed at the enormous consumption of drugs by young people. It has reached such alarming proportions that the public is deliberately not informed about it for fear that it may cause widespread despondency and panic.

But drugs weaken willpower and destroy the ability to make moral judgments. Drug addicts are slaves to a craving. They lose all the dignity and pride of being thinking human beings. What is the future of a community if a high percentage of its schoolchildren are experimenting with dangerous drugs? Can there be any doubt that the future of that community is in jeopardy?

The Western world needs a well-published comprehensive statistical report about the alarming adoption of drugs by the schoolchildren of all nations. The grave social threat overhanging our future generations must be confronted.

The enemy within cannot be combated by an official policy of suppressing unpleasant facts. Every parent will strive to protect their young once they are aware of the terrible danger that threatens them.

* * *

A few years ago it was extremely difficult for even confirmed drug addicts to obtain the narcotics they craved; drugs were extremely expensive. But in the 1970s, drugs of all types are so easily obtainable and so inexpensive in America and Europe that almost any schoolchild can buy them with his or her pocket money.

The authorities cannot prevent enormous quantities of all types of narcotics being smuggled. Drugs are handled so expertly by 'distributors' and 'pushers' that they are as readily available as alcohol was during America's Prohibition.

Refining, smuggling, distributing and pushing drugs is Big Business. It is too widespread for the local police, the Narcotics Squads and Interpol to cope with, and Peking's and Moscow's undercover subverter networks supply the major part of the business. Drugs are too much in demand, and the frontiers between countries too long, for the authorities to control them.

The legal penalties for trading in drugs are severe, and rightly so. The spreading of drug addiction is a crime against humanity, and those who betray mankind for personal gain deserve stern punishment. Drug-traffickers risk long prison sentences and will do so only for abnormally high profits. How is it possible, then, that selling drugs to children can be profitable?

Never before have such enormous quantities of drugs been so expertly smuggled into the Western world and released to a mass-market *at such low prices*. Tons of hard drugs of all kinds are being refined for widespread distribution. The suppliers are not primarily concerned with making profits. They are not deterred by mammoth confiscations by Customs and Narcotics Prevention officers. Their aim is to destroy the morale and structure of the Western democracies, and the funds available for achieving this aim are effectively inexhaustible.

The instigator of 'Drugs for all in the capitalist world' was Peking, but Moscow quickly followed her lead. All the might of the Red Chinese and Soviet Russian states is gathered behind the producing and refining of drugs, their smuggling, distribution and pushing.

Peking's and Moscow's master-subverters and their undercover networks are concentrating upon corrupting the schoolchildren and teenagers of the Western democracies. They have adopted *Cold War* methods more demoralising than any ever before devised by man.

*   *   *

From the late 1960s the consumption of drugs increased alarmingly in America, Britain, France, West Germany, Italy and most other Euro-

pean countries, as well as in Australia, New Zealand, Canada and
South America, and even the Middle East, Africa and Asia. The
smoking of hashish, marijuana and opium has become commonplace
where it was rare before. The more exotic hard drugs—heroin,
pethidine and others—have become known to millions, and are
often slyly praised instead of being condemned. Within a few years of
launching their campaign to destroy the Western democracies with
drugs Peking and Moscow have won much ground. The young of the
free world have been taught to flirt perilously with drugs.

The subverters have never attempted to assume direct control over
drug distribution and pushing, but they give every assistance to the
existing drug-distribution syndicates, while taking care not to become
personally involved.

When 'Operation Drugs' was first launched by Moscow's Special
Division for Subversion, the over-zealousness of some master-subverters in the United States of America resulted in a number of unpleasant
incidents. Attempting to establish their own drug-distribution system
and employ their own pushers, the subverters aroused the hostility of
professional narcotics-traffickers. The latter resented the intrusion into
their territory by outsiders and amateurs. There were shootings and
men died. FBI investigators were puzzled that one dead man, identified
as a Soviet-directed subverter, should have been involved in a shooting
affray with drug-pushers. But subsequently the FBI unearthed information from secret sources which proved that professional criminals
who specialised in narcotics-distribution were being encouraged to
enlarge their corruptive practice by large consignments of drugs sold
to them at giveaway prices. These prices would have been uneconomical
to any supplier wishing to make a profit. Pressing their investigations,
the FBI then learned who the suppliers were, and why they were not
concerned to make a profit . . .

*   *   *

In September 1969 French Security officers in Algiers engaged upon
'special raiding activities', came upon the following directive. It reveals
how deeply Red fifth-column master-subverters and their undercover
networks have penetrated drug trafficking.

September, 1969.

SECRET!   MEMORISE!   THEN BURN!

The distribution of drugs and its supervision by our undercover cadres falls under criticism. The following instructions must be read carefully and carried out:

1. All drugs deposited in dead-drops must be collected within seconds of being deposited. Every minute that a cache remains uncollected increases the possibility of its discovery. Recently a large cache was accidentally discovered after it had been deposited for some hours without being collected. Such an incident *must not* happen again!

2. All supplies of drugs will increase steadily during the course of the following weeks and months. Efficient distribution of this increased quantity of drugs *must* be assured. Suggestions about new ways to smuggle drugs into your country will be considered.

3. Rigid control must be exercised over all drug distributors. They have grown accustomed to the increasing supply of drugs and have become dependent upon it. Any failure of any drug distributor to cooperate fully can be countered by restricting his supplies.

4. The drug distributors, their agents and pushers are all expendable. They should be encouraged to become drug addicts themselves. Extra supplies, without charge, can be granted them for their *personal* use. But caution can never be relaxed. No undercover network subverter shall ever make *direct* contact with drug peddlers.

*   *   *

The war in Vietnam has lasted many years, and provided ample scope for the Red fifth-column subverters to introduce drug addiction into the US Army and Air Force, with such success that drugs have become a weapon of war. The methods used there are so insidious that only recently has Washingon realised the full extent of the danger. Drug addicts make poor soldiers, and at moments of battle-stress could even behave in a way that actively aids the enemy. It has been necessary to appoint special investigators to comb through the American ranks serving in Vietnam, discharge all soldiers affected by addiction and provide medical treatment for others; it has been publicly admitted that conscripts who have served in Vietnam are returning to civilian life with a drug habit they did not possess when they were called up.

Master-subverters often appoint hopped-up drug addicts to lead in rioting and street fighting. They play upon these pawns skilfully, incite them to throw bottles and bricks at the police, smash shop windows, loot, and set fire to buildings. Almost all the Western countries have arrested rioters who have acted under the influence of narcotics. Under-cover subverters cultivate drug addicts. They provide them with regular free supplies until they are completely 'hooked' and dependent upon the subverters, who by these means provide themselves with expendable robots who can be easily encouraged to commit almost any act of violence and lawlessness.

Red China and Soviet Russia are not immune from soiling by the pitch they handle. Addiction is a relatively recent incident in Western society; but Asiatics have a drug-habit tradition. Their opium dens operated publicly at a time when an opium den seemed remote and fantastical to Western minds.

Moscow and Peking have taken elaborate measures to eradicate drug addiction within their borders. The militia and the secret police are constantly smelling out drug-consumers and pushers. Their system of appointing a trusted comrade who is answerable for everyone in his street or block, helps to make this task easy. All citizens who suspect that their neighbours are involved with drugs are obliged to report their suspicions to their street leader; failure to do so can have very serious consequences if it is eventually proved that they withheld this knowledge. As a result, drug addicts pursue their vice in strict and solitary secrecy, and obtaining new supplies of drugs is a perilous operation. The punish-ments for drug addiction are very severe; both Moscow and Peking have adopted a simple and merciless method of dealing with 'hopeless' drug addicts. They are shot, or given death injections. Those addicts who are not totally 'lost' receive corresponding, but nevertheless severe punishments.

Red China and Soviet Russia are using extreme measures to stamp out drug-addiction in their own countries. But in the West their under-cover subverters do their utmost to make it grow and spread swiftly.

15

Air Terrorists

The manifestation of the extremes of violence in the Western world betrays the spreading influence of Red China. The Kremlin calls for the disruption of the Western way of life, where Mao Tse-tung calls for gelignite. Moscow wants rioting, but Peking wants rifles and bombs. Soviet Russia encourages Kangaroo Courts, but Red China instigates hijacking, kidnapping and guerrilla warfare.

Peking's Special Division for Subversion originated 'air terrorism'. It set up training courses for terrorists whose task was to attack and hijack airliners. Cold-blooded men and women have been drilled in the technique of attacking aircraft with submachine guns and incendiary bombs; of concealing plastic hand-grenades and pistols in luggage and upon their persons, and smuggling them through airport checks. These air terrorists are of non-Chinese descent. They are recruited from the ranks of Arab guerrillas and from hard-core communists in all parts of the world.

When Moscow's Special Division for Subversion was informed of Red China's new strategy of assault upon the Western world, it ordered its own master-subverters to recruit and train groups of air terrorists.

Although Moscow and Peking compete for success in undercover subversion, they nevertheless aim at the same broad target. And both Soviet Russian and Red Chinese fifth-column master-subverters plan air terrorism so that aircraft destruction or hijacking appears to be the work of nationalists and fanatics. This is why they always associate such acts with existing crises, such as Middle-East tension.

Terrorism entered a new phase when organised and spectacular terrorist attacks were launched by Peking and Moscow against airliners and their passengers.

*   *   *

On the 28th of December 1968 a Boeing 707 of the Israeli airline
El-Al, with forty-one passengers and a crew of ten aboard, nosed out
on to the runway of Athens Airport in preparation for take-off.
Abruptly, two men, who had been sitting in the transit lounge
after flying in from Beirut, forced their way through the door
to the tarmac, and ran towards the airliner. It was just picking up
speed.

One of the men tore open a holdall, produced a submachine gun
and sprayed the Boeing with bullets. The other man threw incendiary
bombs at it, setting the aircraft's engines on fire. A stewardess broke her
leg and seriously injured her spine while leaping from the burning
airliner, and one of the passengers was subsequently found to have been
shot dead.

Fire-engines sirened out on to the runway and quickly extinguished
the blaze, while airport police arrested the two men. They were
identified as Arabs, aged nineteen and twenty-five. They told the
Greek authorities they had attempted to destroy the Israeli airliner on
orders from the Popular Front for the Liberation of Palestine.

The Popular Front for the Liberation of Palestine promptly issued a
statement in Beirut; it accepted all responsibility for the attack and
added, 'It is a warning to Israel of more to come!'

This statement was intended to convince the world that the outrage
was 'just another move in the Arab-Israeli conflict'. But its real
purpose was to conceal Peking's complicity. The Mao-inspired leaders
of the Popular Front for the Liberation of Palestine had sent the two
Arab air terrorists to a Red Chinese air terrorist training camp, and
had pledged themselves to accept all responsibility for the two men's
subsequent acts of terrorism.

This cold-blooded attack on the Israeli Boeing demonstrated how
vulnerable an airliner can be to air terrorist activity. Another Air
Terrorist Spectacular followed less than two months later.

On the 18th of February 1969, at Zurich Airport, Peking-directed
Arab air terrorists attacked an Israeli airliner as it was about to take off
for Tel Aviv. Four men and a woman, armed with submachine guns
and explosives, drove on to the tarmac in a hired car and opened fire
upon the aircraft. The pilot and co-pilot of the airliner were injured,

and four of the passengers. The aircraft was badly damaged. The terrorists said they were obeying orders given by the Popular Front for the Liberation of Palestine.

The Swiss government was extremely indignant that its neutrality had been violated. The affair was brought to the attention of the UN, and condemned by all the Western democracies. The UN Secretary-General, U Thant, stated:

'If the hitherto peaceful world of civil aviation is to be saved from chaos and anarchy, governments and people, regardless of their political views, must condemn acts of this kind and take all possible measures to prevent them.'

U Thant did not admit that the Peking- and Moscow-directed undercover subverters who plan and instigate such attacks upon airliners aim specifically at spreading chaos and anarchy, nor that passenger-carrying aircraft are a highly exploitable target for political blackmail.

*   *   *

Airliners were easy meat, and from 1969 onwards Red China's and Soviet Russia's air terrorists increasingly concentrated their disruptive influence upon passenger-carrying aircraft.

Every day hundreds of thousands of passengers pass through the busy airports of the Western world. Airliners and travellers all work to a tight timetable. Any minor disruption of the time-schedule causes immense pile-ups of luggage, passengers and airliners. Whenever terrorists plant bombs in aircraft, or even claim to have done so, airport officials are obliged to make security searches of all passengers and luggage. The resulting loss in manpower, time and efficiency is enormous.

But these results were not spectacular enough for the air terrorists. They also wanted world-wide publicity. So the indiscriminating planting of bombs in airliners, and the internationally condemned attacks upon passenger-carrying aircraft, were replaced by the much more risky, but much more spectacular and publicity-producing exercise of hijacking airliners.

The ways and means to hijack airliners had to be studied and the selected air terrorists had to receive specialised training. So it was not until August 1969 that the first skyjacking trial-run was carried out.

* * *

A Boeing 707 belonging to Transworld Airlines, with 113 people aboard, was hijacked over Southern Italy on the 29th of August 1969 while on route to Israel from New York. A young man and a young woman stepped into the pilot's cabin after the airliner had left Rome, and forced the captain to land at Damascus. There the skyjackers ordered the passengers and crew to leave the airliner by the emergency chutes. A few minutes later, they exploded a bomb in the pilot's cabin. The incident seemed motiveless.

America condemned this as an act of international air piracy. But the Syrian government refused to adopt a condemnatory attitude towards the Popular Front for the Liberation of Palestine, which, on instructions from Red China's undercover subverter directors, once again proudly claimed full responsibility for this act of lawlessness. On the contrary, many Israeli passengers on the hijacked airliner were detained by the Syrian authorities, while the Arab skyjackers, twenty-two-year-old Leila Khaled and thirty-year-old Salim Assewy, were both released by the Syrian police.

* * *

The year 1970 began with a determined bid by Peking and Moscow to gain a political stranglehold upon world affairs through the hijacking of airliners.

On the 10th of February 1970 three gunmen attacked a Munich Airport coach and a transit lounge, using hand-grenades and revolvers. Their objective was to hijack an Israeli Boeing 707. Airport police foiled the attempt; one terrorist's hand was blown off by a grenade that exploded prematurely, and a second had both legs riddled with grenade splinters. The responsibility for this abortive skyjacking attempt was claimed by *two* different Arab guerrilla groups.

On the 21st of February 1970 a Caravelle, flying from Frankfurt to Vienna with a consignment of mail for Israel, had its fuselage ripped apart by an explosion. The aircraft managed to land safely in Frankfurt. Four Arabs had prepared a packaged bomb designed to explode at an altitude of 10,000 feet. They had introduced the bomb into the aircraft as registered mail.*

On the same day a Swiss airliner crashed fifteen minutes after leaving Zurich Airport. All its passengers and crew were killed. The Swiss team investigating the crash came to the conclusion that 'The same Arab organisation was at work in Frankfurt and in Zurich.'

At first, the Popular Front for the Liberation of Palestine claimed responsibility for this crash; but subsequently *all* the Arab guerrilla groups issued a joint statement denying any responsibility for the destruction of the Swiss airliner.

The Swiss authorities were not convinced of Arab innocence. They were aware that Arab guerrilla organisations sent terrorists to receive skyjacking training under Peking's and Moscow's supervision. So the entry of Arab nationals into Switzerland was drastically restricted and the Swiss asked the International Civil Aviation Organisation to arrange an emergency conference on international air security.

*   *   *

On the 22nd of July 1970 six Arab terrorists hijacked a Greek airliner at Athens Airport. They threatened to blow it up with all its fifty-five passengers and crew, unless all Arab commandos in Greek custody were instantly set at liberty. Seven hours of negotiations took place by radio-telephone between the hijackers inside the airliner and the Greek authorities. Finally agreement was reached, the passengers were allowed to leave the aircraft and it took off, carrying the skyjackers, its crew and an official of the International Red Cross, who had volunteered to act as intermediary. The airliner was flown to Cairo. When it landed the skyjackers were warmly welcomed and acclaimed heroes by representatives of the Arab Socialist Union. The Greek government honoured its agreement with the skyjackers; it released all Arab prisoners, in accordance with its promise. But while yielding to blackmail, the Greek government extracted a solemn promise from responsible Arab

* Reported by the Federal West German Criminal Police.

diplomats; the diplomats promised that Greece would never again be used as a base for terrorist activities by Arab commandos.

*   *   *

The success of these experiments in destroying or hijacking airliners and in using their innocent passengers as a lever to blackmail governments led to a planned, grand-scale skyjacking operation.

Its objective seems to have been simply the 'act of terrorism'. The demand made by the skyjackers for the release of seven detained Arabs* surely did not merit the enormous expenditure of thought, time and costly planning involved.

But the purpose of the operation becomes patently clear when one realises that it was organised like a military *coup* and carried through by Red Chinese professional undercover subverters. The Arab guerrilla groups, though they supplied their own specially trained members for this action, were mere pawns of Peking's political strategy.

The hijacking of four large airliners in September 1970, which sparked off the war in Jordan, was organised by Red fifth-column master-subverters.

Just before midday on the 6th of September 1970 a Transworld Airlines jet carrying 145 passengers and ten crew, was flying over Belgium en route to New York when armed men burst into the pilot's cabin and ordered the captain to fly to the Middle East.

Two hours later, a Swissair DC-8 jet en route to New York with 143 passengers and twelve crew was hijacked by Arab commandos while flying over central France. The airliner was ordered to change course to Jordan. It landed on the same airfield as the TWA jet.

Almost at the same time, an Israeli airliner was flying from Amsterdam to New York with 145 passengers and ten crew. As the aircraft skimmed along the east coast of England towards Clacton, two hijackers, a man and a woman brandishing revolvers and hand-grenades, ran along the central corridor of the aircraft and attempted to force their way into the pilot's cabin. Israeli security guards intervened and during the skirmish an Israeli steward was shot in the stomach. The man

* One of them would never have been detained at all if the operation had not taken place.

skyjacker was shot dead. The woman attempted to explode a hand-grenade, but an American passenger flung himself on her and threw her to the floor. At once she was seized and held by other passengers. She had pulled the firing pin from the hand-grenade but its mechanism was defective and it failed to explode. This defect saved the lives of all those on board. The airliner made an emergency landing at London Airport, the Arab woman hijacker was taken into custody and the Israeli steward was rushed to hospital, where he later recovered from his wounds.

Only two hours after this abortive effort a fourth aircraft, a Pan-American Jumbo Jet, bound from Amsterdam to New York with 158 passengers and a crew of eighteen was seized by Arab hijackers soon after it left Amsterdam Airport. It was forced to fly to the Middle East and landed at Beirut Airport with its fuel exhausted.

Guerrillas of the Popular Front for the Liberation of Palestine seized the Beirut Airport's control tower and threatened to blow up the Jumbo with everyone aboard if the Lebanese police made any attempt to intervene. The plane was refuelled and then flown on to Cairo; there would not have been room for it at the same airstrip in Jordan which had already received the hijacked TWA and Swissair airliners.

On arrival at Cairo airport, the passengers and crew of the Jumbo were ordered to leave the aircraft as quickly as possible, using the emergency chutes. Passengers were warned that time-bombs had already been planted at strategic points in the airliner's fuselage. These exploded within minutes of the last passenger leaving the plane. The aircraft was engulfed in flames and explosions continued until the jet was completely destroyed. There was no loss of life involved but a number of women passengers broke their legs while making emergency exits from the giant aircraft. The Egyptian government formally arrested the three Arab skyjackers and announced that they would be brought to trial.

Meanwhile, at the desert airstrip in Jordan, later to be known to the world as, variously, Dawson's Field and Revolution Airport, more than 300 passengers in the two hijacked airliners had spent the night as prisoners of the Popular Front for the Liberation of Palestine guerrillas; the Arab guerrillas had cordoned off the airliners with mortars, machine-guns and bazookas. The Jordanian Army, which

represented authority and which had the legal duty to suppress
terrorism, had ringed around the entire area with armoured cars and
tanks; but the Army was helpless. The guerrillas had planted hundreds
of sticks of gelignite in both hijacked airliners and had warned that any
attempt by the Jordanian Army to intervene would result in the aircraft being blown up together with the passengers and crews. Later
that day, a hundred passengers who were not of Israeli nationality
were allowed to leave the airliners. They were handed over to the
Jordanian Army and were escorted to Amman in a convoy of
buses. The remaining passengers and the crews were still detained as
hostages.

Meantime in London, the arrested Arab woman hijacker, who was
detained at Ealing Police Station, had been identified as Leila Khaled—
the same woman who had helped hijack a US airliner the previous
year.*

The plight of the passengers imprisoned in the two airliners at
Dawson's Field was unenviable. By day the temperature inside the
aircraft soared to intolerable heights as the sun beat down upon the
metal fuselages. The passengers included pregnant women and many
children. Conditions in the cramped quarters became increasingly
unbearable and unhygienic. The International Red Cross flew in food,
medical supplies and sanitary equipment—disinfectants, disposable
nappies and stoves for boiling water. Fortunately the Arab guerrillas
did not prevent these relief supplies reaching the hostages. But much
more disturbing than any discomfort was the knowledge that both aircraft had been primed with gelignite. Passengers and crews endured
terrible nervous tension. They were in constant fear that the whim of a
trigger-happy Arab guerrilla would blow them all up. Most of the
passengers sincerely believed they would not come through their
ordeal alive.

On the 9th of September 1970, when they had been prisoners for
three days, a British VC-10 with 108 passengers and ten crew was
hijacked while flying over the Persian Gulf. The pilot was forced to
fly to Dawson's Field. When he landed his VC-10 and lined it up with
the other captured airliners, its arrival brought the total number of

* See page 165.

passengers and crews held hostage by the Arab guerrillas to more than
300.

Inevitably such lawlessness not only shocked the world but caused
immense disruption of air travel. All airlines were acutely concerned
for the safety of their airliners. All airports conducted lengthy searches
of passengers and their luggage.

Meanwhile the civil war was developing in Jordan as Army troops
and guerrillas fought spasmodic battles in Amman and other towns.

The Popular Front for the Liberation of Palestine set a time-limit
for the blowing-up of the airliners, with their passengers and crews
aboard, if its demands were not met. This time-limit was repeatedly
altered as the governments of the Western democracies coordinated
their negotiations in an effort to bring reason and decency into this
area of anarchy and terrorism.

On the 11th of September the Central Committee of the Palestine
Liberation Organisation, representing all the Palestine guerrilla groups
involved in the Dawson's Field action, issued a statement: for humanitarian reasons, all the hostages and crews held at Dawson's Field would
be taken to Amman.

Not all the guerrillas were in agreement with this policy. There were
many dangerous moments while the passengers were leaving the
airliners, when touchy fingers hovered over detonating buttons.

Negotiations continued with the Popular Front for the Liberation of
Palestine, using various intermediaries. Eventually, however, all the
airliners' passengers and crews were taken to Amman in a fleet of buses.
Shortly after the hostages had left the three aircraft, they were ruthlessly
destroyed by the Arab guerrillas; all three were blown up and burned.
But fifty-four passengers and crew remained held as hostages and
were only released subsequently, a few at a time, the last six regaining
their liberty on the 30th of September.

In accordance with the agreements made with the Popular Front for
the Liberation of Palestine, Leila Khaled was released from Ealing
Police Station on the 30th of September. She was put on an RAF
aircraft which flew her to Cairo. En route the aircraft stopped at
Munich and Zurich and picked up the six Arabs who had been arrested
for skyjacking in Western Germany and Switzerland. On the 1st of

October Leila Khaled and her six terrorist comrades were set at liberty, free to begin plotting all over again the hijacking or destroying of yet more airliners.

The Red fifth-column subverters considered this terrorist exercise very rewarding. The Western democracies had suffered a total destruction of four aircraft and great public consternation, and 400 innocent men, women and children being held to ransom. The interruption of flying services and the turmoil caused at airports by the searching of baggage and passengers had created airline chaos.

Law and order had been defeated.

And elected governments had been obliged to set at liberty seven admitted terrorists!

* * *

The hijacking of these airliners was investigated thoroughly by the Intelligence and Security Services of six nations. Their investigations provided factual evidence that the claim by Arab guerrillas that they had masterminded this grand-scale operation was a blatant lie intended to cloak the true sponsors of this skyjacking *coup*. Investigators proved that these acts of air piracy were part of a political plot to destroy the uneasy Suez and Middle East truce. The Popular Front for the Liberation of Palestine had claimed total responsibility for hijacking the airliners brought down at Dawson's Field to avert any suspicion of the complicity of Peking and Moscow. In fact the Popular Front merely provided the subverter-trained skyjackers, an isolated desert airstrip and enough armed guerrillas to maintain control of it. The entire operation was planned by Red fifth-column subverter directors.

The skyjacking conspirators were all undercover subverters, trained by Red China's Special Division for Subversion. They had made their way to the West German city of Stuttgart from different parts of Europe and rendezvous-ed there in the early days of September 1970. Stuttgart was chosen because it is an industrial city possessing excellent air links to the previously selected hijack airports of Amsterdam, Zurich and Frankfurt.

Of these conspirators the best known to the British and international public is Leila Khaled. She arrived in Stuttgart on the 3rd of

September. Her real name is Maria Luna Chaves, and she was born in Honduras on the 9th of April 1941. The conspirator with whom she shared a hotel room in Stuttgart was Celia Martinez Fernandez, who with the aid of Alvero Fuentes, a native of Costa Rica, hijacked the Swissair DC-8 airliner three days later.

On Saturday the 5th of September 1970 these three skyjacking conspirators received their final instructions from a fair-haired, French-speaking European woman who visited them at their hotel. This woman used the name of Dr Maria Reboul. It was a completely ficticious name and was used on just this one occassion. Maria Reboul is also known to Western Intelligence and Security as Madeline Rousseau, Jaqueline Lasalle and Juanita Lopez. She is on the 'Wanted' list of Western security officers and is known to be a Red Chinese master-subverter. She had gone under-ground, but she surfaced long enough to spark off this giant skyjacking operation.

Early on the morning of Sunday the 6th of September 1970 Leila Khaled flew to Holland; she booked in at the four-star Carlton Hotel in Amsterdam. Later she was joined by the mysterious Dr Reboul. In the seclusion of the hotel room Dr Reboul gave her her last-minute instructions: the target was El-Al Flight 219 to New York, the sky-jacking team was to be Leila Khaled and Patrick Joseph Anguello.

Anguello was an undercover subverter from Peking's Special Division for Subversion, he too is well known to Western security officers. He normally operated in Central and South American countries, and the FBI has no record that he has at any time previously had any links with any Arab organisation, or with individual Arabs. All Anguello's previous under-cover activities were undertaken half a world away from the Middle East. It is known that he was employed by Peking's Special Division for Subversion; it supplied him with the skilfully adapted ·22 pistol he carried, most of whose metal parts had been replaced with plastic so that it would escape detection by the airport metal-screening machine.

In the event Leila Khaled was unsuccessful in her skyjacking attempt. She was overpowered before she could do any damage, and Patrick Joseph Anguello was shot dead by an Israeli security guard.

The other skyjacking conspirators were successful, so when the sky-

jacked airliners were landed at Dawson's Field the release of Leila
Khaled was demanded as part of the ransom price for the lives of the
airliners' passengers and crews.

Dr Maria Reboul disappeared mysteriously before security officers
could catch up with her. A search of Anguello's body yielded three
Amsterdam telephone numbers, but a raid by Netherlands police
officers proved only that the suspects had melted away. In West
Germany, Federal authorities investigated the background of a middle-
aged professor who had associations with Middle East students
visiting Germany. These enquiries were dropped for lack of evidence.

This Peking-planned operation was a major undercover subverter
success. Its only cost was the life of one subverter-skyjacker, Anguello,
and he could tell no tales. As a fringe benefit, the air terrorists gained
the distinction of wresting from the hands of British justice a young
woman skyjacker who was undoubtedly guilty. But even British
justice must bow to the threat of force when the lives of many young
children, women and men are menaced by determined fanatics.

16

Terror in Northern Ireland

The pawns who carry out Red China's and Soviet Russia's inhuman policies take refuge in glib phrases that seem to justify the appalling atrocities committed by fanatics, and seem to transform them into heroic martyrs.

There are many young and deluded idealists who proudly quote the words of Régis Debray, a fellow-conspirator of Che Guevara:

> Each one has to decide which side he is on—on the side of military violence or guerrilla violence; on the side of the violence that oppresses, or the violence that liberates. Crimes in the face of crimes. Which ones do we choose to be jointly responsible for, accomplices or accessories to? You choose some, I choose others . . .!*

Those who have difficulty in deciding what violence oppresses and what liberates may have their eyes opened by the following directive, which was transmitted in code from Peking's Special Division for Subversion Headquarters to their master-subverters in Southern Ireland:

> Recent activities in Area One:† *Increased* guerrilla warfare is essential. The population of Area One must be convinced that it is the public's wish to liberate its country from British slavery.
>
> It is not enough to direct guerrilla warfare in Area One from the safe area of Southern Ireland. It is not enough to brief undercover sub-agents, provide them with funds, weapons and explosives and send them into their field of operation without firm instructions and adequate training. It is not enough to rely upon the imagination and

---

* Régis Debray used these words to defend himself at his trial.
† This is the code description for Northern Ireland.

initiative of partly-trained, inexperienced undercover sub-agents. They must be led, trained and given firm orders.

Our objective is to plunge Area One into complete disorder and turmoil. This will be easy if the people are led to believe that the entire population of Area One is determined to force the British to withdraw. To achieve the best and swiftest results, the following tactics must be adopted:

1. All undercover subverters must launch non-stop and widespread agitation throughout Area One. All undercover subverters must be mobilised to initiate demonstrations, rioting, street fighting and terrorism. Money is no obstacle; funds are immediately available.

2. Master-subverters, through network subverters, will select suitable terrorists and instruct them in bomb-making. As mentioned in our preceding Directive 17, nails exploded by gelignite or other explosives are effective weapons and scatter dangerously over wide areas. Time-bombs made from gelignite or other explosives can be concealed in innocent-looking containers, and hidden where they are unlikely to be discovered. It is essential that time-bombs are sited with careful forethought. Refer to our preceding Directive 17. Every bomb must cause the maximum of damage.

3. Master-subverters, through network subverters, must train large numbers of rioters in rifle-firing. Aim at creating a small army of rooftop snipers. Sniping by a few men can tie up the police force and occupy an entire unit of British troops.

4. Children should be encouraged to throw gelignite nail bombs and other explosives at police or troops. Child guerrillas have been used very effectively in Vietnam, Cambodia and other countries. They are easy to recruit for guerrilla activity when they have been impressed by the rioting violence of their fathers and brothers. It was experienced in Vietnam that children are greatly encouraged by money presents. Use money as an inducement for child terrorist acts.

5. Master-subverters have learned that the IRA Provisionals make good network subverter terrorists. Spare no effort or money to recruit as many as possible of these militants. Train them in rooftop sniping and guerrilla warefare, supply them with arms, ammunition

and explosives, and give them all assistance in the manufacture of home-made bombs.

It is confidently anticipated that the situation in Area One will soon respond to the increased activity of all our master subverters and their undercover network sub-agents.

Is *this* the violence that *liberates*?

Peking's master-subverters complied with their directive and speedily set up three guerrilla-warfare training centres in Southern Ireland.* Recruits were smuggled over the border from Northern Ireland to receive training as rooftop snipers and machine-gunners, and were instructed how to make gelignite nail bombs, Molotov cocktails and time-bombs.

One training centre was located in an isolated farm-house north-west of Armagh; a second centre was east of Dromore; and the third centre was to the east of Ballygawley. These training centres were provided with unrestricted funds from Peking.

After several months, all three training centres were swiftly dismantled and their equipment whisked away. The Red Chinese master-subverters who ran these centres had been tipped off that information about the centres' existence had been passed on to the Southern Ireland authorities and they were about to be raided. But this premature closure of the terrorist training centres did not deter Peking's master-subverters from carrying out their Special Division for Subversion directive. New locations were found and the training centres re-opened elsewhere.

*   *   *

* British Counter-Intelligence agents succeeded in infiltrating into an undercover subverter network inside Ireland and learned about these three guerrilla-warfare training centres in Southern Ireland. They informed the authorities of Southern Ireland and were responsible for the raid made by the police of Southern Ireland. The police could find no evidence of guerrilla-warfare training centres, but hundreds of recently fired cartridges revealed that rifle and machine-gun shooting had been practised there not long previously. Other Counter-Intelligence agents have since successfully infiltrated into undercover subverter networks. They are now trying to discover where the new guerrilla-warfare training centres have been secretly set up.

The pattern of spreading and increasing violence in Northern Ireland can be observed by summarising events that occurred in 1969–70.

The Prime Minister of Northern Ireland announced on the 3rd of February 1969 that general elections would be held on the 24th of February. The previous November there had been several violent incidents between Civil Rights supporters and extreme Protestants, when the followers of the Rev. Ian Paisley blockaded Market Street to impede the march of 6,000 Civil Rights supporters. The police, who had the unenviable task of keeping the two groups apart, erected barriers between the opposing forces, whose members were armed with bicycle chains, clubs, pieces of broken chair-legs with nails protruding from them and other dangerous weapons. During the fighting that subsequently developed the police smashed a BBC television camera that was filming a baton charge.

The general elections provided another bone of contention between Protestants and Catholics. Both sides were determined to engage in violent street fighting. Red fifth-column subverters were at work, stirring up intense religious antagonism.

Between the 28th of March and the 20th of April 1969 there were a series of rowdy Civil Rights demonstrations protesting against the principle of Universal Suffrage. The Catholics believed that the election system victimised them. On the 19th and the 20th of April the street rioting became so violent that it caused deep concern. While restoring order the police became the target for the animosity of both sides. A police station was attacked, stones and petrol bottles were thrown, and the police were driven to open fire over the heads of the crowds as a defensive measure. When order had been restored the police occupied a number of strategic points in the Catholic Bogside area which they fortified with water-cannon. All the residents in that area, some 4,000 people, immediately evacuated and reassembled at a neighbouring housing estate. There they armed themselves with pick-handles, iron bars and other weapons and issued an ultimatum to the police to 'retreat from the Bogside within two hours, or be ejected'. The police prudently withdrew and the residents re-occupied the area.

Meanwhile, subverter-directed terrorists among the rioters had exploded bombs and encouraged arson. Fire destroyed an electricity sub-station and caused damage estimated at £600,000; many post offices and bus depots were attacked with petrol bombs, and the main water supply line to Belfast was blown up.

The subverters skilfully aroused the tempers of their impassioned Irish pawns, plied them unstintingly with drink and incited them to even more violence by picking at old political sores. They were so successful that on the 20th of April the Northern Ireland Cabinet announced that it had asked the British government to supply army units to guard key installations within the province. It was the only means by which the country's amenities could be safeguarded.

But rioting continued and the violent clashes between demonstrators and police reached a climax on the 12th and 13th of July. The rioting in Londonderry and Belfast became so widespread, and such a dangerous threat to law and order, that the Minister of Home Affairs took unusual security measures; he strengthened the police force. He said:

> These outbreaks of irresponsible hooliganism—which have been properly condemned by all decent citizens, without regard to religion or political affiliation—could not be condoned by any responsible person in public life, and cannot serve the advance of any political cause. It can best be contained by the cooperation of the community . . .
>
> The police have behaved with exemplary discipline and professional skill in the face of appalling provocation. Since some reference has been made to the use of firearms, it should be understood that a number of warning shots were fired *only* when the lives of policemen on duty were obviously at risk.

The Londonderry Citizens Action Committee was opposed by the introduction of a Special Constabulary. They set up their own Citizens Council, formed with the specific objective of preventing further disturbances. It was quite ineffective. From the 2nd to the 4th of August more violent, bloody clashes took place between Roman Catholics and Protestants. The Roman Catholic area of Hooker Street, Belfast, was transformed into a battleground. Paving stones were crowbarred up and telegraph posts and street lamp standards were torn down and made into barricades to impede the police. Cars were overturned, shops were set on fire and Molotov cocktails exploded.

This violence was not a symptom of public resentment or injustice, or opposition to the government. It was the violence of an impassioned mob inflamed to fury and the lust to destroy by undercover subverters.

The rioting died down, only to break out again on the 12th of August with even greater violence. The government was obliged to order the police to use tear-gas to prevent extensive damage being caused to property and injury to innocent civilians. The police, representing law and order, once again became the target of attack from both Protestants and Catholics. Breeding hatred between the police and citizens is a common subversive tactic, and once again the cry of 'police brutality' was heard in Northern Ireland, as it has been heard in France and America, West Germany and Japan.

*　　　*　　　*

Throughout 1969 and into 1970 the rioting, violence and terrorism increased steadily until May 1970, when the subverter-inflamed rioters were no longer faced by the Constabulary. They now confronted disciplined British troops. But they did so unflinchingly.

On the 17th of May a petrol station was set alight and troops intervened with tear-gas to disperse the rioters. The fighting lasted for four hours, during which time six soldiers and many civilians were seriously injured.

On the 2nd of June an ominous note was sounded. During the fighting between British troops and rioters, a man was shot in the leg by a rooftop sniper.

The 27th and 28th of June became yet another weekend of unleashed violence, inflamed by the six-month prison sentence given to Miss Bernadette Devlin, MP, for her part in inciting riotous behaviour against the police. British troops concentrated in the Bogside area found themselves so heavily outnumbered by rioters that they were forced to retreat under a hail of petrol bombs and other missiles.

On the 28th of June the Irish Prime Minister announced that additional contingents of troops were on their way to Northern Ireland to reinforce the army. This decision had to be taken because of the very serious threats to the lives and livelihood of a very large number of people.

A 'period of emergency' was then fixed by the Government. It started on the 30th of June and would terminate upon a day to be announced by the Governor of Northern Ireland. The Government could not anticipate how long it would need to restore order. Rioting had become completely uncontrollable. The Minister of Development, Mr Faulkner, told in a radio interview why the Government had also introduced strict legislation involving the carrying of firearms. He said:

The trouble that there was yesterday, and last night,* took on quite a new form. New—but yet old. Whereas a year ago, people were talking about defending their homes in various parts of Belfast and in Londonderry, what we saw yesterday was first of all planned arson in various British-owned premises in Belfast. The police have discovered electronic devices that were placed in various stores in Belfast. Then there were gunmen active in one or two parts of Belfast last night, specifically in two places where they were active against the police.

Once again the subverters were using the familiar tactics of transforming street rioting into guerrilla warfare by the introduction of arson, firearms and explosives.

On the 3rd of July British troops in the Roman Catholic area of Belfast were engaged in an all-night battle with armed men. Handgrenades were thrown by rioters and snipers took up positions on rooftops and fired down on the British soldiers. The troops, supported by armoured vehicles, were ordered to occupy the entire area. The fighting was fierce. Buses and lorries were overturned and street barricades were erected to obstruct the soldiers. Two snipers were killed by army marksmen and a third was crushed to death by an armoured vehicle. Sixteen people were injured by rioters' gunshots, and many others by explosions. Extensive damage was caused to a newspaper office, a petrol filling station and a Savings Bank. Acting on information received from Intelligence officers, the army raided

* 27th and 28th of June 1970.

buildings in the Falls Road area on the 3rd of July and seized pistols, rifles, automatic weapons, shotguns, thirty five pounds of explosives and 20,000 rounds of ammunition.

On the 31st of July, in the Roman Catholic area of Belfast, British troops fought a prolonged battle against mobs of demonstrators. A nineteen-year-old electrician was shot dead after being warned five times to stop throwing petrol bombs; when shot, he was holding yet another petrol bomb. The killing inflamed hatred against the disciplined British soldiers, who had fired 328 cartridges above the heads of the crowd. Mr Burroughs, the British government representative in Northern Ireland, said the tension in Belfast was much more distressing than for some time; he added:

'These riots had nothing to do with civil rights and social justice, and little to do with religion. It *appears* to be the cause of republicanism, but there are sinister elements manipulating young people.'

During September 1970 more than seventy bomb explosions took place in Northern Ireland. Among the more important buildings destroyed by bombs were the Carrickfergus Town Hall, an electricity transformer in Newry, the British Army Information Office in Belfast, the Northern Bank in the centre of Belfast, the homes of Lord Justice Curren and the Rev. Smyth, the telephone exchange at Newcastle, County Down, the Customs House in Armagh, the Electricity Board Showrooms at Lurgan, an electricity substation in Belfast, a Customs Post at Killeen, the home of Harry Diamond, a former Labour Member of Parliament, a Royal Navy Recruiting Centre in Belfast and an electricity transformer in Craigabon. This was not the work of political hotheads. This was planned warfare against the State.

*　　*　　*

January 1971 saw the most violent rioting ever to take place between Catholics and Protestants in Belfast. Rioting, killing, arson and destruction reached new heights. Police with water-cannon, and soldiers using rubber bullets, could not quell the disturbances. The Ulster television transmitter was totally destroyed. Forty-eight pounds of gelignite attached to an alarm clock were found by a British soldier,

1. SNIPING: British soldiers must be subjected to around-the-clock sniping. A handful of mobile snipers who shoot to kill can keep a large number of troops constantly on the alert and prevented from carrying out other duties. Take every precaution to prevent killed or wounded snipers falling into British hands. Camouflage all militant action so that it appears to be committed by the I.R.A. or other Irish factions.

2. BOMBING: This should harass the enemy non-stop day and night. Political hot-heads must be pressed into service for planting bombs. No network activist can risk involving himself in this activity. I.R.A.Provisionals and similar Irish fanatics can be found who are eager to plant bombs and rig booby-traps. Youngsters and older children are ideal material for this work. They attract less attention and suspicion than adults, are more sensitive to monetary rewards, and ask no questions. If captured by British Army or Security officers they are unable to provide information about their employer. Children are used extensively in Vietnam, so use them too in your territory.

3. STREET FIGHTING: Whenever this is provoked it should lead up to throwing bricks, stones and bottles at British troops. More gelignite nail-bombs and petrol-bombs must be readily available for use by mobs. Killing British soldiers should be propagated as a praiseworthy target. British Army patrols can be lured into ambushes more easily when children, youngsters and women are the bait.

In August 1971, Peking's Special Division for Subversion transmitt

4. PRECAUTIONS: Every effort must be made to ensure that all acts of terrorism seem to be committed by the I.R.A., the I.R.A.Provisionals, or other Irish fanatics. Nu clue must ever lead to any master operator or his undercover network! Network members must not personally engage in terrorist activity! Their most valuable work is behind the scenes, inspiring obedience to these directives.

5. WEAPONS: To ensure that the I.R.A. etc. are believed to be the instigators and executors of terrorism, only Western-manufactured arms, ammunition and explosives should be used. Easily accessible small caches of arms, ammunition and explosives must be made known to all snipers and Irish militants.

6. BANK RAIDS: Bank and Post Office robberies must be staged, and propagated as fund-raising actions by the I.R.A. and others, to purchase weapons. The supply of funds to network leaders for their networks activity will continue as previously, however.

7. EXPLOSIVES DIRECTIVES: Our directives on how to manufacture gelignite-nail-bombs, petrol-bombs, time-bombs, booby-traps, etc. must be distributed widely. Encourage fanatics to duplicate and circulate them indiscriminately. Every bomb that explodes, no matter how inefficiently, adds to social disruption and harasses the enemy.

━━━━━━━━━━━━━━━━━━━━━━━━━━━━━

THIS DIRECTIVE MUST NOT FALL INTO

UNAUTHORISED HANDS!

MEMORISE!   THEN BURN!
━━━━━━━━━━━━━━━━━━━━━━━━━━━━━

is directive to its master-subverters in Northern Ireland.

who defused the time-bomb with only seconds to spare. Belfast's street rioting was also enlivened by the use of cross-bow bolts, ten-inch feathered metal arrows with steel tips that can kill at 50 yards. Sub-machine-guns fired on army trucks.

By February, the rioting had taken on an even more ominous turn. As had happened during the riots in Chicago and other American cities, many riflemen had taken to the rooftops and were systematically sniping at the police and British troops.

This transformation of rioting into guerrilla warfare caused Authority to accuse the IRA of stirring up trouble in Northern Ireland. A spokesman of the IRA angrily denied this. There existed, he pointed out, a breakaway splinter-group of the IRA which called itself the IRA Provisionals; it was this breakaway group that was responsible for the guerrilla warfare, he alleged. The Provisionals were bitterly opposed to the IRA and responsible for murdering IRA members, he added. This formation of a breakaway group that embraces violence is another familiar subverter tactic. The Black Power group broke away from Dr Martin Luther King in the USA and most countries have known similar violent splinter groups.

Towards the middle of February 1971 terrorism in Northern Ireland had reached a new low. All decent men and women who become involved in the bestiality of war, try to protect children from its evil influence. When cities are attacked, the first responsibility of government is to remove the children to a safe place. But subverters have no moral qualms. In Northern Ireland, on the 8th of February 1971, it was revealed that children between eight and fourteen years of age were being paid fifteen shillings a day to form groups to stone and harass British soldiers and the police. Television screens showed these boys and girls approaching to within a few yards of barriers manned by soldiers, and raining stones and bottles upon them. The soldiers were helpless. They crouched behind their plastic shields and stoically suffered bruised arms and shoulders.

Protestant and Catholic leaders joined in publicly denouncing terrorism. It was, they claimed the worst ever known in Northern Ireland, and a violation of the wishes of the majority of the people living in the province. It did not reflect the religious antagonism between Protestants and Catholics, which was just being used as a flimsy pretext by armed men and terrorists who wished to conduct guerrilla warfare against British soldiers. All the speakers condemned the bombings, and the landmines that had recently destroyed a Land-Rover and killed its four occupants, among whom were two BBC technicians. They regretted the involvement of so many innocent people in the rioting and said all Irish people had been shamed by the methods adopted by the terrorists. They said the IRA had never been afraid to face British troops and fight them honourably.

But the terrorists concealed themselves upon the roofs of tenement buildings, raining fire on British soldiers and thus subjecting all the tenants inside the buildings, men, women and children, to suffer counter-measures by the British forces.

Subverter-inspired terrorism in Northern Ireland follows the pattern of terrorism all over the Western world. A handful of determined undercover subverters seize upon a grievance, inflame passions and encourage rioting that becomes ever more violent until guerrilla warfare holds sway.

* * *

The recent spread of violence and terrorism in Northern Ireland shows how well Moscow's and Peking's subverters succeed in inflaming passions:

5th of June, 1971: A bomb explosion in Roden Street Police Station, Belfast, injured 4 people.

Four occupants of a car driving past an electricity substation were injured when it was wrecked by a bomb.

Another bomb demolished an Army Land-Rover.

8th of June, 1971: An electricity transformer and a clothing warehouse wrecked by bombs.

9th of June, 1971: Three soldiers injured and a civilian shot dead in Springfield Road, Belfast. Householders boarded up windows as bullets swept the streets. Gelignite nail bombs, rockets made from signal flares and dynamite were used by rioting mobs against British soldiers. Cars and buses overturned and set alight.

Two bombs exploded in Bolludumford Power Station.

Two unarmed off-duty British soldiers wearing civilian clothes shot by terrorists in Belfast.

Five soldiers narrowly escaped being blown up by a 150-lb gelignite booby-trap when their Land-Rover approached the Ulster border.

12th of June, 1971: Many people injured in Belfast by a bomb that damaged the Educational Authority Offices in Academy Street.

A second explosion occurred in Belfast College while the first was being investigated.

14th of June, 1971: Nine hundred Royal Scots First Parachute Regiment and four hundred and fifty policemen clashed with Orangemen in Londonderry. Troops used rubber bullets and CS gas.

19th of June, 1971: A new electricity substation in Belfast damaged by time-bomb. Damage estimated at £$\frac{1}{2}$ million.

In Hannahstown, Co. Antrim, four gelignite explosions damaged a new £2 million substation due to start operating in September.

A gelignite bomb damaged Gallaghers' cigarette factory in Henry Street, Belfast.

A stick of gelignite with a burned-out fuse found by staff of a clothing shop.

29th of June, 1971: Two hundred men of the 1st Battalion, Royal Green Jackets, uncovered a key terrorist armoury; material seized included two-way radios, detonators, hand-grenades, gelignite bombs, firearms and ammunition.

4th of July, 1971: Two soldiers of the Royal Green Jackets wounded in the Lower Falls area of Belfast. Their Land-Rover was machine-gunned by a fast-moving private car.

Two civilians were wounded by stray bullets.

The Territorial Army Headquarters was machine-gunned by a speeding car.

Incendiary devices caused fires at a factory in the Ardoyne, the Ulster Bus Depot at Smithfield, Belfast, and at an Orange Hall in Co. Antrim.

9th of July, 1971: Londonderry's bloodiest rioting since August 1969; troops, pelted by gelignite nail bombs, retaliated with rubber bullets and gas canisters and a youth was shot dead.

12th of July, 1971: 3 explosions rocked Royal Avenue, Belfast.

17th of July, 1971: A man shot dead in a public house four miles from Belfast's city centre.

Bombs set fire to a car and damaged a garage in Newry.

18th of July, 1971: Masked gunmen held up the staff of the *Daily* and *Sunday Mirror*'s newspaper printing plant near Belfast; explosive charges were placed in the presses and detonated.

19th of July, 1971: Rioters stoned troops in Londonderry; the soldiers retaliated with rubber bullets. A paratrooper shot in Belfast during a gun battle with terrorists.

A Guinness brewery and a telephone exchange damaged by gelignite bombs.

21st of July, 1971: The caretaker of an Employment Office in College Road, Belfast, injured by a bomb explosion.

22nd of July, 1971: A soldier and a woman hospitalised for bullet wounds during rioting in the Grosvenor Road area of Belfast; there were also incidents of arson.

A man injured in an explosion at Albert Street, Falls Road.

During a night of violence, mobs attacked a patrol of Royal Green Jackets; the troops fired rubber bullets, and submachine-gun bullets wounded an officer and a woman.

24th of July, 1971: The Army winkled out a terrorist headquarters in Ulster; electronic and radio equipment was seized and forty-eight people detained; documents found proved of great assistance to security forces.

Mobs fired shots in the Falls Road area.

Gelignite nail bombs exploded in Leeson Road and Grosvenor Street.

26th of July, 1971: Barricades in Belfast's Casement Park stormed by mobs; nine policemen injured; police patrol bicycles set on fire.

In Adamstown a building burned down.

In Lurgan, troops fired upon a hostile crowd of four hundred and seized crates of petrol bombs.

28th of July, 1971: Five shots fired by a sniper at a unit of the 2nd Battalion Royal Green Jackets, in Londonderry.

29th of July, 1971: Troops fired rubber bullets at youths bombarding them with petrol bombs at Butcher's Gate, Bogside, Londonderry.

Dawn raids by police and sixty troops in Cullingtree Road netted caches of explosives, ammunition and arms.

30th of July, 1971: Troops used water-cannon with blue dye against rioters.

A bomb explosion in Belfast injured eleven.

An explosion damaged the Community Centre at Portadown.

Two private houses were blasted and two of their occupants taken to hospital.

A Customs Post at Muss, a building in Hannahstown and St Cecilia's School in Bogside were also damaged by bombs.

31st of July, 1971: Sticks of gelignite, a detonator and cable found in a club room at St Peter's School, Raglan Street, in Belfast's Falls Road area.

2nd of August, 1971: Mobs attacked Army posts in Londonderry's Bogside; troops used water-cannon.

4th of August, 1971: Three bomb explosions in Londonderry, one thrown from a car; shots fired at an Army post.

One man in Belfast hospitalised after an explosion in Royal Avenue.

5th of August, 1971: Police engaged in relief work following floods in Bogside were stoned by mobs.

6th of August, 1971: Six shots fired from ambush at a patrol of Green Howards in the Ardoyne; one soldier wounded.

7th of August, 1971: A Corporation bus hijacked by terrorists, who fired a submachine-gun at a sandbagged sentry-box in Belfast's Springfield Road; spent cartridges were later found in the abandoned bus.

10th of August, 1971: Today's death toll—eleven! Riots raged in Belfast, Londonderry and Newry.

A boy of fifteen shot by a soldier as he threw a petrol bomb in Belfast.

A soldier shot in the head by a sniper and shot again as he lay on the ground.

Two Belfast women and a priest wounded.

The rioting followed a round-up of 300 IRA suspects.

11th of August, 1971: A soldier shot dead by a sniper in Londonderry, and another wounded.

In Belfast, three soldiers wounded by snipers.

Explosions in Londonderry throughout the night, and a police station besieged by a mob hurling petrol bombs—the police used CS gas.

The bodies of two men found by police in an area of previous fighting. Many fires started in all parts of the city. A helicopter on look-out duty damaged by a sniper's bullet.

12th of August, 1971: Five civilians shot dead in Belfast, four soldiers injured.

An estimated 500 petrol bombs were thrown in Londonderry.

13th of August, 1971: Four armed men entered houses in Belfast and fired the buildings.

In Londonderry sporadic shooting in the Bogside and other districts.

14th of August, 1971: A man, walking along the rain-swept Long Tower Street in Londonderry's Bogside drew a .38 revolver and fired upon an Army patrol. He was killed when troops returned the fire.

15th of August, 1971: A soldier lured to death in Belfast's Crumlin Road. His armoured car stopped to investigate a disturbance involving women, and shots were fired by snipers. An explosion at a house in Twadell Avenue injured four.

16th of August, 1971: A gelignite bomb damaged a supermarket in Londonderry's Waterside. In Bogside troops were showered with petrol bombs.

17th of August, 1971: Troops dismantling barricades in the Bogside area were fired upon.

A gelignite bomb damaged an Army observation post in Bligh's Lane.

Belfast Public Library damaged by an incendiary bomb.

18th of August, 1971: Children badly burned by a petrol bomb in central Belfast.

In the ten days since internment was introduced, gunmen made thirteen raids on Belfast Banks and Post Offices, netting £40,000.

Two police cars damaged by bombs in Co. Tyrone.

19th of August, 1971: 1,300 troops cleared 73 barricades erected in the streets of Londonderry. They were fired upon by snipers.

Armed and masked terrorists raided a flour mill in Belfast's dockland and exploded two bombs.

21st of August, 1971: A gunman in a speeding car shot a soldier in central Belfast. Four masked terrorists with machine-guns stole £2,000 from the Ulster Union Bank in Antrim Road.

Bombs exploded in a car showroom, a garage and a paint factory.

In Londonderry, there were six shooting incidents.

23rd of August, 1971: A bomb destroyed the front gates of Crumlin Road Jail, Belfast, injured two prison officers and two prisoners.

A striptease club, 77 *Sunset Strip*, destroyed by a fifty-pound gelignite bomb. Five other explosions in the city.

24th of August, 1971: A soldier on sentry duty shot dead by a sniper in Belfast.

Bombs exploded in different parts of Ulster.

A Post Office van ambushed and set on fire in the Armagh area.

A bomb damage disrupted power lines in Pomery.

A bomb exploded in the dockyard area of Newry.

In Mowham, Co. Armagh, a family of seven fled from their home, which had been set on fire.

26th of August, 1971: An explosion in Ireland's Electricity Board premises in Belfast killed one man and hospitalised sixteen.

A bomb exploded in Ford car showrooms in Dungannon.

27th of August, 1971: Two soldiers wounded by bullets in a clash with rioters in Armagh.

Troops uncovered 112 grenades, 451 lbs of gelignite and 20 ft of fuse in a cemetery in Newry.

28th of August, 1971: Three raids by masked gunmen in Belfast netted £2,500.

In Armagh 800 people hijacked lorries for use as barricades.

30th of August, 1971: Snipers fired upon soldiers in Belfast; one soldier gravely wounded. Leaflets circulated among Protestants in Belfast, urging them to form armed platoons.

31st of August, 1971: A hardware shop owned by Northern Ireland's Health Minister damaged by a gelignite bomb. Bombs exploded at Guinness premises, a butcher's shop, an electricity transformer and a public house.

2nd of September, 1971: A telephone exchange blown up in Ballygawley.

Three bombs failed to explode in Omagh Town Hall.

Two soldiers shot and wounded by snipers in Belfast.

An unexploded bomb found in the NAAFI building at Holywood,
Belfast.

Snipers fired upon Royal Engineers working near a Constabulary
Station at Forkhill, Co. Armagh.

A transformer damaged in Belfast's Crumlin Road area, causing a
power cut.

A customs post near Strabane blown up; hostile crowds stoned
security forces investigating the incident.

3rd of September, 1971: Forty people injured in a Belfast shopping
centre when four bombs exploded in the space of fifteen minutes.
Rescue work and first aid hampered by 'false alarm' reports of other
bombs.

An electricity transformer blown up in Derry, Co. Tyrone.

Bombs destroyed a customs post in Castleguard.

A petrol station in Belfast's Pentonville Road damaged by a bomb.

A British Army major shot in the stomach by a sniper in Bogside.

A member of the Ulster Defence Regiment shot dead outside a
police station at Kilauley, Co. Fermanagh.

A customs post in Killcoean, Co. Tyrone, blown up by five armed
men.

4th of September, 1971: A bullet fired at a soldier from a speeding
car killed an 18-month-old baby in a pram, in Belfast's Falls Road
area.

A Scots Guard nearby escaped death when a sniper's bullet cut
through his hair, holing his beret back and front.

A part-time member of the Ulster Defence Regiment, on duty at a
police station in Co. Fermanagh, was shot by submachine-guns from
a passing car.

A police sergeant, two constables and two civilians hospitalised after
a police station was blown up in Dundonald, Belfast; a telephone
exchange in the village also damaged.

A bomb blast shattered a Mace Grocery Store in North Belfast.

5th of September, 1971: A bomb thrown from a speeding car injured a soldier and civilians, including an eleven-year-old boy, who was gravely wounded.

Two bodies found in the ruins of a draper's shop set on fire by terrorists.

A soldier killed in an ambush in the Newry–Besbrook Road, Co. Armagh.

6th of September, 1971: A young couple parked a car a few feet from a sentry post behind Queen's Street Police Station and walked away. Shortly afterwards the car exploded, setting fire to a three-storey building.

Troops fired upon in the Springfield Road area.

In Londonderry, rioters set fire to buildings in the Bogside area.

A bomb damaged a police station.

A bomb was thrown at troops in William Street.

In Belfast, the Army seized a cache of ammunition and broadcasting equipment.

Belfast explosions injured children with flying glass.

In Londonderry, a boy of eleven was injured when a gelignite bomb exploded in an Army billet.

7th of September, 1971: A fourteen-year-old girl killed and a civilian wounded in Londonderry's Bogside area during a gun battle between troops and snipers.

A soldier wounded by machine-gun fire in Belfast's Crumlin Road.

Automatic fire directed at troops near the old city walls of Londonderry.

10th of September, 1971: Rioting crowds in Londonderry attacked troops with stones and petrol bombs after a three-year-old boy was killed by an Army lorry.

A bomb exploded in the Comber Police Station, near Belfast. An Army captain was killed while defusing a bomb planted in a Gospel Hall in Belfast.

11th of September, 1971: Four masked gunmen entered a match factory in Domege Road, Belfast, and destroyed it with a fire started by four bombs.

A petrol filling station and a supermarket destroyed by bombs.

In Foyle Road, Londonderry, snipers fired fifty bullets at troops. Nail bombs were used in a concentrated attack upon an Army Post. Shots were fired at troops on the Creggan Estate. A car showroom and a Rates Office were blown up.

12th of September, 1971: Many bombs exploded during the night. Seven shots fired at an Army Post.

13th of September, 1971: Rioting continued in Belfast and Londonderry. Troops used riot shields and armoured cars. A policeman dived down a railway embankment to avoid fire from a submachine-gun.

A bomb damaged a Youth Club. Troops patrolling Crumlin Road fired upon. A bomb hurled at troops from a passing car. In Foyle Road and Bligh's Lane soldiers beat off a mob of 400 with rubber bullets and CS gas. Bombs thrown at armoured cars.

14th of September, 1971: Three men and a pregnant woman badly injured when their house in Belfast's Benn Street blew up. A nurse and a boy injured when a bomb wrecked a library in North Circular Road.

15th of September, 1971: Snipers killed a soldier and seriously injured another at an Army Post in Londonderry.

Two soldiers injured by gunmen in Belfast. An Army vehicle taking the wounded men to hospital came under machine-gun fire. Near Dungannon a soldier was killed in an ambush. Another member of his patrol seriously injured.

16th of September, 1971: A bus carrying thirty handicapped children showered with stones and petrol bombs during rioting—two taken to hospital with burns.

Troops dismantling a barricade were stoned by children, and shot at by terrorists armed with submachine-guns. Troops returned the fire; a gunman fell and was dragged away by companions.

An Ulster policeman kidnapped and taken across the border into Eire. He was later released. The IRA Provisionals recently warned they would kidnap troops, policemen and politicians as hostages.

18th of September, 1971: Snipers in Belfast killed a soldier and wounded two others. A Scots Guardsman wounded by a sniper while on foot patrol in Belfast's Andersonstown area. A gelignite bomb destroyed an Army Post in Seefords Street, wrecked two houses and a betting shop; three soldiers and a civilian injured.

Petrol bombs and explosives thrown at soldiers in Lurgan; a convent in Kilkael evacuated while a bomb was defused.

19th of September, 1971: Another night of violence.

20th of September, 1971: Sporadic sniping. A Belfast Savings Bank damaged by a gelignite bomb.

22nd of September, 1971: Bombing and shooting. A six-year-old girl was injured by snipers' bullets in Belfast. An Army Land-Rover was fired upon.

23rd of September, 1971: A car deposited a bomb on Ulster's M1 Motorway, close by Long Kesh Internment Camp. It blew a 3 ft deep hole in the road.

Troops attacked by a mob in Belfast's Tullymore Gardens.

A Northern Ireland Fishery Board patrol boat was blown up and destroyed. A man and woman died in a Belfast explosion. It was suspected they were manufacturing bombs.

Security forces conducting a search were fired upon by snipers. Nail and petrol bombs were hurled by a rioting mob that also burned a Corporation bus.

A bomb damaged a bottling factory in Londonderry's William Street.

25th of September, 1971: Six children walking to school in Londonderry triggered off a tripwire that failed to detonate 20 lbs of gelignite. The path is used frequently by Army patrols.

26th of September, 1971: Ten shots fired at an Army Mobile Patrol in Belfast's Falls Road. One soldier injured.

Three bombs exploded in the city.

Four masked gunmen held up a bakery in Newry and stole £4,000.

A sentry on duty at an observation post in Londonderry's Bishop's Street area was shot in the head by automatic fire.

A petrol-bomb thrower shot by troops at New Lodge Road, Belfast.

Terrorists set two lorries alight during rioting. A bulldozer clearing the burning lorries was set on fire; the crew was attacked as they abandoned the vehicle. Three soldiers badly burned.

Armed gunmen stole more than £5,000 in simultaneous raids on two Banks and two Post Offices.

3,400 lbs of gelignite stolen from a building site near Brogheda, Eire.

29th of September, 1971: For the second time terrorists launched an anti-tank bazooka rocket. It smashed through a window-frame at Andersonstown Police Station but failed to explode.

Armed gangs in Londonderry and Mallusk stole £19,000 from a bank, a Post Office van and a Post Office.

30th of September, 1971: A 20-lb gelignite bomb exploded in the Fore Street Inn, Shankhill Road, Belfast, killing two and injuring fourteen.

1st of October, 1971: An unexploded bomb found in Ulster Sports Club. Protestants and Catholics clashed on a Wimpey building site. Troops intervened and evacuated 100 Catholics greatly outnumbered by Protestants.

2nd of October, 1971: A soldier on patrol in Chatham Street shot in the stomach by a gunman who stepped out from an alleyway and fired two shots, and died on the way to hospital.

A witness described how a twelve-year-old boy planted a 10-lb gelignite bomb that destroyed a store.

Four armed gunmen entered a distillery and planted two bombs. Soldiers defused them four minutes before they were due to explode.

A bomb exploded in the Northern Bank in Lisburn Road.

A patrol of Green Howards intervened in a fight between youths in the Crumlin Road area and came under snipers' fire. They returned the fire.

An Army patrol ambushed in Norglen Gardens. Twenty shots fired.

Three armed men scooped £30 from the till of a bar in Falls Road.

Armed raiders stole about £6,000 from a bank and Post Office.

3rd of October, 1971: A 10-lb gelignite bomb exploded in a Council Office near Belfast; a man was killed.

Troops were fired upon by a sniper while attempting to retrieve the body.

4th of October, 1971: A bomb thrown from a speeding car at an Army Observation Post in Abecorn Road. The bomb missed and went over a wall before exploding. Troops opened fire at the car. A passenger was seen to slump. Later, a girl aged eight was found in the street seriously wounded.

An Agricultural Inspector was shot dead when terrorists opened fire with automatic weapons on an Army patrol in the Falls Road area.

17

Terrorism 1970–71

1970 and 1971 were the years of guerrilla warfare and terrorism.

Never before in modern history have so many people's lives been disrupted by the action of so few fanatics.

One reason for this is the worldwide news coverage made possible by international and transatlantic television and the use of satellites for communications. An act of terrorism quickly becomes global news. What happens in a remote village in a far-off part of the world is made known to radio listeners and television viewers everywhere—if it is newsworthy. The assassination of a trade union member in a Polish factory would not be reported; but the assassination of a dictator, a highly placed diplomat or a member of a royal family would.

Terrorists want publicity, so during 1970 their activity was directed at targets which gave them worldwide news coverage. The guerrillas in Quebec and Spain achieved international publicity for kidnapping highly placed diplomats, and the Arab terrorists in Jordan by skyjacking airliners loaded with innocent men, women and children.

The planting of time-bombs in aircraft has aroused horror throughout the Western world. But time-bombs planted in an aircraft, though they do get worldwide news coverage, do not gain the terrorists the publicity they desire. The mass-media say ' A bomb has exploded . . .' But what the terrorists want the world to know is that a bomb has exploded for this or that cause. The anonymous planting of bombs in aircraft has been abandoned. Instead, airliners are skyjacked and the motive of the skyjacking is publicly declared. This method exposes individual terrorists to the danger of arrest. But fanatical men and women who will destroy life in furtherance of their cause are equally indifferent to their own personal safety and well-being.

*　　*　　*

Canada, a member of the British Commonwealth, has been deeply involved in terrorist activity of late.

On the 5th of October 1970 Mr James Cross, the British Trade Commissioner in Montreal, was kidnapped. Four armed men forced their way into his house, made him dress at gunpoint, handcuffed him and drove him away in a taxi. Later, ransom demands were made: $500,000 in gold bars; the release of certain political prisoners with a safe conduct to Cuba; and a ban on any police efforts to locate the kidnappers. These demands were to be met within forty-eight hours.

The authors of the crime were an extremist separatist organisation, the *Front de Liberation du Quebec*, or FLQ.*

The Federal government of Canada rejected all ransom demands, but while negotiations were pending, the police refrained from searching for the kidnappers in deference to Mr Cross's safety. The FLQ extended their time limit.

On the 8th of October the Federal government yielded to one of the FLQ's minor demands. It authorised the broadcast of their Political Manifesto. This praised Dr Fidel Castro, the Cuban leader, and denounced many Canadian politicians and businessmen.

Negotiations continued meanwhile for the release of Mr Cross. His release was negotiated between the kidnappers and police inside a house in a Montreal suburb. The house was full of explosives; if the police had acted precipitately at any time, the terrorists would have blown up everyone, including themselves.

On the 10th of October the government offered the kidnappers a safe-conduct to a foreign country if Mr Cross was released. But in the evening of that same day, M. Pierre Laporte, the Quebec Minister of Labour and Immigration, was kidnapped.

He was playing football with his son and nephew in front of his Montreal home when a green car pulled up beside him, two masked men with submachine-guns leaped out, bundled him into the back of the car and drove off. A message from the FLQ said that M. Laporte

---

* This extremist organisation vehemently advocates the principle of separation, which in Canada means independence and self-government for the French Canadian population. These live mostly in the province of Quebec.

would be 'executed' at 10 o'clock that same night unless the authorities replied favourably to the previous ransom demands.

On the 12th of October the Quebec government appointed mediators to negotiate with FLQ representatives the release terms for Mr Cross and M. Laporte (who had apparently not been killed on the night of the 10th), but these negotiations broke down. As a precaution, and as a safeguard to the stability of the State, troops were moved into Montreal and Quebec City.

Four days later, the Federal government evoked the War Measures Act of 1914. This gave them emergency powers to cope with internal insurrection. These powers had never before been invoked in peace-time.

The following day, the 17th of October, the police found M. Laporte's body. He had been murdered.

It was not until the 3rd of December 1970 that James Cross was released from captivity, as a result of an agreement reached between the mediators, the FLQ and the government. The Cuban Consul-General in Montreal assisted in Mr Cross's exchange for the safe-conduct of the kidnappers. He and his kidnappers were driven to the Cuban Embassy and he remained upon this Cuban territory until the kidnappers and their families, flown out by a Canadian military aircraft, reported they had arrived safely in Havana.

*   *   *

Herr Eugen Beihl, a West German diplomat in Spain, was taken captive by a gang calling themselves the ETA.* Herr Beihl was held to ransom to secure the release of a number of Basques who were charged with murdering a police officer.

The Spanish government is well aware that a secret communist undercover force is at work within its frontiers.

During the trial for murder in December 1970 of a number of Basques, violent demonstrations of sympathy broke out in many parts of Spain. This unrest was incited by Moscow's Special Division for Subversion subverters.

Public demonstrations and protest meetings are prohibited by law

* The Basque Freedom Movement.

in Spain, and the disturbances were quelled with a ruthlessness that would be intolerable in a democratic country. The Spanish public were bluntly informed by radio, television and the press that:

'The Basque murderers, the student demonstrations and vandalism, the ETA assaults on military organisations and the kidnapping and holding to ransom of a German diplomat accredited to Spain, were all planned by the Kremlin.' Soviet Russia, it was stated, was entirely responsible for Spain's recent political problems—Moscow had deliberately initiated public strife and lawlessness.

The Spanish government has been convinced of Russian intervention in its affairs since the end of the Spanish Civil War, and combating the Red fifth-column's subversion is built into Spain's political policy. The secret police smell out undercover subverters with all the zeal of Holy Inquisitors intent on discovering witches and burning them at the stake. The Spanish Secret Police assume all the power and protection that the totalitarian state allows them, and use methods that would never be permitted in a democratic country.

Undercover subverters are cunning, and it is extremely difficult to prove anything against them. This does not hinder the Spanish Secret Police, however, who arrest suspects and interrogate them indiscriminately. Such interrogations are not the gentle, civilised exchange of question and answer that would take place in a British police station. However these painful interrogations have often yielded useful information to the Spanish Secret Police and confirmed the existence of widespread Russian-directed undercover subverter networks. There are many innocent and unfortunate Spaniards who had difficulty in convincing their interrogators they are not Moscow-employed subverters, but the Spanish Secret Police believe that the ruffled feelings of a few honest citizens are a small price to pay for political stability.

Captain Manzana of the Spanish *Guardia Civil* smelled out Red undercover subverters with unusual zeal and diligence. His whimsical method of selecting suspects for interrogation aroused bitter hatred. Over several years a great number of suspects endured his interrogation, some of them dying, some merely being crippled in the process. It was useless for the public to protest to a higher authority against Manzana's methods; indeed, any brave, public-spirited person who did protest was turned over to Captain Manzana as a 'suspect'. So, finally, Captain Manzana was warned by anonymous letters that if he did not mend his ways they would be mended for him. Manzana disregarded these warnings. For some months he continued to imprison people without trial, interrogating and torturing them, until one night a knock on his door brought him face to face with masked men who shot him dead.

The murder of Captain Manzana brought sixteen Basques into the international limelight. They were accused of conspiring to kill Manzana, of being members of the revolutionary Basque organisation ETA and of planning to overthrow the Franco régime. Their trial and the subsequent sentences of death issued by their military judges resulted in an outburst of protests from the Western world. General Franco yielded to world opinion; he annulled their death sentences on the 31st of December 1970.

Herr Eugen Beihl was freed as well; secret negotiations had obtained him his liberty just before Christmas 1970. But he suffered agonised weeks of suspense, fearing that his life would be forfeited to prove the determination of his kidnappers.

The leader of the ETA is a refugee from Spain, living in France. When Herr Beihl was kidnapped, and when guerrillas attacked Spanish *Guardia Civil* posts and military installations, he was detained by the French authorities. He strenuously denied that he, or the ETA, were responsible for the kidnapping or the acts of terrorism. They were caused he alleged, by a breakaway group from the ETA, acting on its own initiative, and in direct conflict with the aims and ideals of the ETA. He declared that undercover subverter influences which have been at work within the Basque movement, were responsible for some of its members breaking away and forming a terrorist group. The Spanish Secret Police *know* that Moscow's undercover subverters are at work in Spain, and they never relax their stringent measures to combat them.

*   *   *

As the year 1970 ended and 1971 began, the stepping up of terrorist activity throughout the world paralleled that of industrial strike action.

On the 13th of January 1971 the British Minister for Production and Employment, Mr Robert Carr, was watching television with his wife and thirteen-year-old daughter when a bomb exploded in their London home. A few minutes later a second bomb exploded. Miraculously they escaped injury.

Scotland Yard's Special Branch experts examined what was left of the bombs and confirmed that foreign influences had been at work. A police hunt was started for a young man believed to be the leader of six highly trained men, dedicated to spreading violence and terror. These same undercover subverters had planted a bomb in the Iberia Airline office in London the previous August. The Special Branch knew that these men, who are all experienced in the use of explosives and firearms, are also well provided with finance.

Three hundred Special Branch detectives, the Flying Squad and Regional Crime Squads assisted in the manhunt. The wanted men were identified as having been leading undercover subverters at demonstrations. They had travelled the country and stirred up considerable industrial unrest. The French police were asked to raid an undercover school for bombers where these subverters had received their special training.

The Carr bomb outrage coincided with even more violent rioting in Belfast.

On the 19th of January a Conservative MP, Mr Hugh Fraser, and his family, had a guard placed on them by Scotland Yard. The CID had received an anonymous tip-off that Mr Fraser and his family were to be kidnapped and held to ransom.

The same day, Mr Justice Stevenson was given a police guard when he was told by telephone that a bomb would explode in his home.

On the 28th of January it was revealed that the Attorney General, Sir Peter Rawlinson, and the Metropolitan Police Commissioner had also been victims of bomb attacks earlier in the year.

Further threats against these three personalities were reported in newspapers. A menacing letter had been received, signed by terrorists who called themselves The Angry Brigade.

When the Dean of Johannesburg was brought into court, after being in custody for eight days, it was stated that police had found in his possession communist undercover documents which advocated 'Guerrilla Warfare, Bloodshed and Sacrifice'. These pamphlets also showed how to make hand-grenades and Molotov cocktails.

On the 30th of January Mr Dudley Smith, the Under-Secretary of State at the Department of Unemployment, received a telephone call from The Angry Brigade, threatening him with assassination.

This busy British January of 1971 was accompanied by the most violent rioting ever to take place between Protestants and Catholics in Belfast.

18

The Communist Parties' Influence over Trade Unionists

Cold, bleak, shivering, miserable Britons of the power-cut winter of 1970 will remember three words:

Protest! Demonstrate! Strike!

Sit-downs and sit-ins; work-to-rule, official and unofficial strikes; protests and marches; anti-Springboks and anti-Vietnam demonstrations; riots. All had one objective: to impose the opinions of a minority upon the majority.

The masses are always apathetic. It is often socially essential for a minority to campaign militantly until the majority wakes up and becomes aware that the minority is right. History is rich with examples of individual acts of martyrdom, of men suffering as a result of trying to impose their opinion upon the majority. And they often did so to the ultimate benefits of mankind. But it does not follow that *all* minorities are always right; nor that it is justified for them to impose their *will* upon the majority.

*　　*　　*

The British Communist Party has limited membership and no representation in Parliament; it is undoubtedly a minority group. Britons think it ridiculous to suspect the Communist Party of plotting a Red conspiracy, or of being a source of danger. But during the course of the last few years, the CID, Scotland Yard's Special Branch, the FBI, the *Deuxième Bureau* and many other branches of Intelligence and Security throughout the Western world have unearthed indisputable evidence—most of it undisclosed—proving the complicity of *all* the communist parties of the world in a deliberately engineered and coordinated conspiracy to destroy the Western democracies. This minority political organisation must be regarded everywhere in the free world as one more mask concealing the face of the enemy within.

Many men have not hesitated publicly to make this accusation of a Red Conspiracy; among them is Lord Shawcross, a former Labour Minister; Lord Robens, in his capacity as Chairman of the National Coal Board; Mr Robert Carr,* the Minister of Production; and Mr Harold Wilson, former Prime Minister and present leader of the opposition Labour Party. They are intelligent men, occupying positions of great responsibility and trust. Their words cannot be lightly dismissed when they address a solemn warning to the nation.

Lord Shawcross said: 'There are sinister men in the background who are holding the nation to ransom with unjustified pay demands.'

Lord Robens, during the 1970 unofficial miners' strike, declared: 'You are up against a conspiracy in this country. I accuse the militants, backed by a communist conspiracy, of trying to do what the Russians have not been able to do in this country and in Western Europe.'

Mr Robert Carr, referring to the one-day strike on the 9th of December 1970, held in protest against his Industrial Relations Bill, said: 'The strike had been represented as a spontaneous protest against the Bill. In fact, however, it is being deliberately organised by a body called The Liaison Committee for the Defence of Trade Unions, whose activities . . . are prominently recorded in the newspaper of the Communist Party.'

Mr Harold Wilson, then Prime Minister, said in his 'Red Plot' speech to the House of Commons, during the Seamen's Strike: 'The House will be aware that the Communist Party, unlike the major other political parties, has at its disposal an efficient and disciplined industrial apparatus controlled from Communist Party Headquarters. No major strike occurs anywhere in this country in which that apparatus fails to concern itself.'

The obvious is being stated again and again by responsible men in positions of influence and power. They are repeatedly and publicly warning everyone against the Red plot, conceived by Moscow and Peking, to destroy the Western democracies.

YET THE WARNING IS NOT HEEDED; OR ELSE IT IS NOT BELIEVED.

The trade unions, all the political parties, the Churches, social

* Mr Carr was subjected to a bomb attack at his home. See page 202.

organisations, and all types of public and private organisations, have all been infiltrated by hard-core communist undercover subverters who are intent on pursuing a policy that has been drawn up by the Soviet Russian and Red Chinese political leaders. That policy has one objective: the destruction of the free world.

The efforts of all those who accept Moscow and Peking guidance become devoted to that same end.

The evidence that this Red plot exists is abundant. Yet most people are hard to convince that this great conspiracy is in operation.

Must Britain and the other Western democracies be plunged into complete economic chaos and industrial depression before the danger is seen, recognised and *resisted*?

During the first nine months of 1970 a total of over seven and a half *million* working days was lost in Britain because of strike action. Ninety per cent of these strikes were unofficial. They may have resulted from genuine grievances; but they could have been arbitrated. The crew of a ship should not leave its controls and let the ship cruise onto jagged rocks while they protest against a tea-break grievance. Grievances should be discussed and not allowed to become disruptive and destructive. Production lost by unofficial strikes has caused a serious slump in Britain's economy. This could have been avoided; and *would* have been avoided, if there had been goodwill, and the determination to achieve the best for everyone.

The hard-core communist fifth columnists, directed by master-subverters, have calculatedly fostered an attitude within the worker that is destructive of his means of livelihood. Small grievances are easily converted into explosively dangerous situations that threaten lives and property and cause injustice, arson and death.

Mr Harold Wilson has warned the public against that 'tightly-knit group of politically motivated men'. This 'disciplined apparatus' has the Communist Party at its head.

* * *

The most powerful man in the British Communist Party is the National Industrial Organiser, Mr Bert Ramelson. He is sixty years of age, a Ukrainian-born Canadian barrister. He has a distinguished war record, gained while fighting for Britain. He has not hesitated to express his aims and objectives clearly:

'There is no substitute for political action guided by a revolutionary party for achieving the transformation of society . . . and the establishment of workers' control.'

Mr Ramelson's influence stretches like a web from the Communist Party headquarters in King Street, London, to every shop floor in all branches of industry. He makes no *direct* contact, but relies upon an army of followers who spread 'conscious intention'. These pawns gain results in unity and cooperation because of the general guidance and policy that underlies all their activities.

Mr Bill Jones, of the Transport and General Workers' Union, and a former member of the TUC General Council, has said:

'Workers' control is not the end—it is one of the means to an end. It is no substitute for political power, and in this I agree with Bert Ramelson.'

Mr Jones is one of the Liaison Committee for the Defence of Trade Unions which was formed in 1966. The Committee's Chairman, Mr Kevin Halpin, a shipyard worker, and its secretary, Mr Jim Hiles, are both communists. It is not known who elected these men to the Committee, nor who pays them; but they travel the country from end to end, whipping up resentment throughout industry and instigating strike action.

The 1970 dock strike, which cost the country £37,000,000 *per day* in loss of trade, was led in London by two shop stewards who are known communists: Ernie Rice and Danny Lyons.*

Mr Lou Lewis, a member of the Communist Party's National Executive, was a leader of the building workers' strike in 1967. This strike brought building on the Barbican site in London to a standstill for twelve long months.

Mr George Wake, a member of the Communist Party's forty-one-strong executive, called out the electricity workers on the 5th of January 1971. The Power Workers' Board which he has formed, and

* According to a statement made in Parliament by the Opposition leader Mr Harold Wilson, Danny Lyons was one of the instigators of the Seamen's Strike in 1966.

which is quite unofficial, claims it has the support of 60,000 electricity workers at sixty-three power stations.

Investigations of all unreasonable strike actions always reveal the involvement of militant communists. Yet for every known and declared Communist Party member who openly supports the strike action, there are dozens who are unsuspected undercover subverters directed by Moscow's or Peking's master-subverters. Because they are not suspected they are more effective in their destructive work.

Like an iceberg, the Communist Party that shows above political waters surmounts a submerged and unseen nine-tenth of fifth-column conspiracy.

*   *   *

There are other disruptive political parties. The Socialist Labour League, a Trotskyist organisation, operates from an anonymous shopfront above a supermarket at 186A Clapham High Street, London. Its leader is white-haired Garry Healey, who avoids publicity. The League's organ, *Workers' Press*, sells an astonishing 20,000 copies daily. Although Healey personally shuns publicity the members of the League attract it by their involvement in industrial strife. Notably among them is Mrs Rosemary ('Red Rosemary') Whippe, twenty-two-year-old member of the League, who was sacked from the strike-torn Girling factory in 1970. Factory workers at Girling who were asked to strike in support against her dismissal claimed she was 'planted' on them.* She denied this at the time.

The Socialist Labour League's industrial arm is called the All Trades Union Alliance. In 1969–70 its influence was felt in three key industrial disputes: the Liverpool docks, the Doncaster mines and the motor industry. Its leaders include Mr Alan Thornett, deputy senior shop steward at the Morris car works, Oxford; and Messrs Reg Parsons and John Power, who are both members of the Amalgamated Engineering and Foundry Workers' Union.

Mr Alan English, Secretary of the Liverpool Docks Shop Stewards' Committee, wrote in the newspaper *Workers' Press*: 'I have only once before seen the unity that exists now in the working class . . .

* See page 212.

during the war. Now we are ready for a different kind of war: a war against the Tories.'

An influential member of the Amalgamated Engineering and Foundry Workers' Union is fifty-six-year-old Mr Reg Birch, a lean man of medium height with a dual passion for jazz music and reducing capitalist society to ashes. He is Chairman of the Communist Party of Great Britain (Marxist-Leninist). Although his party is small in numbers, Maoist Mr Birch wields considerable influence as the leader of the Amalgamated Engineering and Foundry Workers' Union's negotiating team with Ford.

An essential factor of Communist–Trotskyist strategy is the indoctrination of workers. Many militant workmen receive their instructions from the Institute for Workers' Control in Gamble Street, Nottingham. Its headquarters are sited in the Bertrand Russell Peace Foundation building, in the cobbled backstreets of the city, where it prints its own literature. The Institute for Workers' Control holds seminars all over the country, at which leading Marxist academics like Mr Ken Coates and Mr Tony Topham, both university lecturers, outline the steps to be taken for workers to gain control of industry. Its 1970 annual conference was held in Birmingham and attended by 1,200 trade union delegates, including many communists.

Mr Albert Martin, the sixty-five-year-old retired Secretary of the Nottinghamshire National Union of Mineworkers—who was beaten up by dissidents in the 1970 unofficial miners' strike—believes the Institute for Workers' Control was behind the 1970 militancy to which Lord Robens referred. The Institute for Workers' Control denied this. But before the strike the Institute for Workers' Control published a plan for a workers' takeover of the mines, devised by a fifty-year-old miner, Mr Arthur Palmer—who was an applicant for Mr Martin's job.

Lecturer Mr Ken Coates is quite open about the aims of the Institute for Workers' Control. He has stated: 'Workers' control begins with simple trade union demands for control of hiring and firing, tea-breaks, hours, speeds of work, allocation of jobs and so on. Pressure mounts through a whole series of demands to the point where the whole of capitalist society meets impasse. At this point . . . one reaches a revolutionary situation.'

Industry has learned to its cost that industrial disruption can be planned by militants. The lessons the militants learn from every strike are studied and reported upon to other branches of militant organisations at regular meetings. After the twenty-two-week strike at the Centrax light engineering factories in Devonshire in 1970, the four key men active in its unofficial strike committee laid it on the line:

> Towards the end of the dispute we met workers from other factory sites. We pooled our experiences and ideas and offered to give help and advice to other workers in a similar predicament. We went all around the country, from factory to factory, organising 'blacking' and 'collection', and explaining what was happening at Centrax.

These four men were: Mr John Webber, Amalgamated Engineering Union Convenor for the Heathfield factory, Mr Dave Ferguson, Amalgamated Engineering Union Convenor, Newton Abbot group, Mr Hugh Gallagher, Electrical Trades' Union Convenor, Newton Abbot, and Mr Jim Robinson, Transport and General Workers' Union Convenor, Newton Abbot. Their words were quoted in the *Red Mole*, a Marxist publication which had Tariq Ali, an extremely active radical, on its editorial board.

Later, the Centrax strike committee used their dispute as a springboard to launch a new, unofficial group of forty-two shop stewards calling themselves The Tolpuddle Group; it meets every month to decide on policy. In the *Red Mole* they claimed credit for helping two other strikes* to keep going.

All militants, and the methods they use, are feared as much by other trade union officials as by the managements—as I have already mentioned. Ninety per cent of all strikes in Britain in 1970 were unofficial. Trade unions and managements tried to cope with the impassioned men responsible, but they were blind to reason.

Two shop stewards, Mr Jock Macrea and Mr Sid Harroway from the Ford motor works, Dagenham, were interviewed in 1970 in

---

* Ottermill and Fine Tubes.

another revolutionary publication, *Black Dwarf*, edited at that time by Tariq Ali.

'The thing I was most worried about during the whole of my career at Fords,' said Mr Macrea, 'was an *official* strike. Because . . . official strikes tend to remove all control, and all the direction away from the workers.'

In recent years few firms in the car industry have been harder hit by wildcat strikes than Ford. Macrea and Harroway told how they operated over those years.

Question: 'Has the Communist Party strength increased in Dagenham during your time?'

Answer: 'Our plant has always been fairly well provided for, and there's always been a lot of our lads who have been party members, and all that.'

Question: 'There must be trouble almost every day?'

Answer: 'Almost invariably. Yes. But we've got built-in procedures. A worker can't be sacked unless it's referred to me. Suspensions come to me if the steward can't resolve them. That is the key to our procedure: *all* plant problems come to the Convenor. So if you've got a good Works Committee and your organisation is working efficiently, it should be good. But in the ultimate . . . you've always got to have workers ready to strike, in my opinion.'

These words from the Ford's Convenors could almost have been printed by the presses of the Institute for Workers' Control.

Question: 'What about outside help during strikes?'

Answer: 'You see, you get this difficulty. You get the students coming to help you during the strikes. They've all got beards and long hair and that sort of thing. They look a bit scruffy. But they say: "We'll go to the gate with you." Then people come along and say: "*They* don't work at Ford's. What are they doing on the bloody gate?" And then you have an issue. It's a terrible problem for us to grapple with. We have to say "We'd love you to help. We'd love you to be on the gates. And we understand what you're trying to do for us. *But the bloody workers don't understand it.*" Recently, we've had leaflets that we should take over the factory, or all sit down, or something. It might appeal to one's adventurous spirit; but of course one has to base all activity on realism. We are certainly not at the stage of being able to take over the factory or effect a sit-down. There may come a day when we say "We'll take over!" But we are certainly not at that level at this stage.'

Mrs 'Red Rosemary' Whippe, the woman at the centre of the Girling brake factory dispute in 1970, betrayed how one small issue can be used to halt production. The Girling factory at Bromborough, Cheshire, is a vital link in the nationwide chain of car production; any strike at Girling's eventually paralyses the entire motor industry.

Mrs Whippe was sacked by a Girling manager after she had taken a day off while working as a trainee. Her dismissal became a rallying call for strike action by the local Amalgamated Engineering and Foundry Workers' Union. But when it was discovered that Mrs Whippe was a member of the Trotskyist Socialist Labour League's youth section, the Young Socialists, her fellow factory workers, refused to come out. Mrs Whippe was a contributor to the Marxist monthly youth publication *Keep Left* under the name of Rosemary Boxall. Her husband, Mr Jan Whippe, is also a Marxist revolutionary.

Mr Frank Barrow, the forty-seven-year-old Electrical Trades Union shop steward, claimed at the time of the Girling dispute that Mrs Whippe had been 'planted at the factory as an agitator'. Mrs Whippe, who holds a second-class honours degree in Social Science from Southampton University, denied the allegation. But there was still no strike.

Violence is occasionally used as a weapon of intimidation. It was used in a 1970 unofficial strike by the Doncaster miners; it has been used on other occasions.

In April 1970 the Pilkington glass factories were hit by a massive unofficial strike—the only major stoppage the firm has suffered for nearly one and a half centuries, apart from the General Strike. It began as a small local dispute but escalated at lightning speed into a bitter and violent affair. Pilkington's group sells products worth more than £100 million each year to a hundred different countries. It is the biggest supplier of glass to the building trade and motor industries in Britain. It is an obvious target for subverters. Lord Pilkington said just before the strike began: 'By watchfulness and initiative, we avoid unnecessary troubles that can arise from allowing quite small local issues to lead to big trouble-spots for us. These troubles are manufactured by those who are very ill-disposed—and we must not forget that there are many such about.'

The Pilkington strike dragged on for seven weeks. At its peak, mobs of workers rampaged through the streets of St Helen's, wrecking offices and smashing windows. Both official trade union leaders and unofficial strike spokesmen received threatening letters. 346,000 mandays were lost, involving 11,000 workmen. Internal differences inside the trade union provoked a breakaway movement that formed a new Glass and General Workers' Union.

Allegations that the trouble was fomented by 'imported' militants could never be proved. But members of Marxist groups, some from nearby building sites and others from Liverpool, were reported to be often at the scene. Since the strike ended the thirty-five-year-old unofficial strike leader, Mr Gerry Caughey, has established links with the All Trade Unions' Alliance.* Prior to the demonstration on the 8th of December 1970 against the government's Industrial Reform Bill, Mr Gerry Caughey was front-paged in *Workers' Press*† as one of the major speakers at Central Hall, Westminster, London.

In every industry in Britain, those who search for them can find minor and fancied grievances. Too often, bad communication between management and workers gives subverters the chance to transform a trivial incident into a dispute that is costly to both workmen and industry.

*   *   *

There are fifty 'front' organisations in Britain controlled by pro-Moscow, pro-Peking and pro-Havana communists. Some of them issue publications.

The Soviet-controlled organisations are, in alphabetical order:

Artists for Peace‡
Authors' World Peace Council‡
Britain-China Friendship Association (BCFA)‡
British-Czechoslovak Friendship League (BCFL)‡
British-Hungarian Friendship Society (BHFS).‡ Monthly publication: *Letter*

---

* The Industrial arm of the Trotskyists.
† The daily organ of the Trotskyist *Socialist Labour League*.
‡ Proscribed by the Labour Party.

British Peace Committee (BPC). ★ British affiliate of *WCP*. Monthly publication: *Peace Monitor*

British–Polish Friendship Society (BPFS)†

British–Romanian Friendship Association (BRFA)†

British–Soviet Friendship Society (BSFS).† Monthly publication: *British–Soviet Friendship*

British–Soviet Society (BSS)†

British–Vietnam Committee (BVC). Monthly publication: *Vietnam Bulletin*

Conolly Association (CA). Monthly publication: *Irish Democrat*

Ex-Servicemen's Movement for Peace;† affiliate of the *International Federation of Resistance Fighters*

International Women's Day:† British affiliate of the *WIDF*

Labour Research Department (LRD).† Weekly publication: *Fact Service.* Monthly publication: *Labour Research*

League for Democracy in Greece (LDG)†

Liaison Committee for the Defence of Trade Unions

Marx House;† the British Communist Party's education centre, with a membership organisation known as *Marx Memorial Library.* Quarterly publication: *Bulletin*

Musicians' Organisation for Peace†

National Assembly of Women (NAW).† British affiliate of the *WIDF*

National Association of Tenants and Residents (NATR)

People's Congress for Peace‡

Scientists for Peace‡

Society for Cultural Relations with the USSR (SCR). Quarterly publication: *Anglo-Soviet Bulletin*

Society for Friendship with Bulgaria (SFB),‡ formerly: The *Committee for Friendship with Bulgaria (CFB)*

Student Labour Federation (SLF).‡ British affiliate of the *WFDY*

Teachers CND;‡ originally *Teachers for Peace*

Welsh Peace Council‡

West Yorkshire Federation for Peace‡

★ Proscribed by the Labour Party.
† *Ibid.*
‡ *Ibid.*

Women's Parliament*
1960 Campaign Committee organised within the *London Co-operative Society*.

The eighteen pro-Peking communist-controlled organisations are, in alphabetical order:

Albanian Society, The; controlled by the *Marxist-Leninist Organisation. for Britain*. Bi-monthly publication: *Albanian Notes*
Britain-Albanian Friendship Society (*BAFS*) controlled by *Friends of China*
Britain-Vietnam Solidarity Front (*BVSF*)
Camden Communist Movement
Camden Marxist-Leninist Group
Caribbean-Latin American, Afro-Asian Committee. Monthly publication: *People's Voice*
Chelsea Young Communists. Publication: *Red Guard*
Committee to Defeat Revisionism for Communist Unity (*CDRCU*) Monthly publication: *Vanguard*
Communist Party of Britain (*Marxist-Leninist*). Bi-monthly publication: *The Worker*
Finsbury Communist Association (*FCA*)
Friends of China (*FOC*)
Internationalists, The; student organisation founded at Dublin University. Bi-monthly publication: *Advance*
London Workers' Committee (*LWC*)
Marxist-Leninist Forum. Monthly publication: *Forum*
Marxist-Leninist Organisation of Britain (*MLOB*). Monthly publication: *Red Front*
Society for Anglo-Chinese Understanding, The (*SACU*). Monthly publication: *SACU News*
Working People's Party of England (*WPPE*). Monthly publication: *Workers' Broadcast*
Working People's Party of Scotland (*WPPS*). Monthly publication: *Scottish Vanguard*

* Proscribed by the Labour Party.

The one pro-Cuban communist-controlled organisation in the United Kingdom is:

Tricontinental Committee, which publishes the monthly *Partisan*

All these organisations are registered and legal. They offer additional opportunities for Moscow's and Peking's master-subverters to cash in on political and industrial disputes.

19

Subverter Target—Trade Unions

The swift growth of technological knowledge and industrial production during the last century has been matched by the rise to power of the trade unions.

A little more than a hundred years ago any working men who dared to meet to discuss ways and means of improving their living conditions were declared dangerous troublemakers and conspirators, who were committing an unlawful act. Many men were sent to prison or transported to Australia and Canada simply for attempting to improve intolerable working conditions.

The growth of the trade unions has corrected gross social injustices, and greatly improved living conditions. It may even have averted bloody revolution.

But the establishment of the unions was not an easy victory for the working classes. At the beginning of the century, industry was not owned by vast combines, but was largely controlled by wealthy families. Battles over wages were between groups of workmen trying to improve their conditions of employment and the individual owners of enterprises whose personal pockets suffered by wage increases. The mill-owner who refused to reduce the twelve-hour day could calculate to a penny how much a reduction in working hours would cost him personally.

The employers vigorously suppressed the workers. The Establishment was often called upon to assist employers, and frequently labour organisers were accused and found guilty of sedition and similar crimes. There was a large pool of unemployed labour, which gave the employers a tremendous leverage. Nobody wanted to be out of work, and the threat of the sack kept wages down. Any man who spoke for the workers was automatically blacklisted; he had no hope of ever finding employment in that industry.

H

If the workers in a factory became too militant, they were locked out—deprived of the right to work. The factory was shut, the owner and his family took a long holiday abroad and often the workmen slowly starved until their spirit was crushed and they pleaded to be allowed to return to work. Thereafter they were extremely careful not to anger their employer. The threat of instant dismissal hung over them all, ensuring uncomplaining obedience and acceptance of minimum working conditions. No man wants his family to suffer hardship and live in abject poverty.

Even in 1939, just before the Second World War, the trade unions were still fighting hard to gain a toe-hold in many industries. The big showdown between Labour and Industry, symbolised by the 1926 General Strike, had badly mauled the trade union movement and sorely depleted its economic reserves. In 1939 there was still great unemployment, and the sack was still an ugly weapon of oppression. References from previous employers were always required from a work applicant, and if his testimonials were not satisfactory, or indicated the applicant was a troublemaker, he was doomed to the dole and the means test.

The need for organised labour to help the war effort changed everything. Men and women had been conscripted, the pool of unemployed had dried up and craftsmen were scarce. The trade unions did not neglect their opportunity; they entrenched themselves strongly. Indeed, many managements, greedy for the lucrative profits obtained from government war contracts, deliberately invited the trade unions to organise the men within their factories; thus they ensured a steady supply of labour with the minimum of industrial disruption.

By the end of the war, trade unionism had a death-grip on industry. In the years that have followed, that grip has never slackened. Britain's economy was badly disrupted by the war; all commodities were in short supply. Labour was switched from war production to rebuilding and to manufacturing the consumer goods everyone so badly needed. There was no unemployment. There was a sellers' market. Everyone wanted to get on the production bandwagon.

The trade unions got on to the bandwagon too. Labour was available to manufacturers, but only on trade union conditions. Any industrialist who refused to accept these conditions could not obtain the labour he required.

Thus, from being defensive organisations that prevented the exploitation of labour, the trade unions grew into powerful negotiators with the monopoly of an essential commodity—labour!

The pendulum has swung—has it swung too far?

The power of the trade unions is enormous. In the 1970s the British trade unions, when united, are more powerful than any government—be it Labour or Conservative. They are more powerful, indeed than the industry that employs their members. If that power is used unscrupulously it can paralyse and destroy the nation. Trade unionism today is not merely the means by which the working man can obtain better working conditions; it has become a powerful weapon that can be used despotically.

This decade can change to the era of dictatorship by the trade unions, if clear thinking does not prevail. Fortunately the men who administer the unions are responsible and intelligent. They have no wish to abuse their power. But the structure of the trade unions leaves them wide open to infiltration by professional Moscow– and Peking-directed master-subverters.

*   *   *

An examination of industrial disputes in the United Kingdom during 1969 shows a total of 3,021 stoppages: this represents a loss of 6,772,000 working days. These were all the results of 'unofficial' disputes, i.e. they were condemned by the official trade union leaders. The industries affected were: the coal mines, the motor industry, the steel industry, the docks, engineering, the post office, road transport, teachers and refuse collectors.

*   *   *

In September 1969 widespread unofficial dock strikes involved some 10,000 workmen and the loss of more than 500,000 working days. The London and Manchester Docks were closed for more than a week and the Merseyside Dock strikers stayed out until the 30th of September.

This strike could easily have been settled by arbitration. But although a government committee was set-up to report upon the dispute, spasmodic striking continued meanwhile until a General Dock Strike decision was taken by a Trade Union Delegate Conference on the 15th of July 1970.

Dockers are key workers. Britain is a small country that cannot support its great population without importing essential commodities. The welfare of the entire British community depends upon the willingness of dockers to unload essential cargoes.

The National Dock Strike began on the 15th of July 1970. The following day the Secretary of State for Employment and Productivity announced in the House of Commons that he had set up a court of inquiry. From Buckingham Palace the Queen made a Proclamation under the 1920 Emergency Powers Act, declaring a State of Emergency.

Eventually the strikers and employers reached an agreement, and the dockers resumed work on the 3rd of August 1970, after a stoppage of nearly three weeks. The State of Emergency was ended the following day. But for these three weeks Britain's docks were paralysed, industry was crippled for lack of essential raw materials, millions of pounds worth of shipping was idle, and the British economy suffered another damaging blow, for the true wealth of any community is not the amount of currency it owns, but the quality of its products and size of its exports.

*   *   *

Big industrial disputes, works-to-rule and strikes may arouse public sympathy or disgust, depending upon how it affects the people at large. A strike in the motor industry or in a steel foundry leaves the average citizen unmoved. He is not affected personally. Only far-sighted citizens realise that continuous wage demands cause higher prices and increase inflation, and that those who demand higher wages are soon trapped by the rise in cost of living and are as badly off as before they made the wage demand.

On the other hand, though it is to be expected that the public opposes a strike that inconveniences it, that is not always the case. The dustmen's strike in Britain in 1970, known as the Dirty Job Strike, had the sympathy of the public, despite garbage piling up in the streets and threatening disease. Many people believed that the dustmen were entitled to a good living wage, and said so.

But when the British coal industry was faced with a shut-down strike in 1970, only small groups of people expressed sympathy for the miners, because people feared the strike would endanger domestic coal supplies during the winter.

Moscow and Peking study public opinion in the Western countries, and issue reports about them to their master-subverters. They are concerned that 'selected' strikes are *not* disapproved of by the population, and that others shall gain the sympathy of the public as well. A very delicate political balance has to be maintained when influencing public opinion, and master-subverters in the field frequently fail to find it.

For many months, for example, the master-subverters and their undercover-network subverters patiently egged on the electric power workers to take drastic action in pursuit of a wage claim. Eventually pressure upon the trade union leaders resulted in an official demand for increased wages. The Electricity Board rejected the claim. Under normal circumstances, strike action would have resulted. But first, to avoid depleting the union's cash reserves by drawing strike pay, a work-to-rule was resolved upon. In practice this comes close to receiving wages while *not* doing the job. The power workers refused to work overtime and received only their basic pay. The public was warned that there would be power cuts. But though the trade union stressed that the power workers did not intend to inconvenience private consumers if it could be avoided, it was nevertheless stated that the work-to-rule by the electricity workers threatened to black out everybody's Christmas holiday.

Power cuts began on the 9th of December 1970; the television shut down; the BBC went off the air; 6,000 broiler chickens died when extractor fans stopped; tons of mail was held up in sorting offices. Signal failures created havoc with railway timetables; houses were plunged into darkness; housewives could not cook; and workmen came home to unheated houses. In the hospitals emergency operations only were carried out; and at Queen Elizabeth Hospital the lives of four-teen new-born babies were endangered when electricity cuts shut down the incubators. The following day a woman died in hospital because power cuts prevented her from receiving the benefits of a heart-stimulating machine.

While management and trade union leaders conducted long-drawn-out discussions the country suffered. It was not until the 15th of December that the work-to-rule was abandoned and the dispute submitted to arbitration.

When the trade union leaders believe their members are not getting a fair deal it is their social duty to negotiate better terms. But when workmen employed in key industries refuse to accept arbitration and resort to work-to-rule and strike action, they victimise the nation.

The British public bitterly resented the electricians' work-to-rule. Many striking power workers were booed at or sent to Coventry; shops and public bars refused to serve them or their families.

Moscow and Peking had hoped the work-to-rule would demonstrate the enormous power vested in the hands of the underpaid electricity workers, and would make the public blame the government for its discomfort. This would result in the government ordering the Electricity Board to yield to the trade union. But the plan misfired. Unpredictably, public opinion condemned the power workers and *they* became the target for the public's animosity. The union saw the red light, the work-to-rule was called off and negotiations entered into with the Electricity Board.

Moscow and Peking learned from this mistake. In December 1970 Moscow transmitted the following directives to her master-subverters in Britain:

The work-to-rule industrial action of the British Electricity Power Workers in December 1970 shows how a successfully worked-up strike campaign may lose its initial momentum. The wage demands of the British Electricity Power Workers was justified and should have had the full support of the British people.

Our undercover network subverters in Britain executed an excellent preparatory job and demonstrated their ability and skill. But they failed in one respect. It was not enough to induce the Electricity Power Workers to take decisive industrial action. The public should have been prepared for the unpleasant results of that action and reconciled to them. If our subverters had used the same care, energy and patience that they practised upon the Electricity Power Workers to condition the British public to suffer the inconvenience of the work-to-rule, success would have been assured. This is a new lesson that must be learned!

In future it is imperative not only to provoke work-to-rule, strikes, demonstrations and riots. Equal care and patience must be given to conditioning the public to support the action taken.

Blueprint-type, detailed instructions were then given to indicate how this should be done.

The electricity maintenance workers had also lodged a wage demand. Had they joined forces with the power workers in an all-out strike, Britain would have been completely blacked out. The Electricity Board's capitulation would have been inevitable. But the maintenance workers were influenced by the public's angry reaction to the power workers. They negotiated their wage demands instead of uniting their action with the power workers.

The fickleness of public opinion was demonstrated during the British postmen's strike, which began in mid-January 1971 and lasted almost seven weeks. Despite the complete blockage of correspondence, the consequent large-scale unemployment, old-age pensioners having to depend upon volunteer workers for their subsistence and great personal inconvenience, the public put up with it and *still* retained sympathy for the underpaid post office strikers.

It is most unlikely that Moscow's subverters engineered this public sympathy in support of the postmen's strike. But Moscow made capital out of it; in a coded directive transmitted in March 1971 it claimed that the British nationwide support for the postmen's cause was a result of their subverters' expert agitation:

> The British Postmen's Strike which was so widely supported by all sections of the public is an excellent illustration of how an industrial action can be popular once the public has been conditioned to support the struggle. Our master-subverters in all countries must keep this unique success of our undercover networks continuously

before their eyes. Whenever far-reaching industrial actions are instigated, they must secure public support for them. Success upon success will follow and the structure of the Capitalist system will rapidly decay.

Our British master-subverters, through their networks of skilled subverters, must continue to condition the minds of the British public. Their example must be followed by all other master-subverters in every Capitalist country. The more public sympathy and support any strike action gains, the more rewarding the outcome . . .

*   *   *

As the year 1970 drew to a close, the indiscriminate and anti-social use of the work-to-rule and strike weapon made itself painfully apparent to the British people.

While the Electricity workers resumed normal duties, working to rule crippled BEA and BOAC. Flights were cancelled, passengers delayed and those travellers lucky enough to get a place on a flight made long journeys without food or drink. Urgent export cargoes were stacked up in warehouses and only perishable goods, or urgent medical supplies, were flown out. Working to rule continued at the airports over the Christmas holidays.

On the 1st of January 1971 the journalists of the *Sun* and the *Daily Mirror* staged an unofficial strike.

On the 6th of January a strike of petrol-tanker drivers threatened to bring public transport to a standstill. By the 7th of January the failure of tanker drivers to supply oil to central-heating customers brought factories and offices to a standstill and many schools had to shut down; children cannot be taught in unheated classrooms in the depths of winter.

By the end of January, the post office strike had obstructed football pool speculation, mail order companies were facing bankruptcy, and old-age pensioners had difficulty collecting their pensions. Now, *all* BEA flights had ceased; every day 12,000 passengers could not fly and the airlines lost £250,000.

Meanwhile the Amalgamated Union of Engineering Workers, with fourteen million members, announced a new series of stoppages—

not because of wage claims or disputes about working conditions, but because it was opposed to the Industrial Relations Bill then before Parliament. This decision was an ominous departure from normal practice: the use of the strike weapon, *not* to improve union members' working conditions, but to attain a political objective.

On the 30th of January, as BEA flights were resumed, shop stewards at the Ford motor plants called for a strike against the management's offer of a £2 per week increase in wages. By the 2nd of February all Ford plants in Great Britain were at a standstill. By the 7th of February the petrol-tanker drivers' strike was threatening to bring London's buses to a standstill.

All this strike action caused direct inconvenience and hardship to the community. It affected children's education, their parents' leisure, enormous financial losses to and closures of some businesses, unemployment and many bankruptcies.

Working to rule and strike action can be weapons of coercion, their victims not just managements but the general public too. Working to rule and strike action can be a cocked pistol, for holding the community to ransom.

The strike of Ford workers coincided with an economic bolt from the blue: the financial collapse of Rolls-Royce. This world-famous enterprise was salvaged by nationalisation on the 23rd of February 1971. Just before this, Ford's management had made a very significant statement; they warned that £2 per week was the maximum wage increase that could be made without endangering the commercial solidity of the Ford Company.

Britain's economic structure is based upon profit-making. Any company that cannot make a profit must pay for its loss out of capital. This is dangerous retrogression, and leads to financial weakness and ultimately to collapse. Is it possible that the unrelenting demands of powerful trade unions can destroy industry?

I believe it is very possible. Many small family businesses have been compelled to close down, or have been forced into bankruptcy, through trade union restrictive practices, which prevented them making a profit, until they could no longer withstand the steady draining away of their capital resources.

Big industry can suffer this fate too. The Ford workers, and others, could strike themselves into unemployment by obstructing the smooth running of industry and putting business in the red. This should be evident not only to the management, but to the man in the street and all wildcat strikers. One of Rolls-Royce's workmen, faced with redundancy and interviewed after the news of Rolls-Royce's failure, said feelingly: 'This might make some of the Ford men think twice about striking!'

The power of the trade unions, if used unscrupulously, can be a serious threat to society and to the workmen themselves. Political decisions made in Parliament by elected politicians should not be resisted by strike action. The economic structure of big industrial concerns should not be jeopardised by unrealistic wage claims.

The delicate balance between rational living and self-destruction can be maintained, but it requires goodwill, commonsense and sincerity between managements, trade unions and the government. The trade union leaders are well aware of their duty to the community, and they are responsible men. But they head a democratic organisation, and many times must reluctantly yield to a majority vote.

This delicate balance is easily destroyed. The professional master-subverters and their undercover networks are well aware of this. The Red fifth column has penetrated and permeated the trade unions.

The trade union's strength is its mass-membership; but there is no way it can guard against penetration by determined subverters and industrial saboteurs. There are a thousand ways for determined subverters to foment unrest in industry and commerce, aggravate uneasy situations and provoke work-to-rule and strikes. Trade union rules and regulations are complicated, because they are designed to allow for *all* possible circumstances. A diligent study of the rule book usually provides subtle subverters with many levers to cause industrial strife. Often the rules are interpreted in ways which were never intended and which are quite clearly nonsensical.

A good illustration is the case of a handful of men who decided to opt out of an *unofficial* strike that involved some 800 workers. The strike had lasted some weeks.

These men sincerely believed they could not be 'blacklegs', since the

strike was unofficial. They returned to work. Subsequently, they were
summoned before a kangaroo court of their fellow factory workers,
were jeered at, taunted for being strike-breakers, and offered the choice
of a £30 fine or expulsion from the Union. A kangaroo court is an
illegal body that acts without official trade union sanction.

The management had stated that the strike was unofficial because the
union did not support the wildcat strikers. In effect, the men who
returned to work and who were accused of being 'blacklegs', were
obeying an official union decision. Nevertheless the management received an ultimatum to dismiss these men, who had conducted themselves in the best interests of good relations between the official trade
union and the management!

Such disputes, misunderstandings and grievances can be manufactured and exploited with ease by Moscow's and Peking's master-
subverters, who are adept in creating industrial unrest. The damage to
industrial goodwill, the economic loss and the personal distress these
subverters can cause is quite out of proportion to their numbers.

In Britain, in January 1971, subverters were holding a great many
industrial dispute aces in their hands. The Post Office workers, BEA
and BOAC, journalists, petrol-tanker drivers, the Amalgamated Union
of Engineering Workers and Ford's were out on strike. Rolls-Royce
collapsed and disaster spread through the shipbuilding yards. It was a
good year for the wreckers of industry.

But Moscow and Peking are relentless taskmasters. Although lavish
with praise for their agents, they never cease to demand more and
bigger successes. So in mid-May 1971 Moscow's Special Division for
Subversion sent the following directive to its master subverters in the
United Kingdom:

The recent slackness of revolutionary industrial activity in Britain
must be condemned. The forces of reaction must not be allowed a
breathing respite. Intensify all efforts on all fronts. Do not concentrate solely upon large industrial plants or factories. Every minor industrial dispute contributes to the achievement of the main objective.
Disrupt production everywhere! And ensure that even the smallest
industrial dispute receives wide publicity.

All undercover network members must seize upon even the smallest grievance to inflame the workers to resentment against employers. Time and again it has been shown a skilful operator can kindle workmen's indignation into flames of anger, causing strike action of very considerable dimensions. Persist with the proven methods that have yielded excellent results. If it is impossible to stir up discontent among workmen employed in a large factory, then fall back upon the 'key-worker' method. Locate the life-centre of the plant, where only a handful of men are employed, but upon whose production the rest of the factory depend. Find, or manufacture, a grievance that will cause them to ban overtime, work to rule, or strike.

The Common Market is a new, controversial issue that can easily give rise to grave misgivings in the minds of the British workmen. Labour displacement, rocketing prices and fear of the future can be very valuable propaganda ammunition. Opposition to the Common Market can be channelled into dissatisfaction with existing employment conditions and can lead to industrial disruption.

It must always be apparent that demonstrations, strikes or riots, etc., are spontaneous. It must *never* be suspected that political influences have inspired them!

The subverters-networks acted upon these directives as though they had been issued by God. The following extract of events shows the astonishing parallel between the Kremlin's orders and what happened inside the United Kingdom:

8th of June, 1971: A strike of skilled maintenance men at British Leyland's Oxford (Cowley) plant halted production of the new Morris Marina and Austin Maxi. 4,360 workmen were laid off.
For the 15th time in nine weeks an unofficial strike brought Manchester docks to a standstill—nineteen ships idle.

9th of June, 1971: Paint-shop workers walked out on strike at Ford's Halewood Plant. This strike action stopped production on vehicles valued at £1½ million. The total loss of production caused by strikes at Ford's Merseyside plant since January 1971 is estimated at £35 million.

11th of June, 1971: Coventry Corporation bus crews voted for weekly one-day stoppages.

10,000 Coventry car workers banned overtime for a month. This disrupted car production at Chrysler, British Leyland and Rolls Royce.

12th of June, 1971: 380 fitters at Swan Hunter's ship repair yards, Wallsend, resumed work after a sixteen-week stoppage.

14th of June, 1971: Seventy paint-shop workers resumed work at the Cowley car factory. 7,000 workers had been laid off by the strike, costing production of 5,000 vehicles.

15th of June, 1971: 1,300 assembly workers walked out on strike at Ford's Halewood Plant.

900 workers walked out at British Leyland's Swindon Plant.

16th of June, 1971: 3,000 workers manufacturing gearboxes at Ford's Halewood Plant were asked to support the assembly workers' strike. A shut-down of the transmission department could seriously disrupt production at Ford's Dagenham and other factories.

17th of June, 1971: Ford's transmission department workers joined the strike. At Dagenham 24,000 workers faced lay-offs.

Dockers and crane drivers at Manchester Docks staged their fortieth unofficial stoppage in ten weeks.

18th of June, 1971: Coventry Corporation bus crews staged a second unofficial one-day strike.

Ford's Halewood Plant at a standstill. 9,000 workers on strike or idle. Since April 1971 a total of nine disruptions at the plant has cost production of 13,000 cars costing £9 million.

British Leyland threatened with strike action by 3,000 foremen at sixteen plants.

10,000 workers at the Hawker–Siddeley Aviation Factory at Brough started an unofficial strike.

22nd of June, 1971: At 2.25 a.m., Mr William Batty and his wife awakened by an explosion that wrecked the lower part of their house. Mr Batty is Managing Director of Ford's. At 2.50 a.m. The Press Association in Fleet Street received a telephone call from the Angry Brigade 'Communique 14. We've just got Ford's and the Bosses!' (Earlier in the year the Angry Brigade claimed a similar bombing at a Ford administrative building in East London.) A second telephone call from the Angry Brigade claimed the destruction of an electricity substation at Dagenham.

25th of June, 1971: The Jaguar plant in Coventry brought to a standstill by strike action.

29th of June, 1971: 150 workers at the Birmingham factory of Wilmot Breeden Ltd downed tools. This company supplies bumpers, locks, handles and window winders to the motor industry.

1st of July, 1971: A labour dispute by assembly workers, lasting one day, cost the production of 140 Triumph cars at Coventry.

2nd of July, 1971: The Minister of Employment stated in Parliament that, for the year ending 31st of May 1971, 2,878 strikes caused a loss of 17,337,000 working days.

6th of July, 1971: Jumbo jet services were disrupted by lack of fuel when a petrol company was 'blacked'.

8th of July, 1971: A hundred more men on strike at Wilmot Breeden's Birmingham factory.

A thousand workers laid off at British Leyland's Solihull factory because of lack of supplies of (Breeden's) window winders.

A thousand workers laid off at the Triumph factory in Coventry because of an overtime ban by toolroom workers.

10th of July, 1971: ITV blacked out for ten minutes by an unofficial strike.

A strike of 100 maintenance workers at British Leyland's Longbridge plant halted production and caused 2,500 men to be laid off.

At British Leyland's Cowley plant 190 men were laid off, in addition to 1,200 laid off in Solihull, due to lack of supplies by Wilmot Breeden.

12th of July, 1971: Stoppages caused to ITV in Yorkshire by strike action. Strike representatives said the stoppage might spread.

13th of July, 1971: All production at British Leyland's Longbridge plant brought to a standstill by an unofficial strike action. 7,500 workmen laid off.

14th of July, 1971: The three-week-old strike at the Fisher–Bendix factory, Kirkby, Liverpool, declared official by the AEUW.

Television workers voted to withdraw labour from ITV within ten days.

22nd of July, 1971: Every major hospital in England and Wales affected by one-day strike of hospital technicians.

23rd of July, 1971: Publication of *The Times* delayed by an industrial dispute.

29th of July, 1971: Nine people arrested outside Fine Tubes factory, Plymouth. It had been picketed by strikers for thirteen months.

1st of August, 1971: The housekeeper of Mr John Davies, Secretary for Trade and Industry, treated in hospital after a bomb explosion in Mr Davies' London flat. The Angry Brigade telephoned Associated Newspapers, claiming responsibility.

2nd of August, 1971: Seven hundred senior Giro operators withdrew their labour. This action at Post Office Computer Centres can disrupt wages for 150,000 Post Office staff.

2,800 Tyneside shipbuilding workers employed in Swan Hunter yards voted to strike.

5th of August, 1971: A walk-out of airlines staff disrupted flights at London Airport.

15,000 steel blast furnacemen issued strike notices.

7th of August, 1971: Overtime on the Concorde project banned by 1,000 draughtsmen. A similar ban by 800 electricians took effect earlier in the week, following their one-day strikes.

13th of August, 1971: End of the brewery strike. It closed a hundred public houses in Lancashire alone.

16th of August, 1971: The Angry Brigade telephoned the Press Association, claiming that they planted the bomb which damaged an Army drill-hall in Holloway, North London.

17th of August, 1971: 90% of the clerical staff at the British Steel Corporation's Abbey Works, Port Talbot, South Wales, on un-official strike.

18th of August, 1971: 300 lorry drivers from nine firms in the Bir-mingham area stayed on strike after the previous day's one-day token strike by more than 1,000 drivers.

21st of August, 1971: Because of a month-old strike by 390 boiler-makers, 168 men were laid off in the Brooke Marine Shipyard at Lowestoft.

22nd of August, 1971: Special Branch detectives investigating the Angry Brigade detained two girls and four men. A large quantity of explosives and firearms, including two machine-guns, seized from a flat in Amhurst Road, Stoke Newington.

24th of August, 1971: 300 engineers on strike at nine Lucas factories threaten the complete shutdown and laying-off of 20,000 workers. 10,000 toolmakers banning overtime brought Chrysler *Avenger* production to a standstill. 3,000 other workers idle.

27th of August, 1971: Disputes in Birmingham's motor industry have brought 22,000 workers to a standstill. Lucas, British Leyland and BSA factories seriously affected.

31st of August, 1971: At British Leyland's Triumph works at Coventry, 2,000 men idle as a result of a go-slow by ninety drivers.

4th of September, 1971: After six hours discussion, talks broke down between Lucas representatives and strikers. The stoppage had lasted two weeks and threatened the jobs of hundreds of thousands of workers in the car industry.

Jaguar of Coventry unable to start production again until the following Tuesday's night shift, following a dispute involving 10,000 toolroom workers.

6th of September, 1971: Because of labour troubles, British Leyland forced to postpone showing a new Triumph car at October's Motor Show.

British Leyland and Chrysler factories laid off 10,000 workers and lost £1 million in production. The Triumph Coventry plant lost £½ million.

7th of September, 1971: 836 men struck unofficially at Swan Hunter's Neptune Shipyard at Newcastle-upon-Tyne. They demanded a 'travel allowance' for walking 22 yards. They were joined by sheet-metal workers, crane-men and labourers from other unions.

A work-to-rule ordered by the General and Municipal Workers Union, The Amalgamated Engineering Union and the Electrical Workers Union at the Rank Xerox factory at Micheldene, Gloucester. When Mrs Peggy Pollock refused to obey these orders, six hundred co-workers walked out.

8th of September, 1971: National two-day strike of Hospital Technicians. Four hundred engine fitters walked out at Triumph's Coventry factory.

2,000 workers at the Rank Xerox factory voted to stay on strike until Mrs Peggy Pollock joined the Union or was dismissed.

14th of September, 1971: A second one-day strike by 8,000 key workers stopped production of cars in Coventry. Laying-off brought the total of workless to 25,000.

15th of September, 1971: Industrial action by printing trades workers severely reduced the editions of all national newspapers. Total loss: four million copies.

16th of September, 1971: Trade union pickets outside the British Aircraft Corporation's Concorde works at Filton, Bristol, battled with workmen who defied the strike call.

17th of September, 1971: HM Stationery Office in High Holborn, London, closed when warehouse and bookshop assistants stopped work.

Twenty-nine diecasters on strike at Fry's Diecasting, Jarrow, Durham, because Mr William Tankard worked too hard and regularly exceeded his machine quota.

18th of September, 1971: Disputes of printing workers caused a loss of production of national newspapers totalling nine million copies and a financial loss of £100,000. This was mainly caused by NGA members holding union meetings during working hours.

The Rolls Royce plant at Filton, Bristol, brought to a standstill by six thousand men on unofficial strike. This is the second of a series of stoppages planned to take place every Friday.

19th of September, 1971: All national newspapers closed down when printing workers continued meetings during working hours.

24th of September, 1971: All national newspapers started publishing again after a five-day stoppage. It had cost the industry eighty million copies and £½ million.

26th of September, 1971: Strike began at Merseyside docks. Coventry car production disrupted by the third in the series of one-day strikes by toolroom workers.

At Cowley, Oxford, 1,000 skilled car workers began work-to-rule and banned overtime.

Merseyside docks resumed full working.

27th of September, 1971: A one-day strike by 20,000 members of the Association of Scientific Technical and Managerial Staff. A hundred and sixty General Electric Company plants will be affected.

* * *

The vast influence of subverters at work within the trade unions cannot be doubted.

Can the men who administer the trade unions find a way to control the enemies who work from within their organisations? Or will the destructive influence of subverters bring some union leaders and their unions to disaster? If industry collapses and unemployment is widespread, the trade unions will share industry's fate.

20

300,000 Died!

In June 1971 the world was shocked by reports of genocide in East Pakistan. It is estimated that 300,000 East Pakistanis died a violent death in the space of a few weeks. The victims were men, women and children; peasants and tribesmen. They were slaughtered by modern firearms, by wooden clubs and by torture. Women and young girls were raped by West Pakistani soldiers and afterwards had their breasts cut off. Children, including babies in arms, were massacred as ruthlessly as adults.

Hundreds of thousands of East Pakistani refugees, seeking to evade the horror of genocide, swamped over the border into India. The mass migration created such a dangerous threat of a cholera epidemic and mass starvation that the resources of all the world Powers were spontaneously united in a gigantic rescue operation.

A detailed report explaining why this calamity occurred would have to take into account not only nationalism and patriotism, but also politics, religious conflicts and tribal superstitions.

It is possible, however, to oversimplify the major events and incidents, and present them so readers can understand the basic causes of the widespread suffering in East Pakistan in May and June 1971.

*   *   *

Pakistan consists of two separate territories with India driven like a wedge between them. West Pakistan holds the reins of government and is five times the size of East Pakistan. But the population of the eastern part is larger than the western. East Pakistan, an overpopulated and impoverished area, has for a long time been campaigning for self-rule. Failing this, it demands proportional representation in the federal government. On the 7th of December 1970 general elections for the first time gave East Pakistan a majority vote. But the West Pakistani

politicians in power were reluctant to knuckle under to this new
alignment of government control. They repeatedly deferred the date
fixed for the opening of the new Assembly. This prevarication finally
exasperated East Pakistan so much that it stepped up its demands for
self-rule.

Once again a new date was set for the first meeting of the Assembly—
the 25th of March 1971. But on that same day, West Pakistani troops
stationed in East Pakistan were ordered out to take all steps necessary
to forestay an 'anticipated' East Pakistani revolt. This they did, with
considerable violence and little consideration for justice.

East Pakistani guerrilla troops retaliated against this act of intimidation. But so involved and intermingled are politics and religion that
the guerrillas picked as their main target the minority of East Pakistanis
who shared the same (Muslim) religious beliefs as the major proportion of West Pakistanis. A minor massacre of these religious devotees
took place.

Between the 28th of March and the 12th of April the West Pakistan
Government flew two divisions of troops into East Pakistan. Their
military objective was to restore public order, but what these troops
effectively embarked upon was genocide. Many objective observers
who talked to the West Pakistani officers and their men learned that
they were determined to wipe out every expression of the wish for
self-rule in East Pakistan. They were achieving this objective by ruthlessly killing and burning, and were disposed, if necessary, to massacre
two million people and transform East Pakistan into a mutely suffering colony.

*   *   *

There is little doubt that Pakistan became involved in this horrifying
bloodbath because of the clever manipulation of its politicians and
populace by Red China and Soviet Russia.

For many years Red China's master-subverters have been operating
in West Pakistan, which Peking considers its own zone of influence.
Russian subverters meanwhile were operating in East Pakistan and
India. Both communist countries were competing for influence over
this divided territory. They employed the usual subverters' tactics:

guerrilla groups were formed and trained, arms and explosives were smuggled into guerrilla bases, religious conflicts were sharpened and every smouldering grievance was fanned into flames of violent revolt.

The conflicting religions of Pakistan provide excellent opportunities for subverters to foment riots and bloodshed. But East Pakistan, Soviet Russia's baby, yielded the most spectacular results. Its people were poor and underprivileged, religious feelings ran high, and they felt bitterness towards the central government. Subverters have always exploited nationalistic zeal to the full, as is indicated by their violence-provoking success with the Basques, the terrorism raging in Northern Ireland, the bombings and kidnappings in French-speaking Canada led by Quebec-French nationalists, and the fighting in Indo-China.

But Pakistan was especially unfortunate. It became doubly plagued by subverters. Red China grew concerned about the success of Russian subverters in East Pakistan, so Peking therefore equipped and sent its own army of subverters into East Pakistan. Their instructions were to build up guerrilla forces that would be directly controlled by Red Chinese master-subverters. Whenever possible they were to penetrate already existing guerrilla groups, usurp the control of their Russian master-subverters and transfer control to Red Chinese master-subverters.

The man placed in charge of Peking's 'Operation East Pakistan' was Jeje Khan. He had previously been master-subverter in Karachi, where he had posed as a prosperous businessman since 1963. His opposite number in West Pakistan was Abdul Hind, who posed as a prosperous exporter while he operated a parallel subverter network to Khan's. Each man, under guidance from Peking, controlled approximately seventy undercover subverters whose activities they coordinated. Each undercover subverter commanded a network of thirty-five to fifty subverters, giving a total of between five and seven thousand trained undercover subverters!

While Khan's network sowed hatred in East Pakistan towards West Pakistan, Hind's subverters in West Pakistan whipped up bitter hostility against East Pakistan.

I

Hind's subverters penetrated deeply into the higher strata of West Pakistan's Government and Military Command. Their influence and positions enabled them to play a decisive role in the events of May-June 1971.

*   *   *

When the West Pakistani government showed itself reluctant to concede governmental power to East Pakistan, both the Chinese and the Russian subverters seized the opportunity to provoke bloody riots in East Pakistan in support of the demands for self-rule. Meanwhile in West Pakistan Peking's subverters spread the word in official circles that East Pakistan was ripening for revolt and that there would be an attempt to take over West Pakistan by force. They did their work so successfully that the West Pakistani Government panicked. It ordered the troops it had stationed in East Pakistan to take defensive measures against the anticipated uprising.

The violent, oppressive measures adopted by the West Pakistani troops provided the fuse with which the subverters in East Pakistan triggered off the explosive retaliation of East Pakistani guerrilla groups.

This open activity on the part of East Pakistani guerillas of course confirmed the West Pakistani High Command's fear of a revolt, and it sent two divisions to East Pakistan to suppress the uprising.

There would have been no genocide at this juncture had it not been for the cold-blooded tactics adopted by Red China's subverters. They launched a widespread campaign throughout West Pakistan, spreading 'reports' about atrocities committed by the East Pakistanis. The anger and passions of the East Pakistanis had been inflamed, and they had indeed committed atrocities, but the Red Chinese subverters magnified them enormously. Atrocity stories are always embellished as they are passed on, and the subverters bolstered them up by circulating forged evidence and testimony. Over and again there were new 'reports', apparently confirmed, that West Pakistani troops on routine marches had been ambushed by East Pakistani guerrillas, mercilessly tortured, mutilated and ignominiously slaughtered.

When the West Pakistani troops were flown into East Pakistan they were thirsting for vengeance. Their superior officers had not failed to brief them about the East Pakistanis' ruthlessness. The troops were warned: 'Never trust the treacherous East Pakistani civilians! Shoot first and ask questions afterwards!' And as for atrocities, West Pakistani soldiers couldn't be blamed if they gave the East Pakistanis what they thought was a taste of their own medicine.

The resulting killings and atrocities committed by West Pakistani troops might have carried on much longer, but Moscow inexplicably failed to provide the East Pakistani guerrillas with the quantities of arms and explosives they needed. This shocking Soviet failure later caused heads to roll in Moscow, for the Kremlin is unwilling to relinquish East Pakistan to Red China. But by failing to provide adequate arms to East Pakistan, the prolonged, large-scale guerrilla warfare which would have developed, simply withered away. Thus, instead of Pakistan being involved in a major revolutionary conflict, with Pakistani pawns fighting to decide whether control should fall to Moscow or to Peking, the conflict dissolved into an extermination operation carried out by West Pakistani troops.

Moscow fell back upon a weak second line of attack to counteract Peking's influence in West Pakistan. It launched an immense propaganda drive to bring to the attention of the world the terrible atrocities committed in East Pakistan by West Pakistani troops. Soviet Russia claimed to be the foremost big Power to rush relief to East Pakistani refugees in India.

The Red Chinese subverters retaliated defensively. They stepped up the anti-East Pakistani atrocity propaganda and in every way sought to justify the West Pakistani troops' orgy of slaughter. They claimed it was the only way possible to stop the widespread massacre of innocent people by East Pakistani terrorists.

Thus did Moscow and Peking spread confusion and terror in Pakistan. Such fighting, terrorism, murder and atrocities do not spring from intelligent thinking; they are spawned by inflamed passion, fanaticism and emotional instability. People en masse easily fall victim to inflamed passions and blind emotion, and it is this weakness in human nature that subverters play upon.

*   *   *

The following passage is a coded Peking directive transmitted in May 1971, and seized in June 1971 from one of Abdul Hind's network agents:

All arms and explosive supplies must be distributed quickly to our specially trained guerrillas in Bangladesh. It is imperative that all previous consignments of armaments made in Czechoslovakia are also distributed. This will later serve a purpose of considerable political significance.

East Pakistani guerrillas and West Pakistani troops must now be brought into open conflict. Intensify our propaganda until all East Pakistani guerrillas and civilians are completely convinced that West Pakistani troops have committed countless atrocities. Our master-agents in West Pakistan must convince the West Pakistani divisions due to be sent to East Pakistan that their comrades have been ambushed, tortured and mutilated by East Pakistani guerrillas and civilians. Even though such incidents are considerably exaggerated, neither side will be able to check their authenticity because of communication difficulties.

All terrorist acts in West Pakistan should be committed in popular centres where public attention and publicity can be easily focused upon them. It is imperative that such terrorist acts shall appear to be ruthlessly planned and executed by East Pakistani terrorists.

Concentrated agitation must also be launched among the West Pakistani troops stationed along the Indian border. Hatred and hostility must be whipped up between West Pakistani and Indian troops. The situation here is sensitive, shootings and border incidents can be easily provoked and will involve India in the conflict. Action can be taken now to provide evidence that the Indian troops are trigger-happy and encouraged to excesses by their officers.

The zeal with which Peking and Moscow subverters carried out this directive caused deaths and suffering throughout Pakistan.

The deliberate incitement of war between countries is so alien to civilised thinking that this directive might be thought to be the work of raving lunatics. But staging border incidents and provoking wars are important steps toward achieving the subverters' main objective.

In Pakistan and India they have concentrated all their efforts behind this directive. Their unceasing fomentation of trouble in East Pakistan and on the Indian–Pakistani border has led to the recent crisis. War between Pakistan and India became inevitable, and the precise role Moscow and Peking have adopted towards the combatants is of headline importance.

21

The Future?

Major Peter Johnson of the Scots Guards was driving along Belfast's Springfield Road in a Land-Rover when two small boys aged about thirteen and wearing short trousers stepped out from cover and levelled Thompson submachine-guns at him.*

The major was grimly amused. Kids at play! But the next moment the submachine-guns hammered, bullets cut through the air and the vehicle shuddered under the clanging impact of lead.

Major Johnson stared in shocked astonishment as the two diminutive figures scampered away, and suppressed the defensive reflex to fling up his gun and shoot down these two young would-be murderers. Civilised adults do not make war on children!

The civilised code of the Western democracies renders them vulnerable to the anti-civilised tactics adopted by subverters. A thief can only thrive in a community where most men are honest, and do not steal from *him*. A subverter can only foment industrial strife because democracy respects freedom of thought and allows him scope to stir up discontent.

The nations that most respect liberty are the biggest victims of subversion. Brute force and contempt of moral values are the weapons of primitive savages. Barbarians can destroy culture and civilisation. Subverters deliberately create and spread barbarism. The Red fifth column intends to destroy the Western world!

A public warning is useless if it is not heeded. But history shows that it is difficult to alert the public to impending danger. The menace of the Red fifth column cannot easily be proved, and a public bombarded by newspaper, radio and television sensations is sceptical by nature. Many refuse to believe that a Red world-wide conspiracy is feasible.

* Belfast, 26th of October 1971.

How can a few thousand trained subverters spread such chaos, terrorism and violence throughout the world?

Subverters have studied mass psychology and take advantage of the herd instinct: where one sheep leads, the others will follow. Market traders plant stooges in the crowd who rush to buy when 'bargains' are offered; the herd follows. Ambitious playwrights seat their friends in the front row to cheer and stamp their feet; the herd applauds. Private enterprise has spent a fortune researching mass psychology; the pleasant, average housewife who tells on television why she uses such and such a soap powder leads a great herd of housewives to the shop-counter. Subverters know that if they provoke a few men to take militant action the herd will follow. Most strikes are launched by a few strikers, and the rest of the herd follows suit, albeit half-heartedly. Subverters *know* that if a few angry men throw rocks at the police there is every chance that violent rioting will result.

The subverter uses skill in selecting his stooges to lead the herd. His most willing tools are sincere idealists. Many terrorists in Northern Ireland are self-sacrificing idealists who are convinced that their cause is good and worthy. So are the workmen who down tools, the saboteurs who destroy factories, the guerrillas who train in the jungles and the terrorists who hijack airliners. The weakness of all idealists is the broad streak of fanaticism in their make-up. Fanaticism destroys their judgment. Subverters have studied psychology; they know how to play upon the emotions and convert misguided idealists into anti-social fanatics.

Subverter-duped 'idealists', 'stooges' or 'ringleaders' can be provoked into leading the herd. But how can subverters influence so many ringleaders in so many places in so many walks of life?

The subverter uses the normal business method of efficient delegation of labour. Through his networks he can have the right man in the right place at the right time. Obtaining information about who is to be the 'ringleader' in the right place presents few problems. A parallel organisation in the business world is the Agency which can supply a Credit Rating about anybody! Within a few days a Credit Agency can give an estimate of anybody's financial standing; it is probably more accurate than the subject himself could provide at such short notice. The Agency employs only a handful of men and women who work as discreetly as any spies. Like the subverter, they have numerous contacts and can penetrate every branch of industry, banking and social life. If a private business with limited capital and staff can operate so efficiently, what can be achieved with the unlimited finances and manpower of Moscow and Peking! When a factory is marked down for strike action, or a Northern Ireland power station is to be bombed, the subverter can quickly know the best idealist to make the 'ringleader' of the operation; if he wished, he could also know his credit rating!

The subverter has only one objective: to destroy the capitalist system of the Western world. This gives him wide scope. *Anything that directly or indirectly impoverishes a nation* brings it closer to economic disintegration. Riots and wars, sabotage and destruction of private and public property, public disorder and declining morality, all contribute to the subverters' main objective.

The trained Russian or Red Chinese subverter has his finger in every pie. He delegates work to members of his undercover network, which is composed of the nationals of the country in which he is operating. He controls this network with an iron hand. Through him and it Moscow or Peking wield decisive influence over such widely diverse organisations as the Anarchists, the Angry Brigade, Church Committees, Trotskyists, Tenants' Associations, the Black Panthers, the IRA, Students' Union, and scores of other organisations. By jig-saw planning of these stooges' actions within these organisations, the subverter can synchronise public disturbances. He can even create friction between organisations and poison uneasy situations, as when clashes between rival student organisations started the French students' wave of violence in 1968.

*   *   *

In Great Britain and in the US the subverter leans heavily upon the democratic privileges that the law grants all citizens. In these countries it is not a crime for men to demonstrate, to make public speeches or to go on strike. A citizen is free to urge key-workers to strike for any reason, however absurd, and even though thousands of other workmen may be laid off as a result. In totalitarian Spain such trouble-makers are instantly singled out for police investigation. But demo-cratic countries respect the law. Troublemakers can build molehills into mountains, foment discontent, inflame industrial incidents into shock-ing injustices and bring entire industries to a standstill without coming into conflict with the law.

Unhappily, some employers are so exasperated by agitators' time-wasting quibbling they make over-hasty decisions and provide the troublemaker with a more substantial grievance. And when workmen have a *genuine* grievance, a good subverter will inflame it into a national crisis. This occurred with the 1966 Seamen's Union strike, which paralysed Britain's docks, and the Miners' strike in 1970.

Again and again during strikes that are causing grave national and economic damage, security officers have found evidence that trouble-makers have caused or aggravated the dispute, acting on orders from abroad. But it is not a crime in law to sway men's opinions, and it is impossible to prove that these men's true motive is social sabotage.

Master-subverters and their undercover networks, like the official communist parties legally established in the Western world, remain scrupulously aloof from violence and disorder. They never risk legal censure. It is the IRA, the Provisionals, the Black Panthers, the Angry Brigade and dozens of other organisations infiltrated by subverters that practise violence and reap the blame.

★   ★   ★

The Western world is being assaulted by not one but two armies of subverters, directed by Moscow and Peking. They have the same major objective; but while competing for domination within the country of their operations, they attack the same targets. Peking was the first to introduce terrorism into political sabotage, but Moscow is no laggard in the use of violence and murder, as the Attorney-General, Sir Peter Rawlinson, reminded the House of Commons on the 18th of October 1971.

The Attorney-General made reference to the well-documented case of Dr Vladimir Katchenko, who had sought political asylum in London. Moscow guessed his intentions and he was intercepted and made prisoner by Russian Embassy officials. Later, they attempted to smuggle him aboard an Aeroflot airliner and return him to Moscow. But vigilant British Security officers intervened and rescued him by taking him into custody. Their efforts were frustrated, however. Katchenko was seriously ill, and the British doctors who were called in finally discovered he had been injected with a slow-working, fatal poison. In a race to save the Russian defector's life, a team of specialists researched to find an antidote for the poison. Time was running out fast, and little progress had been made when the Soviet Embassy blandly offered to 'cure' Katchenko if he was handed over! Any uncivilised state would have devoted all its efforts to extracting information from the Russian before he died, instead of trying to save his life. But British culture yielded to Russian barbarism. To save Katchenko's life, he was handed over to the Soviet Embassy. As things turned out this act of humanity may well have been abortive, for Katchenko has never been heard of since.

When diplomats behave in this way, what acts of barbarism are committed by less educated operatives? Can it be doubted that the directives issued to subverters are intended to result in the loss of life?

It is this murderous state attitude that provides the IRA with the funds to pay a bounty of £70 for each Ulster policeman killed,* places lethal weapons in children's hands and explodes bombs among shoppers.

Subverter-inspired political sabotage has reached a low that repudiates all civilised human values. Such violent passions have been provoked in Northern Ireland that cold-blooded murder there has become praiseworthy. Young men in uniform, sent out from Britain to undertake an unpleasant chore, are being murdered with telescopic-sight rifles. There are few crimes worse than shooting a man between the shoulder-blades from a safe hideout, but many Irish patriots' emotions have been aroused to the point where they consider murder honourable!

Mr Reginald Paget, Labour MP for Northampton, impassionedly voiced his opinion about these murders in the House of Commons on

---

* Official report from Belfast, published in the *Daily Telegraph* on the 20th of October 1971.

the 19th of October 1971 when the House was discussing allegations that interned Irishmen had been interrogated by torture. Mr Paget commented:

'Is it not a fact that information has been obtained from these internees which has resulted in our being able to save the lives of a number of our troops? One cannot fight urban guerrillas with kid gloves, and it is unfair to ask our troops to do so.'

This outbreak from Mr Paget demonstrates the widespread moral conflict provoked by subverter-inspired atrocities. A great humanitarian, Mr Paget was grappling with the awful reality that brutality and torture had saved young soldiers from being murdered. He was asking if brutality should be punished if it prevents murder. But he undoubtedly also supports the principles later expressed by Mr Callaghan, who said:

'Whether the inquiry is conducted in private or in public, is it not the case that whatever methods are being practised upon our troops, and however much murder is being committed, we could not agree to depart from civilised standards in this matter? Otherwise we would become no better than those committing the murders.'

It is a measure of the subverters' success that such moral dilemmas have been raised in Parliament. These are not normally the dilemmas of civilised peoples. They only arise because barbarism has been set loose within a domain where liberty, freedom and justice have prevailed for so many years.

* * *

The Red fifth column operating in the Western world is a terrible and destructive force. Can it be combated? Many have tried to answer this question, and failed. It may be there is no answer. Is there a remedy for a killing virus that rages ever more furiously?

But *some* measures can be adopted to diminish the evil corruption of subverters:

To prevent the kidnapping of diplomats and the hijacking of airliners and their passengers, the governments of the world can swear agreement *never* to submit to the demands of kidnappers or hijackers.

This could lead to a planeload of passengers and crew being blown up by fanatics, but governments have taken graver decisions. This action would make kidnapping and skyjacking futile, if blackmail is the motive. An additional deterrent could be an agreement by all governments that kidnappers and skyjackers should suffer the severest penalty the law permits.

The least violent activity of subverters is instigating sit-ins, working-to-rule and strikes. The latter, especially lightning strikes, seriously damage industry and cause loss of profits. This loss compels employers to resist wage increases. It is a vicious circle. All strikes inevitably reduce, instead of improve, the workers' wage-increase prospects. Strikes organised on a national scale and involving basic industries lead to serious inflation, large losses, industrial depression and subsequent large-scale unemployment. Rolls-Royce and the depressed British shipyards are awful warnings. Workmen and employers suffer equally from any breakdown in production.

In Britain, the government has introduced legislation to reduce unofficial strikes. The motives are sound but the method is resented by those who can benefit most. Their resentment is understandable. Many working men remember how legislation once victimised them. Such men can easily be convinced by subverters that the new legislation is a menace instead of a protection for them and their families. But all workmen have a safeguard: their own common sense. Industry can pay high wages and workmen's families can live in comfort, but *only* if industry booms and spreads prosperity. Workmen have a duty to reason for themselves, and to resist being stampeded by emotional appeals to their destructive impulses. Strike action is a last resort when arbitration fails. At this extreme of disagreement the gloves must come off and the might of capital confronts the strength of labour. But such trials of strength achieve nothing.

Capital needs labour as much as labour needs capital. In this year of 1971, when grave industrial depression menaces Europe and many other countries, they cannot afford to be class-enemies, for they have too many interests in common. Employers must adopt all reasonable measures to wipe out their workers' discontents and make them happy at work. The workman has perhaps an even greater responsibility—to safeguard the business that employs him from economic collapse, and thus ward off his own redundancy. He must ever be on guard against hotheads who aggravate minor grievances and urge hasty, destructive action, and who may well be the innocent tools of subverters. Every war, or trade dispute, eventually concludes with peace talks to decide future policy. Common sense argues that it is better to hold the peace talks *without* undergoing the privations of battle.

When subverters operate in areas of explosive emotionalism, they find it easy to provoke violence. It happened during the negro and students' riots in America, with the Guevarists in Bolivia and Ceylon, with the Bengali guerrillas in East Pakistan, and with the French students in Paris. Much closer to Britain, the violence in Northern Ireland has reached new extremes of inhumanity, which *nothing* can justify.

The most poignant feature of the Irish tragedy is that the most militant terrorists have only very vague objectives. The ideals of liberty, patriotism, freedom from oppression, and independence cannot condone murder, and the terrorists can only justify themselves by citing the violence used against them. But the Irish violence is self-regenerating. It is fuelled by the desire for revenge against reprisals that followed their earlier act of violence. It is easy for subverters to heap more fuel upon such fierce flames. They eagerly provide the militants with finance and gleefully supervise the abundant flood of armaments from all parts of Europe.

In Holland, on the 16th of October 1971, the Dutch Security forces intercepted a consignment of more than three tons of mortars, rocket launchers and small arms. It was just a small part of a much larger consignment of arms manufactured in Czechoslovakia, and purchased by David O'Connell, Chief of Staff of the IRA Provisionals. Two days later, British Special Branch officers intercepted six weighty suitcases being unloaded from the liner *Q.E. II* in Southampton. They contained a new type of urban guerrilla weapon that can be assembled and dismantled in a few minutes. An enormous quantity of ultra-modern weapons are reaching the terrorists in Northern Ireland. Those 'idealists' who come into possession of them have been convinced by subverters that they must spread Ireland's troubles, just as trouble is being inflamed by subverters between India and Pakistan. Detachments of Irish terrorists are deliberately instigating border incidents which are intended to bring Britain and Eire into armed conflict. The bombing in November 1971 of London's Post Office Tower was intended to provoke the British to retaliation.

It may be many years before the violence raging in Northern Ireland finally ceases, but by then a great many people will have suffered, and many more will have been killed. This expenditure of individual lives is of no importance to the subverter. His objective is to DESTROY the Western world. The reasons why terrorists wage guerrilla warfare, or how many of them die, do not interest the subverter.

*   *   *

The monetary system of the Western world is wide open to swift erosion by subverters. Soviet Russia and Red China have nothing to fear from world-wide inflation; inside their frontiers, currency serves simply as a means to exchange goods. Capital is NOT the mainspring of their economic system. They can forge Western currency and ease it into circulation, knowing that world-wide inflation can have no depressing effect upon their own internal economic systems. It is only recently that Britain adopted the decimal currency system; yet forged 50p coins that can be detected only by experts using laboratory equipment are already in circulation.

Enormous stores of counterfeit currency and official documents are cached all over Europe and the USA. They are held ready for distribution at a critical moment of international tension. Only very costly and elaborate defensive counter-measures can be adopted by the Western democracies. They must hoard a complete issue of new currency to replace the old if it is made valueless overnight by an overwhelming flood of counterfeits. Printing plates must be made and held in reserve so that all government stationery can be overprinted with government crests never previously used, and therefore not forgeable —for the time being. This will counteract the circulation of forged call-up and demobilisation orders and other vital official documents. But it is all very costly and complex. It requires an army of technicians constantly planning means and ways. Even if 'Counterfeit Warfare' is never used, the energies of Western democracy are being sapped by safeguarding against such threats.

* * *

The vilest of subverter tactics is the deliberate spread of drug addiction. This threatens our future generations more than the present, for it attacks our children.

Red China has openly adopted the spread of drug addiction as a method of warfare in Vietnam. Chou En-lai told about Red China's plan to make drug addicts of American troops when he met President Nasser in Alexandria six years ago. Chou En-lai added: 'The more troops they [the Americans] send to Vietnam, the happier we shall be. We shall then have them in our power and can have their blood.'

The threat has been fulfilled. The Pentagon is shocked by the extent of drug addiction among American soldiers, and appalled by the upsurge of heroin addiction. The men behind the spread of drug addiction, both in Vietnam and in the West, are the subverters. They arrange that the pushers get their supplies from abroad at rock-bottom prices.

But when the Western democracies are confronted by the deliberate spread of drug addiction among school children and adolescents, it is essential that decisive and rapid action be taken. If it could be proved that marijuana is no more habit-forming than alcohol, it could be legalised. This would enable Narcotics Prevention officers to concentrate upon stamping out the lethal 'hard' drugs. Severe punishment for pushers, plus large cash rewards for information leading to their arrest, are in fact under consideration.

* * *

Subverters are protected by a very efficient intelligence service. Recently, when a Soviet Control Agent flashed a top-priority high-speed radio message to Moscow Secret Service Headquarters that Oleg Lyalin had just defected to the West, the Special Division for

Subversion issued the following directive to its master subverters throughout the free world:

STRICTLY SECRET! MEMORISE! THEN BURN!
THIS MUST NOT FALL INTO UNAUTHORISED HANDS!

British agent-provocateur action has culminated in the pending expulsion of Soviet diplomats. This is a plot to undermine our agents' confidence in our security. Western Intelligence is making a concerted effort to penetrate our undercover networks. Strict compliance with routine security measures is our only safeguard.

Under no circumstances can there be personal contact between master operators, network leaders and undercover activists! All communications must be confined to the foolproof contact methods detailed in previous Security Orders:

1. Communicate through private codes inserted in specified newspapers.

2. Use private codes, written on picture postcards, which are sent to cover addresses and transmitted from there in the prescribed manner.

3. Use Dead-Drops.

4. When urgent contact is essential, use the specially designed telephone signals, with or without the use of a Black Box, but only in extreme emergency.

5. Whenever the slightest suspicion is aroused that Security agents suspect any network member or agent, the warning signal must be flashed and the *entire* network must immediately cease activity and go underground.

The only safeguard for master-operators and undercover networks against Western agents is rigid compliance with the security measures!

This is a warning!

STRICTLY SECRET! MEMORISE! THEN BURN!
THIS MUST NOT FALL INTO UNAUTHORISED HANDS!

* * *

Mankind is divided against itself. The ideals that one group of people cherish are despised by an opposing group that embraces conflicting ideals. Mankind's hope for the future can only be that intelligence and reason will triumph over blind emotion.

To defend its culture and its ideals, the West must always be on guard against the Red fifth-column enemy within!

But all men, irrespective of their nationality, their colour, their religion or political opinions, must always be on guard against the enemy that dwells within themselves!

Index